# The Penguin B
# of Australi

**Phillip Adams** has been a controversial columnist for 45 years and has presented the ABC's prestigious 'Late Night Live' for more than a decade. His serious books range from *Adams Versus God* to *Retreat from Tolerance* and *A Billion Voices*, and he has co-presented two TV series on science – everything from quantum mechanics to cosmology – with Professor Paul Davies. Add to this his filmmaking activities and his chairing of dozens of major governmental bodies and you'll understand that he has a constant problem with stress and depression. Which is why he works on joke books as an alternative to electroconvulsive therapy.

Following glamorous careers in modelling and television, **Patrice Newell** switched to farming – running a 10 000 acre cattle and sheep property in the Upper Hunter. She told her story recently in the autobiographical bestseller *The Olive Grove*. Coping with the dramas and difficulties of farming – and with Phillip – she too seeks the light relief of joke collection. 'After a typical day of droughts, floods and bushfires there's no better therapy,' she says, 'apart from increased beef prices.'

Other collections by
Phillip Adams and Patrice Newell

*The Penguin Book of Australian Jokes*
*The Penguin Book of More Australian Jokes*
*The Penguin Book of Jokes from Cyberspace*
*The Penguin Book of Schoolyard Jokes*
*Pocket Jokes*
*What a Joke!*
*What a Giggle!*
*The Penguin Book of All-New Australian Jokes*

# THE PENGUIN **BUMPER** BOOK OF AUSTRALIAN JOKES

Collected by Phillip Adams

and Patrice Newell

PENGUIN BOOKS

Penguin Books Australia Ltd
487 Maroondah Highway, PO Box 257
Ringwood, Victoria 3134, Australia
Penguin Books Ltd
Harmondsworth, Middlesex, England
Penguin Putnam Inc
375 Hudson Street, New York, New York 10014, USA
Penguin Books Canada Limited
10 Alcorn Avenue, Toronto, Ontario, Canada M4V 3B2
Penguin Books (NZ) Ltd
Cnr Rosedale and Airborne Roads, Albany, Auckland, New Zealand
Penguin Books (South Africa) (Pty) Ltd
24 Sturdee Avenue, Rosebank, Johannesburg 2196, South Africa
Penguin Books India (P) Ltd
11, Community Centre, Panchsheel Park, New Delhi 110 017, India

First published by Penguin Books Australia Ltd 2001

1 3 5 7 9 10 8 6 4 2

Copyright © Phillip Adams and Patrice Newell 2001

The moral right of the authors has been asserted

All rights reserved. Without limiting the rights under copyright reserved above, no part of this publication may be reproduced, stored in or introduced into a retrieval system, or transmitted, in any form or by any means (electronic, mechanical, photocopying, recording or otherwise), without the prior written permission of both the copyright owner and the above publisher of this book.

Cover illustration by Ned Culic
Design by Cathy Larsen, Penguin Design Studio
Typeset in Sabon 10/16 by Midland Typesetters, Maryborough, Victoria
Made and printed in Australia by McPherson's Print Group, Maryborough, Victoria

National Library of Australia
Cataloguing-in-Publication data:

The Penguin bumper book of Australian jokes.

Includes index.
ISBN 014 100689 7.

1. Australian wit and humor. I. Adams, Phillip, 1939– .
II. Newell, Patrice, 1956– . III. Title : Bumper book of
Australian jokes.

A828.02

www.penguin.com.au

**FOR RORY**

# INTRODUCTION

Thanks to impeccable biblical scholarship we know that the world was created in 4000 BC. Not billions and billions of years ago, as scientists suggest, but shortly before the Egyptians built the pyramids.

Archbishop James Ussher, by studying the Old Testament in forensic detail and counting all the 'begats', backtracked over the millennia to define this epic event in cosmic chronology.

Inspired by the archbishop, vice-chancellor of the University of Cambridge, John Lightfoot, decreed that the final act of creation – the animation of Adam – had occurred at 9 a.m. on Sunday, 23 October. In, yes, the vintage year of 4004 BC.

Amongst the other hard data provided by biblical scholars are the exact dimensions of Heaven, calculated from Revelations 21:16. Extrapolating from Testamental data, the first edition of *Pear's Shilling Cyclopaedia* (1897) tells us: A cube of 12 000 furlongs is 496 793 088 000 000 000 000 cubic feet. If half of that is reserved for the Throne of God and the Court of Heaven, and a quarter of it for the streets of the city, there is still enough space to provide 30 321 843 750 000 000 000 ordinary-sized rooms. That would give one room apiece to all the inhabitants of a million worlds as thickly peopled as the earth is now.

The news that there's plenty of room in Heaven is important because, sadly, there's about to be a rush for accommodation. For it is the sad news of your editors to report that the world that began some sixty centuries ago is doomed to end next Tuesday afternoon, at around 3.30 p.m. Eastern Standard Time.

Perhaps it is God's judgement upon us. For throwing too many parties. For having too much fun. We popped the champagne cork for the Bicentennial of the First Fleet's arrival in 1988. We exploded fireworks to salute a new century and, yes, a new millennium in January 2000, though many scholars suggested that we were jumping the gun by 365 days. We celebrated Sydney's Olympics that same year – and have just completed rejoicing in the Centenary of Federation.

In short, a good time was had by all. Now the good time is over.

# The Penguin Bumper Book of Australian Jokes

The giant asteroid that will shortly pocket us in the ongoing game of celestial billiards will do us in as absolutely as its predecessor did the dinosaurs. Oddly, we can't be entirely sure when that calamity occurred. For some strange reason the dinosaurs didn't get a mention in the Old Testament – nor did they get a guernsey from Archbishop Ussher. But that doesn't change the fact that our days, indeed our hours, are numbered. Our collective goose is cooked. We are about to kick the bucket.

Hence the publication of this book. Its purpose is to smooth the pillow on our deathbed, to dull our pain, to give us a few hours of good-humoured distraction before the destruction. This book contains humanity's last laugh. Or rather, last laughs, given that you may find more than one of the jokes amusing.

That's always been the function of humour. If we believe in evolution, which fans of Archbishop Ussher and John Lightfoot most emphatically do not, we'd acknowledge that humour and laughter are amongst its most ingenious inventions. Embodied in the joke we have a tool, a mechanism, an *exorcism* for all unpleasantness. The joke is the equal of electro-convulsive therapy, of long-term psychoanalysis, of Prozac, in its ability to bring relief from moments

# The Penguin Bumper Book of Australian Jokes

of mental and spiritual anguish. Moments like the end of the world, currently approaching us at incomprehensible speed.

Whenever things are dark and gloomy for humans, humans tell jokes. That is why Jews, on the receiving end of bigotries for almost all of Archbishop Ussher's 4000 years, have been so masterful at creating ironic humour. Victims of pogroms, herded into ghettos, confronted by a doom as implacable as the asteroid, Jews have responded with the greatest jokes in creation. They have made a completely disproportionate contribution to human comedy.

During what George W. Bush's dad so engagingly describes as 'deep do-dos', the same phenomenon occurs. A space shuttle explodes just after launching. We make a joke about it. The world is breeding lawyers even faster than cane toads. We make jokes about them. We fear ill-health and impotence, mothers-in-law and politicians and, lo and behold, there are appropriate jokes. Or inappropriate jokes, given the tenets of political correctness.

So make yourself comfortable and enjoy this book as, thanks to asteroidal proximity, your final seconds evaporate. And in doing so, join us in thanking the countless and anonymous authors who invented

# The Penguin Bumper Book of Australian Jokes

these jokes, recycled them from previous incarnations (in our years of collecting we've found very little evidence of truly new jokes) and put them back into circulation.

The joke is, truly, the most democratic form of literary work. We give them to each other more generously than greetings or kisses. Indeed, kisses are a good parallel. People spread jokes like kisses spread germs – or like computers spread viruses through cyberspace.

Whilst the identity of our authors cannot be known we would like to thank the hundreds of people who have contacted us with examples – particularly Claudia Gaber, Mark Evans and Christian Raith, whose anthropological efforts have been heroic. And special thanks, too, to Bob Christie, for his scrutiny of biblical texts.

We would also like to thank ... but there's no time. A great, dark shape is filling the heavens. It is accompanied by the smell of sulphur. Our canary has just died.

Enjoy.

**T**wo swaggies are sitting outside a pub in a small country town, hundreds of miles back o' Bourke. They're not talking much. Just sitting. A blue-tongue lizard is basking in the sun nearby. A couple of blowies are circling their heads. One of the men has a dog which is lightly snoring by his feet.

An old farmer riding an ancient horse hovers into view, and slowly plods by.

'Well, I'll reckon I'll be moving on,' says one swaggie to the other, 'as soon as the traffic dies down.'

**I**t's their wedding night and the young bride is setting the ground rules. 'This is how I want to arrange our sex life. In the evening, if my hair is done, it means that I don't feel like sex at all. If my hair is somewhat undone, a little loose, it means I may or may not want sex. But if my hair is completely undone, that's your signal. That means I want sex.'

'Fine by me, darling,' said the groom. 'And here's my set of signals. When I come home, I'll usually hit the bottle. If I have just one drink, that means I don't want sex. If I have two, I may or may not want sex. And if I have three drinks, your hair doesn't matter.'

**Q**antas flight 256, Sydney to Melbourne, has boarded. The passengers are all sitting patiently in their seats and the cabin crew are hanging up the last of the jackets and checking seatbelts. But the passengers can see – thanks to the door of the flight deck being open – that neither pilot nor copilot has arrived.

Then, suddenly, just seconds before the scheduled take-off time, they appear in the doorway. Resplendent in their uniforms, one has hold of a seeing-eye

Labrador, whilst the other tap-taps away with a white cane. Both are wearing dark glasses.

Nervous laughter spreads through the cabin. The passengers are convinced that this is some kind of joke.

The pilot follows the Labrador into the cockpit, and the copilot follows the pilot, tap-tapping away with his white stick. The door closes. The engines start.

After the usual admonishments about safety procedures, the airbus is positioned for take-off. It begins to move faster and faster down the runway, towards the waters of Botany Bay.

It starts to look as though the plane will never take off – that it will plunge off the tarmac and into the drink. Screams of panic fill the cabin.

At that exact moment, the plane lifts smoothly into the sky.

Up in the cockpit, the copilot turns to the pilot and says, 'You know, Arthur, one of these days they're going to scream too late and we'll all die.'

'Doctor, I can't pronounce my F's, T's and H's.'
*'Well, you can't say fairer than that then.'*

A wealthy woman walked along Knox Street, Double Bay, flaunting her suede jacket. An animal liberationist came up to her and said, 'Don't you know a little calf was murdered for that jacket?'

To which the woman replied, 'I didn't know there were any witnesses. Now I'll have to kill you, too.'

I poured Spot remover on my dog. Now he's gone.

I used to have an open mind but my brains kept falling out.

I couldn't repair your brakes, so I made your horn louder.

**Shin**: a device for finding furniture in the dark.

**How** do you tell when you run out of invisible ink?

**Join** the Army, meet interesting people, kill them.

**Once** upon a time, in the Kingdom of Heaven, God went missing for six days. Michael, the archangel, searched high and low for him. But mainly, given God's exalted status, he searched high. Finally he found him, on the seventh day, resting. And he inquired of God, 'Where have you been?'

God sighed a deep, contented, satisfied sigh and proudly pointed downwards through the clouds. 'Look what I've done, Michael.'

And Michael looked. And saw a new planet.

'I called it earth,' said God, 'and I put life on it. And it's going to be a great place of balance.'

'Balance?' inquired Michael.

And God began to explain, by pointing at the Northern Hemisphere. 'For example, northern Europe will be a place of great opportunity while southern Europe will be poor. The Middle East over there will be a hot spot ... but down there, at the South Pole, things will be very cold.'

God continued to point to different parts of the planet. 'Over there I've created a continent of white people ... and over there a continent of black people.'

Michael began to see what God was getting at.

'See that place? That's America. North America will be rich, powerful and cold while South America, down there, will be poor, powerless and very warm. Can you see the balance?'

'Yes, God,' said the archangel, very impressed. 'But what about that place?' And Michael pointed to a vast continent between Africa and South America.

'Ah,' said God, 'that's Australia, the most glorious place on earth. There are beautiful mountains, lush rain forests, fine rivers, bubbling streams and endless beaches for people to enjoy. And the locals? They're good-looking, intelligent and humorous. It will be popular all over the planet. You see, they'll be very sociable, hardworking, egalitarian yet high achieving, and they'll be known throughout the world for their hospitality. And I'm going to give them superhuman, undefeatable cricket and rugby players who'll be admired and feared by all who come across them.'

Michael shook his head in wonderment and admiration. But then he said, 'God, you said there would be balance. How will you balance Australians?'

And God replied, 'Wait till you see the ugly, whining, sheep-fucking Kiwis I'm putting next to them.'

**F**or countless generations a prestigious Melbourne ladies college had been educating the daughters of the well-to-do and influential. It was particularly proud of the girls in its athletics team. But what the headmistress and the board didn't know was that the team's ambitious coach had been giving her squad steroids. As a result, the team's performance soared.

They won countless championships and some of the girls were being considered for the 2004 Olympics in Athens.

Whereupon Fiona, a 16-year-old hurdler, visited the coach and said, 'Miss, I have a problem. Hair is starting to grow on my chest.'

'What!?' said the coach in a panic. 'How far down does the hair go?'

Fiona replied, 'All the way down to my balls.'


An optimist thinks that this is the best possible world. A pessimist fears that this is true.


During negotiations between the Australian and the European Commission to allow for increased imports of Australian produce, particularly BSE-free beef, among the many clauses in the long contract were undertakings to respect the EU's view on human rights; as well as an undertaking to abide by the Commission's views on English as the common language.

The Australian negotiators pointed out that Australians spoke English, so this shouldn't present any difficulties. Brussels pointed out that Europe was insisting English be improved and simplified so that it was more comprehensible to EU member nations.

To this end, Her Majesty's government accepted a five-year phase-in plan that would be known as 'Euro-English', and Australians would be expected to comply.

The alternative to simplified English was that the EU would adopt German as its lingua franca – but given Germany's behaviour in the 20th century, this had been overruled by most member nations.

Following is the relevant section from the EU contract submitted to Canberra for signing.

'In the first year "s" will replace the soft "c". Sertainly, this will make the sivil servants jump with joy. The hard "c" will be dropped in favour of the "k". This should klear up konfusion and keyboards kan have one less letter. There will be growing publik enthusiasm in the sekond year, when the troublesome "ph" will be replaced with "f". This will make words like "fotograf" 20 per sent shorter. In the third year, publik akseptanse of the new spelling kan be ekspekted to reach the stage where more komplikated

# The Penguin Bumper Book of Australian Jokes

changes are possible. Governments will enkourage the removal of double letters, which have always ben a deterent to akurate speling. Also, al wil agre that the horible mes of the silent "e" in the language is disgraseful, and they should go away. By the fourth year, peopl wil be reseptiv to steps such as replasing "th" with "z" and "w" with "v". During ze fifz year, ze unesesary "o" kan be dropd from vords kontaining "ou" and similar changes vud of kors be aplid to ozer kombinations of leters. After zis fifz yer, ve vil hav a reli sensibl riten styl. Zer vil be no mor trubl or difikultis and evrivun vil find it ezi to understand ech ozer. Ze drem vil finali kum tru! And zen ve vil tak over ze world.'

There will always be death and taxes; however, death doesn't get worse every year.

The early bird gets the worm, but the second mouse gets the cheese.

**T**elevangelists: The pro-wrestlers of religion.

**E**agles may soar, but weasels don't get sucked into jet engines.

**W**hy are ABC management executives buried four-metres deep?
*Because deep down, they're really nice people.*

**A**fter a week in her new job, which involved making the coffee, taking dictation and slowly tapping out simple business letters with two fingers on a word processor, the blonde secretary is told late on Friday night, by a less than impressed employer, 'Don't come Monday.'

Her response, as bright as a button: 'Okay, I'll see you on Tuesday.'

# The Penguin Bumper Book of Australian Jokes

An old man lies back on his plumped-up pillows. He's in his early 80s and has had every imaginable illness and ailment – including a kidney transplant, a triple bypass and two hip replacements. And now, on top of everything else, he has pneumonia.

His wife, 20 years his junior, discusses his plight in whispers with the GP. 'Is there anything more you can do for him?' she asks.

'No,' replies the doctor, 'I'm afraid that he's only got a few days left. A week at most.'

'So what will I do if he asks for a cigarette?'

'I'd let him have one.'

'And what will I do if he asks for a drink?'

'Why not. Just do whatever you can to make him happy in these final hours.'

Having shown the doctor out, the wife goes to the kitchen and starts mixing up a batch of chocolate-chip cookies. The delicious aroma drifts from the oven, down the hall and into the old bloke's bedroom. When it reaches his nostrils he stirs a little, opens one eye, then the other, sniffs the air, and sniffs again. His dry, parched mouth begins to moisten with saliva. Chocolate-chip cookies have always been his absolute favourite.

Somehow the old bloke finds the strength to sit

up, turn back the doona and lower his withered legs to the floor. His feet find his slippers and he manages to slip them on. Then he begins to totter towards the kitchen. But after a few steps, he loses his balance and falls to the ground. But he remains resolute. The scent of the cookies keeps urging him on.

Finally, he makes it to the kitchen and there, on the table, is a plate of his all-time favourites. He reaches up and takes a cookie in trembling fingers.

At this moment his wife comes into the kitchen, grabs a wooden spoon from the mixing bowl and hits him on the knuckles.

'Leave those alone, you greedy old bugger,' she says. 'They're for the wake.'

Four blokes get casual work at a building site. The foreman tells the first that his job will be to lug bricks. The second will have to mix gravel. The third will have the task of moving wheelbarrows full of sand. And the fourth, who happens to be Chinese, will be responsible for coordinating. He'll have to make sure there's lots of bricks, lots of sand and a wheelbarrow.

An hour later, the foreman returns to find that none of the four recruits is working. Not only is there no sign of the Chinese bloke, but the other three are simply sitting on the ground looking confused. 'What the hell's going on?' asks the foreman. 'Where's the sand? Where's the bricks? Where's the wheelbarrow? Where's the Chinese bloke who's meant to be looking after supplies?'

Whereupon the Chinese bloke jumps out from a nearby shed. He's got a great big grin on his face and is yelling: 'Suplise! Suplise!'

**A** bloke has picked up a young woman at a bar and persuaded her to accompany him to a motel. Once there he tries some foreplay which is so fumbling that the woman's response is less than enthusiastic.

He tries this, he tries that. Whatever he tries, he's discouraged. Finally the woman manages to get off the bed and, straightening her clothing, prepares to depart.

'Please don't go. Please. At least, not without giving me a 68.'

'What a dickhead. You mean a 69,' she says contemptuously.

'No, a 68. You give me a blow job and I'll owe you one.'

'Welcome to the Twilight Nursing Home,' said the matron. 'I'm sure you'll be very happy here, provided you follow our rules.'

'Thank you,' said the new nurse, looking around at the impressive facilities.

'Yes, we have the *crème de la crème* of elderly folk here. We provide very good food – and we've never, never used kerosene in our bathrooms.'

'No kerosene,' echoed the new nurse.

'On the other hand, we do give our elderly gentlemen guests just a little Viagra.'

'Viagra? Aren't they too old?'

'Yes. But we only give them a little.'

'Why?'

'To stop them rolling out of bed.'

**The Penguin Bumper Book of Australian Jokes**

**O**LD IS WHEN: your girlfriend says, 'Let's go upstairs and make love,' and you answer, 'Honey I can't do both!'

OLD IS WHEN: your mates compliment you on your new alligator shoes and you're barefoot.

OLD IS WHEN: a woman catches your attention and your pacemaker opens the garage door.

OLD IS WHEN: going braless pulls all the wrinkles out of your face.

OLD IS WHEN: you are cautioned to slow down by the doctor instead of the police.

OLD IS WHEN: 'getting a little action' means you don't need to take any fibre today.

OLD IS WHEN: 'getting lucky' means you find your car in the parking lot.

OLD IS WHEN: an 'all-nighter' means not getting up to pee!

**O**nce upon a time there was a Jewish pirate, whose name was Abby. He plied his piratical trade up and down the Gold Coast where he preyed on Jewish retirees who kept powerboats moored by their condos at Surfers Paradise or Noosa. He would strip the women of their necklaces and bracelets, and the men of their gold Rolexes. And with the passing of years, he became more and more famous. Until, inevitably, there was talk of making a feature film about him.

One day, whilst visiting his ship's chandlers, Abby was accosted by Al Clark, the producer of *Priscilla, Queen of the Desert* and, more recently, *Chopper*. Clark told Abby that he wanted to make a film like *Chopper*, based on a real-life criminal, and that he'd cut Abby in for a percentage.

Abby was flattered and readily agreed.

'I'd like to begin with some research,' said Clark. 'I'd like to ask you some questions.'

'Sure, ask away.'

'Well, how did you get the wooden leg?'

'The stump? Like Captain Hook in *Peter Pan*, my leg was bitten off by a crocodile. A dirty great croc about 30 foot long.'

'And what about the hook?'

'Another crocodile,' said Abby. 'Not as big, only 20 foot long. But it bit off my arm, so I had to get a metal hook to go with the wooden leg.'

'And what about the eye patch?'

'A seagull pooped in my eye.'

'Well, it's very photogenic,' said Clark. 'Like the wooden leg and the metal hook, it'll look great on the big screen. But I don't understand. A bit of seagull poop shouldn't blind you.'

'It will,' said Abby sadly, 'if it happens the very first day you have a hook.'

In Adelaide a group of Scots organised a day of highland games, bagpipe playing and haggis eating. MC for the spectacle and excitement was an elderly Scot, inevitably called Jock.

As the day progressed, those sampling Scotch whisky in the sponsors' tent became increasingly inebriated. The drunkest of them all was a dignified woman who, under the influence, became wildly enamoured of Jock.

'Jock, have you got anything up your kilt?' she asked, breathing fumes all over him.

'Put your hand up and find out.'

Which, without hesitation, she did.

'Oh Jock,' she said, clearly shocked. 'It's gruesome.'
'Put your hand up there again,' said Jock, 'and it will grew some more.'

**G**ive a man a free hand and he'll run it all over you.

**B**eauty is in the eye of the beer holder . . .

**T**wenty-four hours in a day . . . Twenty-four beers in a case . . . Coincidence?

**I**f everything seems to be going well, you have obviously overlooked something.

**M**any people quit looking for work when they find a job.

**D**ancing is a perpendicular expression of a horizontal desire.

**A** very old bloke turned up at a doctor's surgery and sat patiently in the waiting room, leafing through battered copies of the *Women's Weekly* and the RACV journal. Finally he was ushered into the GP's presence.

'Doctor, I want some Viagra.'

'Some Viagra? At your age? Are you still sexually active?'

'No, I'm a widower. I haven't had a fuck for 20 years.'

'Then why do you want some Viagra?'

'Well, I only want half a dose.'

'Half a dose? Why half a dose?'
'I want to stop peeing on my shoes.'

Two blokes were sitting side by side at a bar. Both were staring into their drinks. Neither was talking. One was of Chinese origin, and owned a local restaurant. The other was Jewish and ran a menswear shop.

After 20 minutes of sitting side by side, the Chinese restaurateur accidentally spilled some of his beer on the Jewish businessman.

'Typical! Typical!' said the Jewish bloke. 'First Pearl Harbor, now this!'

'Excuse me, I'm not Japanese. I'm Chinese. It was the Japs who bombed Pearl Harbor.'

'Japanese, Chinese! They're all the bloody same,' said the Jew as, quite deliberately, he poured his drink on his Oriental neighbour.

'You bastards!' yelled the Chinese restaurateur. 'Absolutely typical! First you sink the *Titanic*! Now this!'

'Sink the *Titanic*? Sink the *Titanic*? It wasn't a Jew who sank the *Titanic*, you Chinese twit. It was an iceberg!'

'Goldberg. Iceberg. It's all the same thing.'

At the end of his long, triumphant career, Sir Robert Menzies, preparing to leave the Lodge for Haverbrack Avenue, East Malvern (via a quick trip to the Cinque Ports), called young Harold Holt, his nominated successor, into his office.

'My boy,' said Sir Robert, 'I want to give you the benefit of my accumulated political wisdom.' And he handed Harold two white envelopes, both bearing the prime-ministerial seal.

'These are for you to use when you're in terrible, terrible trouble. The first time you find yourself in a corner from which you cannot escape, open the first envelope. It will show you how to cope, how to escape, how to survive.'

'Thank you, sir,' said Harold, 'thank you very, very much.'

'The second envelope,' Sir Robert continued, 'is

for when you find yourself in an even worse situation, when the political walls are closing in, when the hyenas and the vultures are circling.'

'Thank you, thank you, sir,' said Harold.

The great man stood, shook the younger man's hand, and showed him to the door.

A few months later, just after the visit of Lyndon Johnson, when Harold Holt said 'All the way with LBJ', the political circumstances were extremely difficult. Feeling desperate, Harold went to the safe, unlocked it and extracted the first of the two white envelopes.

He opened the envelope, unfolded a sheet of paper and read the words Sir Robert had written: 'Blame everything on your predecessor.'

So he did. And it worked. And for a time, all was well for the relatively inexperienced prime minister.

Then, inevitably, came an even worse crisis and, yes, it did seem as if the walls were moving in to crush him. So Holt went back to the safe and withdrew the second envelope. With trembling fingers he opened it, unfolded the paper, and read: 'Hand your successor two white envelopes . . .'

# The Penguin Bumper Book of Australian Jokes

The art critic arrived at the Paddington gallery to review the works of an up-and-coming Aboriginal artist. Instead of doing bark paintings or dot paintings, the artist used canvas and the latest high-tech paints – and painted portraits of proud, naked blackfellas standing on a blistering Australian landscape.

Every painting was a variation on the same theme. Tall black warriors holding spears, woomeras and boomerangs, posed defiantly in the endless deserts.

But there was one painting that was just a little different. It showed three blackfellas standing by a gum tree, but one of them had a bright white penis.

The critic stared and wondered, wondered and stared. What was the symbolism of the white penis? So he speculated about it in his review for the *Sydney Morning Herald*, submitting any number of hypotheses.

The day the review appeared the phone rang. It was the painter. 'Brother, you got that entirely wrong. You see, those three blokes weren't blackfellas. They were whitefellas who worked in a coalmine. And the one in the middle, the one with the white dick? He'd gone home for lunch.'

A bloke wanted to purchase a present for his new girlfriend. They'd only been going out together for a few weeks so, after careful consideration, he decided that a pair of gloves would strike the right note. Not too romantic, not too personal.

Accompanied by his girlfriend's sister, he went to Grace Bros and bought a really charming pair of white gloves. At the same time, the sister bought a pair of panties for herself.

During the wrapping, the shop assistant mixed up the items – so the sister got the gloves and the girlfriend got the panties. And she also got the little card that the bloke had written.

'Darling, I chose these because I know that you're not in the habit of wearing any when we go out in the evening. If it hadn't been for your sister, I would have chosen the long ones with the buttons. But she wears short ones that are easier to get off.

'I know they're a pale colour, but the lady told me you could wear them for weeks and they wouldn't look soiled at all.

'I had her try yours on for me and they looked really good, even though they were a little tight on her. She also told me that her pair helps her to keep her ring clean and shiny. In fact, she hadn't had to wash it since she'd begun wearing them.

'I wish I were there to put them on for you the first time as, no doubt, many other hands will touch them before I have a chance to see you again.

'When you take them off, remember to blow into them before putting them away. They'll naturally be a little damp from wearing. And just think how many times my lips will kiss them during the weeks ahead. I hope that you will wear them for me on Friday night.

'All my best.

P.S. The latest style is to wear them folded down with a little fur showing.'

Once upon a time there was a shepherd looking after sheep on the edge of a deserted road. Suddenly a brand-new Jeep Cherokee screeches to a halt next to him. The driver, a young man dressed in a Zegna suit, Cerutti shoes, Rayban sunglasses, Rolex wristwatch and a Pierre Cardin tie, gets out and asks the shepherd, 'If I guess how many sheep you have, will you give me one of them?'

The shepherd looks at the young man, then looks at the grazing sheep, and replies, 'OK.'

The young man parks the car, connects his notebook and mobile fax, enters a NASA website, scans the ground using his GPS, opens a database with 60 Excel tables filled with logarithms, then prints out a 150-page report on his high-tech mini-printer. He turns to the shepherd and says, 'Exactly 1586 sheep here.'

The shepherd answers, 'That's correct, you can have your sheep.' The young man picks out what he thinks is the best-looking specimen and puts it in his jeep.

The shepherd looks at him and asks, 'If I guess your profession, will you return my animal to me?'

The young man answers, 'Yes, why not.'

The shepherd says, 'You're a consultant.'

'How did you know?' asks the young man.

'Very simple,' answers the shepherd. 'First, you came here without being called. Second, you charged me a fee to tell me something I already knew. Third, you don't understand anything about my business. Now – can I have my dog back?'

**T**wo fat blokes in a pub. One says to the other, 'Your round.'
　　The other says: 'So are you, you fat git.'

**T**wo cannibals were eating a clown. One says to the other: 'Does this taste funny to you?'

**P**olice arrested two children today. One was drinking battery acid, the other was eating fireworks. They charged one and let the other off.

### The Penguin Bumper Book of Australian Jokes

**A** blind bloke walks into a shop with a guide-dog. He picks up his dog and starts swinging it around his head. Thoroughly alarmed, the shop assistant says, 'Can I help, sir?'

*'No thanks,' says the blind bloke, 'just looking.'*

**I**t's strange, isn't it? If you stand in the middle of a library and go 'AAAAGHHH!!' everyone will just stare at you. But if you do the same thing on an airbus, on a flight between Adelaide and Perth, everyone joins in.

**A** bloke was hitchhiking on the F3. He'd been thumbing away for hours and no-one had as much as slowed down. Then, all of a sudden, there was a squeal of brakes and there, right in front of him, was a BMW being driven by a thirty-something yuppie.

'Could you give me a lift?' said the hitchhiker.

'Sure,' said the yuppie. 'You look great! The world's your oyster! Go for it!' And he drove off.

'Somebody complimented me on my driving today,' said one blonde to another.

'Really?'

'Well, actually it was on my parking.'

'Really?'

'Yes, they left a little note on the windscreen. It said "Parking Fine". Wasn't that nice?'

So I got home and the phone was ringing. I picked it up and said, 'Who's speaking please?' And a voice said, 'You are.'

So I rang up my local swimming baths. I said, 'Is that the local swimming baths?' He said, 'It depends where you're calling from.'

So I rang up a local rubbish removal firm. I said, 'I want a skip outside my house.' He said, 'I'm not stopping you.'

He said, 'I'm going to chop off the bottom of one of your trouser legs and put it in the library.' I thought, 'That's a turn up for the books.'

So I went to the dentist. And he said, 'Say

"Aaaah".' I said, 'Why?' He said, 'Because my dog's died.'

Most dentist chairs go up and down. The one I was in went backwards and forwards. I thought, 'This is strange.' And the dentist said to me, 'For Christ's sake, get out of the filing cabinet.'

So I was in my car, driving along, and my mobile rang. It was my boss. 'You've been promoted.' And I swerved. Then he rang up a second time and said, 'You've been promoted again.' And I swerved again. He rang up a third time and said, 'You're managing director.' And I swerved into a tree. And the policeman said, 'What happened to you?' And I said, 'I careered off the road.'

**A**pparently, one in five people in the world are Chinese. And there are five people in my family. So one of them must be Chinese. It's either my mum or my dad. Or my older brother Colin. Or my younger brother, Ho-cha Chou. But I think it's Colin.

# The Penguin Bumper Book of Australian Jokes

## WOMEN'S BUMPER STICKERS

So many men, so few who can afford me.

If they don't have chocolate in heaven, I ain't going.

My mother is a travel agent for guilt trips.

Princess, having had sufficient experience with princes, seeks frog.

Coffee, chocolate, men. Some things are just better rich.

Don't treat me any differently than you would the queen.

If you want breakfast in bed, sleep in the kitchen.

I'm out of oestrogen – and I have a gun.

Guys have feelings too. But like . . . who cares?

Next mood swing: 6 minutes.

## The Penguin Bumper Book of Australian Jokes

AND YOUR POINT IS?

WARNING: I HAVE AN ATTITUDE AND I KNOW HOW TO USE IT.

OF COURSE I DON'T LOOK BUSY . . . I DID IT RIGHT THE FIRST TIME.

DO NOT START WITH ME. YOU WILL NOT WIN.

YOU HAVE THE RIGHT TO REMAIN SILENT, SO PLEASE SHUT UP.

ALL STRESSED OUT AND NO-ONE TO CHOKE.

I'M ONE OF THOSE BAD THINGS THAT HAPPEN TO GOOD PEOPLE.

HOW CAN I MISS YOU IF YOU WON'T GO AWAY?

SORRY IF I LOOK INTERESTED. I'M NOT.

IF WE ARE WHAT WE EAT, I'M FAST, CHEAP AND EASY.

DON'T UPSET ME! I'M RUNNING OUT OF PLACES TO HIDE THE BODIES.

# The Penguin Bumper Book of Australian Jokes

An older Jewish gentleman marries a younger lady and they are very much in love. However, no matter what the husband does sexually, the woman never achieves orgasm. Since a Jewish wife is entitled to sexual pleasure, they decide to ask the rabbi.

The rabbi listens to their story, strokes his beard, and makes the following suggestion. 'Hire a strapping young man. While the two of you are making love, have the young man wave a towel over you. That will help the wife fantasise and should bring on an orgasm.'

They go home and follow the rabbi's advice. They hire a handsome young man and he waves a towel over them as they make love. But it doesn't help and she is still unsatisfied.

Perplexed, they go back to the rabbi.

'Okay,' says the rabbi, 'let's try it reversed. Have the young man make love to your wife and you wave the towel over them.'

Once again, they follow the rabbi's advice. The young man gets into bed with the wife and the husband waves the towel. The young man gets to work with great enthusiasm and the wife soon has an enormous, room-shaking orgasm.

The husband smiles, looks at the young man and says to him triumphantly: 'You see, THAT'S the way to wave a towel!'

I intend to live forever. So far, so good.

I love defenceless animals, especially in a good gravy.

If Barbie is so popular, why do you have to buy her friends?

If you ain't makin' waves, you ain't kickin' hard enough!

**M**ental backup in progress – Do Not Disturb!

**M**ind Like a Steel Trap – Rusty and Illegal in all States.

### THE TONG-MASTER

**G**riff was at the barbecue and Joel was at the barbecue and I was at the barbecue; three men standing around a barbecue, sipping beer, staring at sausages, rolling them backwards and forwards, never leaving them alone.

We didn't know why we were at the barbecue; we were just drawn there like moths to a flame. The barbecue was a powerful gravitational force, a man-magnet. Joel said the thin ones could use a turn, I said yeah, I reckon the thin ones could use a turn. Griff said, yeah they really need a turn. It was a unanimous turning decision.

Griff was the Tong-Master, a true artist, he gave a couple of practice snaps of his long silver tongs, SNAP SNAP, before moving in, prodding, teasing, and with an elegant flick of his wrist, rolling them onto their little backs. A lesser tong-man would've flicked too hard; the sausages would've gone full circle back to where they started.

Nice, I said. The others went yeah.

Kevin was passing us, he heard the siren-song-sizzle of the snags, the barbecue was calling, beckoning, Kevinnnnn . . . come. He stuck his head in and said any room? We said yeah and began the barbecue shuffle; Griff shuffled to the left, Joel shuffled to the left, I shuffled to the left, Kevin slipped in beside me, we sipped our beer. Now there were four of us staring at sausages, and Griff gave me the nod, my cue.

I was second-in-command, I had to take the raw sausages out of the plastic bag and lay them on the barbecue, not too close together, not too far apart, curl them into each other's bodies like lovers – fat ones, thin ones, herbed and continental. The chipolatas were tiny, they could easily slip down between the grill, falling into the molten hot-bed-netherworld below. Carefully I laid them sideways ACROSS the grill, clever thinking.

Griff snapped his tongs with approval; there was no greater barbecue honour. P.J. came along, he said looking good, looking good – the irresistible lure of the barbecue had pulled him in, too. We said yeah, and did the shuffle, left, left, left, left.

He slipped in beside Kevin, we sipped our beer.

Five men, lots of sausages. Joel was the Fork-Pronger; he had the fork that pronged the tough hides of the Bavarian bratwursts and he showed a lot of promise. Stabbing away eagerly, leaving perfect little vampire holes up and down the casing. P.J. was shaking his head, he said I reckon they cook better if you don't poke them.

There was a long silence, you could have heard a chipolata drop. This newcomer was a rabblerouser, bringing in his crazy ideas from outside.

He didn't understand the hierarchy: first the Tong-Master, then the Sausage-Layer, then the Fork-Pronger – and everyone below was just a watcher. Maybe eventually they would move up the ladder, but for now – don't rock the Weber.

Dianne popped her head in; hmmm, smells good she said. She was trying to jostle into the circle; we closed ranks, pulled our heads down and our shoulders in, mumbling yeah yeah yeah, but making no room for her. She was keen, going round to the far side of the barbecue, heading for the only available space . . . the gap in the circle where all the smoke and ash blew. Nobody could survive the gap; Dianne was going to try. She stood there stubbornly, smoke blinding her eyes, ash filling her nostrils, sausage fat spattering all over her arms and face. Until she couldn't take it any more. She gave up, backed off.

Kevin waited till she was gone and sipped his beer. We sipped our beer, yeah. Griff handed me his tongs. I looked at him and he nodded. I knew what was happening, I'd waited a long time for this moment – the abdication. The tongs weighed heavy in my hands, firm in my grip. Was I ready for the responsibility? Yes, I was. I held them up high and they glinted in the sun.

Don't forget to turn the thin ones Griff said as he walked away from the barbecue, disappearing toward the house. Yeah, I called back, I will, I will. I snapped them twice, SNAP SNAP, before moving in, prodding, teasing, and with an elegant flick of my wrist, rolling them back onto their little bellies.

I was a natural. I was the Tong-Master.

But only until Griff got back from the toilet.

The Sheriff said: 'I'm looking for a man with a brown paper hat, wearing brown paper clothes and riding a brown paper horse.'

'What do you want him for?'

'Rustling.'


A nun, wearing the non-nunny mufti gear favoured since Vatican II, was walking back to the convent through a local playground when a bloke came lumbering up to her and demanded her purse.

Opening it, he found nothing inside but some rosary beads – so he chucked the lot onto a garden bed. 'Come on, where's your money?' he said, and began running his hands all over her clothing.

Shuddering slightly, the nun rolled her eyes to heaven.

'Come on! Come on! Where's your bloody money?' By now he was exploring her girdle.

'Keep looking,' said the nun, 'and I'll send you a cheque.'

### The Penguin Bumper Book of Australian Jokes

A couple of bushies had finished their fencing contract back o'Bourke and were heading towards town when they were overcome by thirst. So they parked the ute at the front of a lonely little pub and went inside to breast the bar.

'What's the beer like?' they asked a stockman, who'd arrived a few minutes earlier and was tying his blue heeler to a fence post out the front.

'The beer here? It's bloody awful,' said the stockman. 'I'll be glad when I've had enough.'

---

The scene is Camberwell – a nice, upper-middle-class suburb in Melbourne. Four GPs work together in a medical practice. The surgery is nicely decorated, with nice prints on the wall and nice, fresh, up-to-date magazines for the patients to read. Magazines like *Country Life* and *Harper's Bazaar*.

And business is booming when a bloke walks in and fronts the receptionist.

'Yes sir, may we help you?'

'There's something wrong with my willy,' he replies.

You can hear the sharp intake of breath in the waiting room, as the nice, middle-class patients look up from their nice magazines.

'I beg your pardon?' says the receptionist.

'There's something wrong with my willy,' the bloke repeats.

The receptionist is aghast. She puts her finger to her lips and says, 'Sshhh,' adding, 'you can't come into a place like this and say things like that.'

'Why not? You asked me what was wrong and I told you.'

'Sir, we do not use language like that at this practice,' she hisses at him. 'Please go outside and come back in and say . . .'

'Say what?'

'Well, say there's something wrong with your ear or something.'

The man shrugs and walks out. He waits several minutes and re-enters.

The receptionist smiles icily and asks: 'Yes sir, may we help you?'

'There's something wrong with my ear,' he says.

The receptionist nods with approval. 'And what is wrong with your ear, sir?'

'I can't piss out of it,' he replies.

It was New Year's Eve and the local pub was full as a bull's bum. As midnight approached, a lady stood up on the bar and said that it was time to get ready for the celebration.

'At the stroke of midnight I want every husband here to stand next to the one person who makes his life worth living.'

There was an expectant hush in the pub. Then, after what seemed an eternity, the old wall clock over the bar began to chime. And the crowd began to chant the countdown.

'Twelve, eleven, ten, nine, eight, seven, six, five, four, three, two, ONE!'

Suddenly there was a lot of movement as the husbands made sure they were standing next to the one person who made their life worth living. And as everyone began to sing 'Should auld acquaintance be forgot,' the bartender was almost crushed to death.

**A** ten-year-old swaggered into the pub and demanded of the barmaid: 'A double Scotch on the rocks.'

'A double Scotch on the rocks? What do you want to do? Get me into trouble?' the barmaid asked.

'Maybe later,' the kid said. 'Right now, I just want the Scotch.'

**A** couple of blokes were standing in line at a fast-food restaurant, waiting to order their burgers and fries.

There was a sign posted over the till: 'No bills larger than $20 will be accepted'.

And one bloke said to another, 'If I had a bill larger than 20 bucks I wouldn't bloody well be eating here.'

### The Penguin Bumper Book of Australian Jokes

A couple of kids were wandering around Darling Harbour, looking at the lights and the boats and the passing parade, when suddenly one was attacked by a vicious Rottweiler. Responding in an instant, the other boy grabbed the Wok Pool's sandwich board and beat the dog to death with it.

A reporter from the *Daily Telegraph* was strolling by and witnessed the incident. He rushed over to interview the brave child.

'SYDNEY BOY SAVES FRIEND FROM VICIOUS ANIMAL', he started writing in his notebook.

'But I'm not from Sydney,' the little hero said.

'Sorry, I just assumed you were.' He started to write again, 'MELBOURNE VISITOR RESCUES BOY FROM HORRIFIC ATTACK'.

'I'm not from Melbourne either,' the boy said.

'Well, where are you from?'

'I'm from Brisbane,' said the boy.

The reporter started a new sheet in his notebook and wrote, 'YOUNG REDNECK MANIAC KILLS BELOVED FAMILY PET'.

**The Penguin Bumper Book of Australian Jokes**

Four proud fathers are playing a round of golf at Royal Melbourne. Three of them head to the first tee whilst the fourth goes into the clubhouse for a quick pee.

The three men start talking, boasting about their sons.

'My son is a home builder,' says the first, 'and so successful that he gave a friend a new home for nothing.'

The second man says, 'My son is a car salesman and now owns a multi-line dealership. He's so successful that he gave a friend a new Mercedes, with all the options.'

The third man, not wanting to be outdone, boasts that his son is a stockbroker, 'And he's doing so well that he gave his friend an entire stock portfolio.'

The fourth man returns from his pee and one of the blokes says, 'We've just been talking about our sons. Incidentally, how is yours doing?'

The fourth man replies quietly, almost sadly, 'Well, my son is gay and dances in a gay nightclub. Look, I'm not totally thrilled about it. But he's doing really well. His last three boyfriends gave him a house, a brand-new Mercedes and an entire stock portfolio.'

**The Penguin Bumper Book of Australian Jokes**

**A** group of girlfriends is on vacation when they see a five-storey hotel with a sign that reads: FOR WOMEN ONLY. Since they are without their boyfriends and husbands, they decide to go in.

The bouncer, a very attractive guy, explains to them how it works.

'We have five floors. Go up floor by floor, and once you find what you are looking for, you can stay there. It's easy to decide since each floor has a sign telling you what's inside.'

So they start going up, and on the first floor the sign reads: 'All the men here have it short and thin'.

The friends laugh and without hesitation move on to the next floor.

The sign on the second floor reads: 'All the men here have it long and thin'.

This still isn't good enough, so the friends continue on up.

They reach the third floor and the sign reads: 'All the men here have it short and thick'.

They still want to do better and so, knowing there are still two floors left, they continue on up.

On the fourth floor, the sign is perfect: 'All the men here have it long and thick'.

The women get all excited and are going in, when they realise that there is still one floor left.

Wondering what they're missing, they head on up to the fifth floor.

There they find a sign that reads: 'There are no men here. This floor was built only to prove that there is no way to please a woman.'

**A** dinner speaker was in such a hurry to get to his engagement that when he arrived and sat down at the head table, he suddenly realised that he had forgotten his false teeth. Turning to the man next to him, he said, 'I forgot my teeth.'

The man said, 'No problem.' With that, he reached into his pocket and pulled out a pair of false teeth. 'Try these,' he said.

The speaker tried them. 'Too loose,' he said.

The man then said, 'I have another pair . . . try these.'

The speaker tried them and responded, 'Too tight.'

The man was not taken aback at all. He then said, 'I have one more pair of false teeth – try them.'

The speaker said, 'They fit perfectly.'

With that he ate his meal and gave his address. After the dinner meeting was over, the speaker went to thank the man who had helped him.

'I want to thank you for coming to my aid. Where is your office? I've been looking for a good dentist.'

The man replied, 'I'm not a dentist. I'm the local undertaker!'

**C**orduroy pillows: They're making headlines!

**B**lack holes are where God divided by zero.

**A**ll those who believe in psychokinesis raise my hand.

**E**xcuses are like arses, everyone's got 'em and they all stink.

**The Penguin Bumper Book of Australian Jokes**

I tried sniffing Coke once, but the ice cubes got stuck in my nose.

A salesman telephoned a household, and a four-year-old boy answered.

The conversation went thus:

Salesman: 'May I speak to your mother?'

Boy: 'She's not here.'

Salesman: 'Well, is anyone else there?'

Boy: 'My sister.'

Salesman: 'OK, fine. May I speak to her?'

Boy: 'I guess so.'

At this point there was a very long silence on the phone. Then:

Boy: 'Hello?'

Salesman: 'It's you. I thought you were going to find your sister.'

Boy: 'I did. The trouble is, I can't get her out of the playpen.'

# The Penguin Bumper Book of Australian Jokes

**A** woman from Victoria purchased a piece of timberland in New South Wales. There was a large gum tree on one of the highest points in the tract. She wanted to get a good view of her land so she started to climb it. As she neared the top, she encountered a wedge-tailed eagle, which attacked her.

In her haste to escape, the lady slid down the tree to the ground and got many splinters in her private parts. In considerable pain, she hurried to the nearest doctor. He listened to her story, then told her to go into the examining room and he would see if he could help her. She sat and waited for three hours before the doctor reappeared.

The lady, now angry, demanded, 'What took you so long?'

The unperturbed doctor replied, 'Well, I had to get permits from the Environmental Protection Agency, the National Parks people and the Bureau of Land Management before I could remove old-growth timber from a recreational area.'

**The Penguin Bumper Book of Australian Jokes**

**A** guy walks into a petrol station and buys a pack of cigarettes. He pulls one out and starts smoking it.

The cashier says, 'Excuse me, sir, but you can't smoke in here.'

The guy says, 'Don't you think it's kind of dumb that I can buy them here but can't smoke them here?'

And the cashier replies, 'Not at all . . . we also sell condoms.'

**A** young bloke walks into a post office one day to see a middle-aged, balding man standing at the counter methodically placing 'Love' stamps on bright pink envelopes with hearts all over them. The balding man then takes out a perfume bottle and starts spraying them all.

His curiosity getting the better of him, the young bloke goes up to the balding man and asks him what he's doing. The balding man says, 'I'm sending out 1000 Valentine cards signed, "Guess who?"'

'But why?' asks the young man.

'I'm a divorce lawyer.'

**A** blonde went to her letterbox several times before it was even time for the postman to make his delivery.

A neighbour asked about her repeated trips.

She said, 'My computer keeps telling me I have mail.'

**E**very year at the state fair Paul entered the lottery for the brand-new truck – and lost. This year, he told his friend David he wasn't going to bother entering.

'What kind of attitude is that?' asked David.

He leaned closer and whispered, 'What you need, pal, is faith. Look around and see if the good Lord sends you a message.'

Strolling around the fair, Paul grew more and more despondent as the drawing neared. Nothing struck him – no divine inspiration, no sign from God.

Finally, while he was passing old Mrs Kelleher's pie stand, he glanced over and saw the woman bending down. She wasn't wearing any panties, and suddenly her arse began to glow. All of a sudden, a finger of flame came from the skies and, without her even knowing it, used her arse as a table. The fiery finger etched a seven on each cheek.

Thanking God, Paul rushed to the raffle booth and played the number 77. A few minutes later, the draw was held. And once again Paul lost.

The winning number was 707.

A dyslectic cop is severely reprimanded by his captain because the spelling on his police reports is incomprehensible. 'How can you expect anyone to read this? If you file just one more document with any – and I mean ANY – words misspelt, you are going on report!' screamed the captain.

The cop vows not to make any more mistakes. The next day he is in his patrol car when a report of a traffic accident comes over his two-way radio. He arrives at the scene to discover a head-on collision. The cop takes out his notebook and begins to write, taking care to spell each word correctly.

'One, O-N-E. Ford, F-O-R-D. In the ditch, D-I-T-C-H.'

'That's good,' thinks the cop, as he walks across the street to the other vehicle.

'One, O-N-E. Holden, H-O-L-D-E-N. In the ditch, D-I-T-C-H.'

'I'm doing OK,' says the cop out loud as he confidently walks to the middle of the highway – and discovers a decapitated head.

'One, O-N-E. Head, H-E-A-D. In the boulevard, B-O-L . . . B-L-U . . . B-O-L-L . . . B-I-L . . .'

Finally, he looks around, kicks the head with his boot, and writes, 'One head in the D-I-T-C-H'.

**A** bloke was forced to take a day off from work to appear for a minor traffic offence. He grew increasingly restless as he waited hour after endless hour for his case to be heard.

When his name was called late in the afternoon, he stood before the magistrate only to hear that the court would be adjourned for the rest of the afternoon and he'd have to return the next day.

'What for?' he snapped at the magistrate.

His honour, equally irked by a tedious day and the sharp query, roared out loud, 'Twenty dollars contempt of court! That's why!'

Then, noticing the man checking his wallet, the magistrate relented, 'That's alright. You don't have to pay now.'

The young man replied, 'I know. But I'm just seeing if I have enough for two more words.'

**A** recently married minister went to his congregation, informed them of his wife's pregnancy and asked for a raise that would allow him a reasonable salary for his new circumstances.

After deliberation, it was agreed that the increase in family size warranted the raise.

After six births in six years, the congregants called a meeting to complain that the cost was becoming burdensome.

Things got contentious.

Finally, the minister stood at the altar and said, a little angrily, 'Having children is an act of God!'

'Snow and rain are acts of God too,' a man at the back of the room said, 'But most of us wear rubbers.'

**A** prominent young lawyer was on his way to court to begin arguments on a complex lawsuit, when he suddenly found himself at the Gates of Heaven. St Peter started to escort him inside when he began to protest that his untimely death must be some sort of mistake.

'I'm much too young to die! I'm only 35!' St Peter agreed that 35 did seem a bit young to be entering the pearly gates, and agreed to check on his case.

St Peter returned, and said to the attorney, 'I'm afraid that the mistake must be yours, my son. We verified your age on the basis of the number of hours you've billed to your clients, and you're at least 108.'

**A** successful businessman flew to Melbourne's Crown Casino for the weekend to gamble. He lost the shirt off his back and had nothing left but a dollar and the return-half of his round-trip ticket. So if he just got to Tullamarine, he could get himself home to Sydney.

He went out to the front of the casino where there

was a taxi waiting. He got in and explained his situation to the cabbie and promised to send the driver money when he arrived home. He offered him his credit-card numbers, his driver's-licence number, his address, etc. But to no avail.

The cabbie said, 'If you don't have $30, get the hell out of my cab!'

So the businessman was forced to hitchhike to the airport, and was just in time to catch his flight.

A year later the businessman, having worked long and hard to regain his financial success, returned to Crown Casino, and this time won big. Feeling pretty good, he went out to the taxi rank, and who should he see at the end of a long line of cabs, but the bloke who'd refused to give him a ride when he was down on his luck.

The businessman thought for a moment about how he could get back at the bastard.

He got in the first cab in the line, 'How much for a ride to Tulla?' he asked.

'Thirty bucks,' came the reply.

'And how much for you to go down on me on the way?'

'Get out of my taxi, you poofter!'

The businessman got into the back of each cab in

the line and asked the same questions with the same result, getting kicked out of each taxi.

When he got to his 'friend' at the back of the line, he jumped in and asked, 'How much for a ride to the airport?'

The cabbie replied, 'Thirty bucks.'

'The businessman said, 'OK,' and off they went.

Then, as they drove slowly past the long line of cabs, the businessman gave a big smile and the thumbs-up sign to each driver.

**P**roudly showing off his new apartment to friends late one night, the bloke led the way to his bedroom, which had a big brass gong on the wall.

'What's that big brass gong for?' asked one of the guests.

'That's the talking clock,' the man replied.

'How does it work?'

'Watch,' the man said, giving it an ear-shattering pound with a hammer.

And someone on the other side of the wall

screamed, 'For fuck's sake, it's ten past three in the fucking morning!!'

A primary teacher starts a new job at a school in Canterbury and, trying to make a good impression on her first day, explains to her class that she is a Canterbury-Bankstown fan. She asks her students to raise their hands if they, too, are Bulldogs fans.

Everyone in the class raises their hand except one little girl. The teacher looks at the girl with surprise and says, 'Mary, why didn't you raise your hand?'

'Because I'm not a Bulldogs fan,' she replied.

The teacher, shocked, asked, 'Well, if you're not a Bulldogs fan, then who are you a fan of?'

'I'm a Dragons fan, and proud of it,' Mary replied.

The teacher could not believe her ears.

'Mary, why, please tell, are you a Dragons fan?'

'Because my mum and dad are from Kogarah and my mum is a Dragons fan and my dad is a Dragons fan, so I'm a Dragons fan too.'

'Well,' said the teacher, in an obviously annoyed tone, 'that's no reason for you to be a Dragons fan. You don't have to be just like your parents all the time. What if your mum was a prostitute and your dad was a drug addict and a car thief – what would you be then?'

'Then,' Mary smiled, 'I'd be a Bulldogs fan.'

### RULES FOR MY BOSS

**1.** Never give me work in the morning. Always wait until four o'clock and then bring it to me. The challenge of a deadline is refreshing.

**2.** If it's really a rush job, run in and interrupt me every ten minutes to inquire how it's going. That helps. Or even better, hover behind me, advising me at every keystroke.

**3.** Always leave without telling anyone where you're going. It gives me a chance to be creative when someone asks where you are.

**4.** If my arms are full of papers, boxes, books or supplies, don't open the door for me. I need to learn how to function as a paraplegic, and opening doors with no arms is good training in case I should ever be injured and lose all use of my limbs.

**5.** If you give me more than one job to do, don't tell me which is the priority. I'm psychic.

**6.** Do your best to keep me late. I adore this office and really have nowhere to go or anything to do. I have no life beyond work.

**The Penguin Bumper Book of Australian Jokes**

**7.** If a job I do pleases you, keep it a secret. If that gets out, it could mean a promotion.

**8.** If you don't like my work, tell everyone.

**9.** If you have special instructions for a job, don't write them down. In fact, save them until the job is almost done. No use confusing me with useful information.

**10.** Never introduce me to people you're with. I have no right to know anything. In the corporate food chain, I am plankton. When you refer to them later, my shrewd deductions will identify them.

**11.** Be nice to me only when the job I'm doing for you could really change your life and send you straight to manager's hell.

**The Penguin Bumper Book of Australian Jokes**

**12.** Tell me all your little problems. No one else has any and it's nice to know someone is less fortunate. I especially like the story about having to pay so much tax on the bonus cheque you received for being such a good manager.

**13.** Wait until my yearly review and THEN tell me what my goals SHOULD have been. Give me a mediocre performance rating with a cost of living increase. After all, I'm not here for the money.

**NOTICE OF REVOCATION OF INDEPENDENCE, PUBLISHED ON THE OCCASION OF THE TIED VOTE IN FLORIDA . . .**

To the citizens of the United States of America:
In the light of your failure to elect a president of the USA and thus to govern yourselves, we hereby

give notice of the revocation of your independence, effective today.

Her Sovereign Majesty Queen Elizabeth II will resume monarchical duties over all states, commonwealths and other territories. Except Utah, which she does not fancy.

Your new prime minister (the Rt. Hon. Tony Blair, MP, for the 97.85 per cent of you who have until now been unaware that there is a world outside your borders) will appoint a Minister for America without the need for further elections. Congress and the Senate will be disbanded. A questionnaire will be circulated next year to determine whether any of you noticed.

To aid in the transition to a British Crown Dependency, we have introduced the following rules with immediate effect:

**1.** You should look up 'revocation' in the Oxford English Dictionary. Then look up 'aluminium'. Check the pronunciation guide. You will be amazed at just how wrongly you have been pronouncing it. Generally, you should raise your vocabulary to acceptable levels. Look up 'vocabulary'. Using the same

### The Penguin Bumper Book of Australian Jokes

27 words interspersed with filler noises such as 'like' and 'you know' is an unacceptable and inefficient form of communication. Look up 'interspersed'.

**2.** There is no such thing as 'US English'. We will let Microsoft know on your behalf.

**3.** You should learn to distinguish English and Australian accents. It really isn't that hard.

**4.** Hollywood will be required occasionally to cast English actors as the good guys.

**5.** You should relearn your original national anthem, 'God Save the Queen', but only after fully carrying out task one. We would not want you to get confused and give up halfway through.

**6.** You should stop playing 'American football'. There is only one kind of football. What you refer to as 'American football' is not a very good game. The 2.15 per cent of you who are aware that there is a world outside your borders may have noticed that no-one else plays 'American football'. You will no longer be allowed to play it, and should instead play proper football. Initially, it would be best if you played with the girls. It is a difficult game. Those of you brave enough will, in time, be allowed to play rugby (which is similar to 'American football', but does not involve stopping for a rest every twenty seconds or wearing full Kevlar body armour like nancies). We are hoping to get together at least a US rugby sevens side by 2005.

**7.** You should declare war on Quebec and France, using nuclear weapons if they give you any 'merde'. The 97.85 per cent of you who are not aware that there is a world outside your borders should count yourselves lucky. The Russians have never been the bad guys. 'Merde' is French for shit.

# The Penguin Bumper Book of Australian Jokes

**8.** The fourth of July is no longer a public holiday. The eighth of November will be a new national holiday, but only in England. It will be called 'Indecisive Day'.

**9.** All American cars are hereby banned. They are crap and it is for your own good. When we show you German cars, you will understand what we mean.

**10.** Please tell us who killed JFK. It's been driving us crazy.

— *For and on behalf of Her Majesty's government.*

**A** man is walking home alone late one night when he hears a BUMP . . . BUMP . . . BUMP . . . behind him.

Walking faster, he looks back and makes out the image of an upright coffin banging its way down the middle of the street towards him.

BUMP . . . BUMP . . . BUMP . . .

Terrified, the man begins to run towards his home, the coffin bouncing quickly behind him . . .

BUMP . . . BUMP . . . BUMP . . .

He runs up to his door, fumbles with his keys, opens the door, rushes in, slams and locks the door behind him.

However, the coffin crashes through his door, with the lid of the coffin clapping . . .

Clappity-BUMP . . . clappity-BUMP . . . clappity-BUMP . . . on the heels of the terrified man.

Rushing upstairs to the bathroom, the man locks himself in. His heart is pounding; his head is reeling, his breath is coming in sobbing gasps.

With a loud CRASH the coffin breaks down the door, bumping and clapping towards him.

The man screams and reaches for something, anything . . . but all he can find is a bottle of cough syrup!

Desperate, he throws the cough syrup at the coffin . . .

. . . the coffin stops.

The LAPD, FBI and the CIA were all keen to prove that they were the best at apprehending criminals. The President decided to give them a test. He released a white rabbit into a forest and each of them had to catch it.

The CIA went in. They placed animal informants throughout the forest. They questioned all the plant and mineral witnesses. After three months of extensive investigations, they concluded that rabbits do not exist.

The FBI went in. After two weeks with no leads they bombed the forest, killing everything in it, including the rabbit. They made no apologies; the rabbit had it coming.

The LAPD went in. They came out after just two hours with a badly beaten bear. The bear was yelling, 'OK, OK, I'm a rabbit, I'm a rabbit!'

The Australian Prime Minister heard about this and decided to test Australia's law enforcement agencies. So he released a white rabbit into the forest just outside Canberra.

The Victorian police went in. They returned

15 minutes later with a koala, a kangaroo and a tree fern all shot to pieces. 'They looked like dangerous rabbits, we had to act in self-defence,' was their explanation.

The NSW police went in. Surveillance tapes later revealed top-ranking officers and rabbits dancing naked around a gum tree stoned out of their brains.

The Queensland police went in. Shortly afterwards, they came out driving a brand-new Mercedes, scantily clad rabbits draped all over it. The Queensland premier congratulated them on maintaining traditional family values.

The NCA couldn't catch the rabbit, but promised that if they were given a budget increase they could recover 90 million dollars from the rabbit in unpaid taxes and proceeds of crime.

The WA police went into the forest and caught the white rabbit, but the rabbit inexplicably hanged itself in the cell when the attending officer 'slipped out momentarily' for a cup of coffee.

The NT and SA police joined forces to belt the crap out of every rabbit in the forest except the white one. They knew the black ones caused all the trouble.

The AFP refused to go in. They examined the issues, particularly cost, and decided that because of the low priority, and cost to the organisation as a whole, the matter should be rejected and returned to the referring department for investigation.

ASIO went to the wrong forest.

'My father is better than your father!' said Billy.

'No, he's not!' replied Johnny.

'My brother is better than your brother!' Billy said.

'He is not! He is not!' yelled Johnny.

'My mother is better than your mother!' Billy bellowed.

A long pause ensued, then Johnny said, 'Well, you've got me there. I've heard my Dad say the same thing.'

A gorilla escapes from the zoo and after three weeks, the zoo keepers give up looking for him. Some time later, a man calls the zoo complaining of a gorilla in a tree in his backyard. The zoo keeper rushes right over. When he arrives, he has a net, a baseball bat, a shotgun and a dachshund.

The man asks what the items are for. He's told, 'I'm going to climb the tree and hit the gorilla on the head with the baseball bat. When he falls out of the tree, you throw the net over him, and the dachshund will go straight for his balls.' The man asks, 'But what's the shotgun for?'

The zoo keeper answers, 'If I miss the gorilla and fall out of the tree, you shoot the dachshund.'

## A PROCLAMATION FOR THE AUSTRALIAN REPUBLIC

We, the people of the broad brown land of Oz, wish to be recognised as a free nation of blokes, sheilas and the occasional boong. We come from many lands although a few too many of us come from New Zealand and, although we live in the best country in the world, we reserve the right to bitch and moan about it whenever we bloody like.

# The Penguin Bumper Book of Australian Jokes

We are One Nation but we're divided into many States.

First, there's Victoria, named after a queen who didn't believe in lesbians. Victoria is the realm of Mossimo turtlenecks, caffelatte, grand final day and big horseraces. Its capital is Melbourne, whose chief marketing pitch is that it's 'livable'. At least that's what they think. The rest of us think it's too bloody cold and wet.

Next, there's New South Wales, the realm of pastel shorts, macchiato with sugar, thin books read quickly and millions of dancing queens. Its capital, Sydney, has more queens than any other city in the world, and is proud of it. Its mascot is the Bondi lifesaver, who pulls his Speedos up his crack to keep the left and right side of his brain separate.

Down south we have Tasmania, a state based on the notion that the family who bonks together, stays together. In Tassie, everyone gets an extra chromosome at conception. Maps of the state bring smiles to the sternest faces. It holds the world record for a single mass-shooting, which the Yanks can't seem to beat no matter how often they try.

South Australia is the province of half-decent reds, festivals of foreigners and bizarre axe murders.

SA is the state of innovation – where else can you so effectively reuse country bank vaults and barrels as in Snowtown, just out of Adelaide (also named after a queen). They had the Grand Prix, but lost it when the views of Adelaide sent Formula One drivers to sleep at the wheel.

Western Australia is too far from anywhere to be relevant in this document. Its main claim to fame is that it doesn't have daylight saving because, if it did, all the men would get erections on the bus on the way to work. WA was the last state to stop importing convicts, and many of them still work there in government and business.

The Northern Territory is the red heart of our land. Outback plains, sheep stations the size of Europe, kangaroos, jackaroos, emus, Ulurus and dusty kids with big smiles. It also has the highest beer consumption of anywhere on the planet, and its creek beds have the highest aluminium content of anywhere too. Although the Territory is the centrepiece of our national culture, few of us live there and the rest prefer to fly over it on our way to Bali.

And then there's Queensland. While any mention of God seems silly in a document defining a nation of half-arsed agnostics, it is worth noting that God probably made Queensland. Why he filled it with dickheads remains a mystery.

Oh yes, and then there's Canberra. The least said the better.

We, the citizens of Oz, are united by the Pacific Highway whose treacherous twists and turns kill more of us each year than die by murder. We are united in our lust for international recognition, so desperate for praise we leap in joy when a ragtag gaggle of corrupt IOC officials tells us Sydney is better than Beijing.

We are united in a democracy so flawed that a political party, albeit a redneck, gun-toting one, can get a million votes and still not win one seat in Federal Parliament while bloody Brian Harradine can get 24 000 votes and run the whole country.

Not that we're whingeing. We leave that to our Pommy immigrants. We want to make 'no worries, mate' our national phrase, 'she'll be right, mate' our national attitude and 'Waltzing Matilda' our national anthem. (So what if it's about a sheep-stealing crim who commits suicide.)

We love sport so much our newsreaders can read the death toll from a sailing race and still tell us who's winning. And we're the best in the world at all the sports that count, like cricket, netball, rugby, AFL, roo-shooting, two-up and horseracing.

We also have the biggest rock, the tastiest pies, the blackest Aborigines and the worst-dressed Olympians in the known universe. We shoot, we root, we vote. We are girt by sea and pissed by lunchtime. And even though we might seem a racist, closed-minded, sports-obsessed little people, at least we're better than the Kiwis.

The CIA had an opening for an assassin. After all the background checks, interviews and testing, there were three finalists: two men and a woman.

For the final test, the CIA agents took one of the men to a large metal door and handed him a gun. 'We must know that you will follow instructions, no matter what the circumstances. Inside this room you will find your wife sitting in a chair. Kill her!'

The man said, 'You can't be serious. I could never shoot my wife.'

The agent said, 'Then you're not the right man for this job.'

The second man was given the same instructions. He took the gun and went into the room. All was quiet for about five minutes. Then the man came out with tears in his eyes. 'I tried, but I can't kill my wife.'

The agent said, 'You don't have what it takes. Get your wife and go home.'

Finally, it was the woman's turn. She was given the same instructions to kill her husband. She took the gun and went into the room. Shots were heard, one shot after another. The agents heard screaming, crashing and banging on the walls.

After a few minutes, all was quiet. The door opened slowly and there stood the woman. She wiped the sweat from her brow and said, 'This gun is loaded with blanks. I had to beat him to death with the chair.'

**S**teve went to confession and told the priest that he had been with five different women the night before, each woman another man's fiancée or wife.

The priest told Steve to go home and squeeze three lemons and two limes into a cup of water and drink it.

Steve asked the priest if that would give him absolution.

The priest replied, 'No, but it should wipe that grin off your face.'

**T**hree old men are at the doctor for a memory test. The doctor says to the first old man, 'What is three times three?'

'Two hundred and seventy-four,' is his reply.

The doctor worriedly says to the second man, 'It's your turn. What is three times three?'

'Tuesday,' replies the second man.

The doctor sadly says to the third man, 'OK, your turn. What's three times three?'

'Nine,' says the third man.

'That's great,' exclaims the doctor. 'How did you get that?'

'Jeez Doc, it's pretty simple,' says the third man, 'I just subtracted 274 from Tuesday.'

A little old couple walked slowly into McDonald's one cold winter evening.

The little old man placed an order, received his food – one cheeseburger, a small fries and a Coke – and then took it to their table. He unwrapped the burger and carefully cut it in half. He placed one half in front of his wife. Then he carefully counted out the fries, divided them into two piles and neatly placed one pile in front of his wife.

He took a sip of the Coke. His wife took a sip. She set the cup down between them. The man began to eat his few bites of burger then turned to his fries.

Young Kevin had been watching and went to their table to offer to buy them another meal. 'No, no,' said the little old man. 'We're fine. We're used to sharing everything.'

Then he noticed that the little old lady hadn't eaten a bite. She just sat there watching her husband eat and occasionally taking a sip of the Coke.

'Why aren't you eating?' Kevin asked. 'What are you waiting for?'

She smiled, 'The teeth.'

A wealthy businessman decides to go on a safari in Africa. He takes his faithful pet dog along for company. The dog starts chasing butterflies and before long is lost. Wandering about he notices a leopard heading rapidly in his direction with the obvious intention of having lunch.

The dog thinks, 'Oh damn, I'm in deep shit now.' Then he notices some bones on the ground close by, and immediately settles down to chew on the bones with his back to the approaching cat.

Just as the leopard is about to leap, the dog says loudly, 'Jesus, that was one delicious leopard. I wonder if there are any more around here.'

Hearing this the leopard halts his attack and slinks away into the trees. 'Whew!' says the leopard, 'that was close. That dog nearly had me.'

A monkey watches the whole scene from a nearby tree. He reckons he can put this knowledge to good use. So, off he goes. The monkey catches up with the leopard and spills the beans. The leopard is furious at being made a fool. 'Here monkey, hop on my back and see what's going to happen to that bloody dog.'

The dog sees the leopard coming with the monkey on his back, and thinks 'What the hell am I going to do now?' Instead of running, the dog sits with his back to his attackers pretending he hasn't seen them. And when they get close enough to hear, the dog says, 'Where's that damn monkey? I just can't trust him. I sent him off half an hour ago to bring me another leopard, and he's still not back!'

**A** bloke buys several sheep, hoping to breed them for wool. After several weeks he notices that none of the sheep are pregnant, and calls a vet for help. The vet tells him that he should try artificial insemination. The bloke doesn't have the slightest idea what this means but, not wanting to display his ignorance, only asks the vet how he will know when the sheep are pregnant. The vet tells him that they will stop standing around and will, instead, lie down and wallow in grass.

The bloke hangs up and gives it some thought. He comes to the conclusion that artificial insemination means he has to impregnate the sheep. So, he loads the sheep into his truck, drives them to a lonely place, has sex with them all, brings them back and goes to bed.

Next morning, he wakes and looks out at the sheep. They are all still standing. So he loads them in the truck again, drives to a secluded paddock, bangs each sheep twice for good measure, brings them back and goes to bed. Next morning, he wakes to find the sheep still standing around.

'One more try,' he tells himself. He spends all day shagging the sheep and, upon returning home, collapses into bed.

The next morning, he cannot even raise his head from the pillow to look at the sheep. He asks his wife to look out and tell him if the sheep are lying in the grass. 'No,' she says, 'they're all in the truck and one of them is honking the horn.'

William went to a psychiatrist. 'Doc,' he said, 'I've got trouble. Every time I get into bed, I think there's somebody under it. Then, when I get under the bed, I think there's somebody on top of it. Doc, you've gotta help me, I'm going crazy!'

'Just put yourself in my hands for two years,' said the psychiatrist. 'Come to me three times a week and I'll cure your fears.'

'How much do you charge?'

'My fee is $100 per visit.'

'That's awfully expensive, Doc,' reckoned William. 'Let me sleep on it and I'll get back to you.'

Six months later the doctor and William crossed paths. 'Why didn't you ever come back to see me again?' asked the psychiatrist.

'For $100 a visit? Heck, a bartender cured me for $10.'

'How did he do that?' asked the psychiatrist.

'He told me to cut the legs off the bed!'

**The Penguin Bumper Book of Australian Jokes**

## NEW ENTRIES FOR THE MACQUARIE DICTIONARY

ABDICATE: to give up all hope of ever having a flat stomach.

ESPLANADE: to attempt an explanation while drunk.

WILLY-NILLY: impotent.

FLABBERGASTED: appal over how much weight you have gained.

NEGLIGENT: describes a condition in which you absentmindedly answer the door in your nightie.

LYMPH: to walk with a lisp.

GARGOYLE: an olive-flavoured mouthwash.

COFFEE: a person who is coughed upon.

FLATULENCE: the emergency vehicle that picks you up after you are run over by a steamroller.

BALDERDASH: a rapidly receding hairline.

TESTICLE: a humorous question on an exam.

SEMANTICS: pranks conducted by young men studying for the priesthood, including such things as gluing the pages of the priest's prayer book together just before vespers.

RECTITUDE: the formal, dignified demeanour assumed by a proctologist immediately before he examines you.

OYSTER: a person who sprinkles his conversation with Yiddish expressions.

CIRCUMVENT: the opening in the front of boxer shorts.

SARCHASM: the gulf between the author of sarcastic wit and the reader who doesn't get it.

REINTARNATION: coming back to life as a hillbilly.

GIRAFFITI: vandalism spray-painted very high.

FOREPLOY: any misrepresentation about yourself for the purpose of obtaining sex.

### The Penguin Bumper Book of Australian Jokes

INOCULATTE: to take coffee intravenously.

OSTEOPORNOSIS: a degenerate disease.

KARMAGEDDON: it's like, when everybody is sending off all these really bad vibes, right? And then, like, the earth explodes and it's like, a serious bummer.

GLIBIDO: all talk and no action.

DOPELER EFFECT: the tendency of stupid ideas to seem smarter when they come at you rapidly.

INTAXICATION: euphoria at getting a refund from the taxation office, which lasts until you realise it was your money to start with.

**T**ommy Shaughnessy enters the confessional box and says, 'Bless me Father, for I have sinned. I have been with a loose woman.'

The priest asks, 'Is that you, little Tommy Shaughnessy?'

'Yes, Father, it is.'

'And who was the woman you were with?'

'Sure and I can't be tellin' you, Father. I don't want to ruin her reputation.'

'Well, Tommy, I'm sure to find out sooner or later, so you may as well tell me now. Was it Brenda O'Malley?'

'I cannot say.'

'Was it Patricia Kelly?'

'I'll never tell.'

'Was it Liz Shannon?'

'I'm sorry, but I'll not name her.'

'Was it Cathy Morgan?'

'My lips are sealed.'

'Was it Fiona McDonald, then?'

'Please, Father, I cannot tell you.'

The priest sighs in frustration. 'You're a steadfast lad, Tommy Shaughnessy, and I admire that. But you've sinned, and you must atone. Be off with you now.'

Tommy walks back to his pew. His friend Sean slides over and whispers, 'What'd you get?'

'Five good leads,' says Tommy.

A couple of blokes are heading up the Birdsville Track in their Land Cruiser when they blow a tyre. At the same time, they blow a radiator hose. And a head gasket. They realise they're in a bit of trouble.

But they do the right thing and stick with the vehicle. They know that, sooner or later, someone will be along. And that the worst thing they could do is head off in what might well prove to be the wrong direction.

Trouble is, nobody comes. And they run out of drinking water. There's only a few drops left in their radiator, which are bright green with coolant.

The sun beats down on their heads and, desperate and faintly delirious, they start walking.

Soon the road has disappeared and they're climbing up and down sand dunes, the situation getting worse and worse. And the thirst! Intolerable.

Then, on a distant sand dune, they see an extraordinary sight. A row of brightly coloured tents. If they didn't know better they'd swear they'd stumbled upon a bazaar.

They go to the first tent where they're welcomed

# The Penguin Bumper Book of Australian Jokes

by a couple of belly dancers and an old gentleman in a burnous. 'Water! Water!' they croak.

'Sorry, effendi, but we only have custard and jelly.'

'Custard and bloody jelly!?? What use is that when you're dying of dehydration?'

So they go to the next tent where they're greeted by more dancing girls and another charming Arab.

'Water! Water!'

'Forgive me,' says the Arab, 'but I can't offer you water. On the other hand, you are welcome to share my jelly and custard.'

'Jelly and bloody custard!?'

And they use their last atom of strength to get to the third tent where, once again, there's a warm welcome . . . and custard and jelly.

'Look, we'll pay anything. Anything!!! But for God's sake, give us some water!'

By now all the belly dancers and Arabs are clustering around them, tut-tutting sympathetically. 'We are very, very sorry. But all we have is custard and jelly, jelly and custard.'

So the two blokes stagger off towards inevitable death.

'That was very, very strange, wasn't it,' says one bloke to the other.

'It certainly was a trifle bazaar.'

**J**ust before the presidential election, Al Gore was out jogging (followed by jogging cameramen and jogging secret agents) when he saw a little boy sitting on the kerb with a cardboard box. In the hope of getting a good photo opportunity, he ran to the child and said, 'What's in the box?' And the little boy said, 'Kittens. They're brand-new kittens.'

Al Gore laughed and said, 'What kind of kittens are they?'

'Democrats,' the child said.

'Isn't that cute?' said Al, and jogged off.

A couple of days later, Gore was running with Bill Clinton – followed by an even bigger contingent of media and security. And he saw the same little boy with the same box sitting on the same kerb. And Al said to Bill, 'You've gotta check this out.'

And they jogged over to the child. 'Look in the box, Bill, isn't that cute? Look at those little kittens. Hey, kid, tell the President what kind of kittens they are.'

The boy replied, 'They're Republicans.'

'Woooo,' said Al, 'I came by here the other day and you said they were Democrats.'

'Well,' the kid said, 'their eyes are open now.'

## GEORGE W. BUSH'S LIPS ARE WHERE WORDS GO TO DIE

The Bush administration is going to be called the Wizard of Oz Administration, because Dick Cheney needs a heart and George W. needs a brain!

- Thousands of people are expected for the 15th annual Burning Man festival this year in Black Rock Desert near Reno, Nevada. This is the big hippie festival where people run around naked, drink and get stoned, or as George W. Bush likes to call it, get ready to run for president.

- While campaigning in South Carolina, George W. Bush made a surprise appearance at a meeting of high school football coaches. It was a real surprise because Dubya wasn't much of a football player in high school. While the rest of the team was practising for the big game, he was on the bench trying to sort the out-of-bounds lines.

- Doctors attending a conference in New Orleans sponsored by the American Stroke Association saw a demonstration of a new device that uses laser beams to break up blood clots deep inside the brain. The procedure works great but it's still pretty dangerous. One slip of the laser and the patient can turn into a Texan president.

- George W. Bush raised twice as much money from the entertainment business as Bob Dole did when he ran for president in 1996. Hollywood types love George W. Between the coke, the booze and the naked dancing on the bar, he's the first candidate who represents their family values.

- George W. Bush says that illiteracy among school children amounts to a 'national emergency' and he'll spend $5 billion over five years to address the issue. George W. Bush and illiteracy. This is the new definition of 'the blind leading the blind'.

- After Boris Yeltsin resigned as president of Russia, the candidates had only three months to get ready for the election to choose his successor. Three months! It took George W. Bush three months just to figure out that there were no fraternities to join in the Electoral College.

- George W. Bush targeted America Online users with interactive banner ads that appeared automatically on top of Web pages. Bush didn't have anything to do with the ad. His idea of appealing to people who use the Internet was to change his name to George WWW Bush.

- George W. Bush continues to mangle the English language. He told parents worried about too much profanity and violence on TV to 'Put the "off" button on.' It's getting so bad, the 'W' in his name now stands for 'What'd he say?'

- Executives at Britannia.com say the free online encyclopaedia is no longer crashing every time too many people try to access the website. In fact, now the only time the system gets overloaded is when a reporter asks George W. Bush a question about world affairs.

- According to a new survey, the United States is the third-happiest country in the world overall, behind Denmark and Australia. When asked why he thought the US was behind Denmark, George W. Bush said he didn't know, 'But we're ahead of Wal-mark and K-Mark.'

- According to the Islamic Republic News Agency, authorities in Iran have executed seven drug traffickers and seized more than 1.5 tonnes of illegal narcotics in the past six months. In a related story, Iran is the first foreign country George W. Bush was able to name the leader of.

**A**n Anglican minister had a kitten that climbed up a tree in his backyard and was afraid to come down. The minister coaxed, offered warm milk etc. The kitten would not come down. The tree wasn't sturdy enough to climb, so the minister decided that if he tied one end of a rope to his car, another to a branch, and drove till the tree bent down, he could reach up and get the kitten.

He did all this, checking his progress in the mirror frequently, then figured if he went just a little bit further, the tree would bend sufficiently for him to reach the kitten. But as he moved a little further forward . . . the rope broke.

The tree went 'boingg!', and the kitten instantly sailed through the air and out of sight. The minister felt terrible. He walked all over the neighbourhood asking people if they'd seen a little kitten, but nobody had.

So he prayed, 'Lord, I commit this kitten to your keeping,' and went on about his business.

A few days later he was at the grocery store and met one of his church members. He happened to look into her shopping trolley and was amazed to see cat food. Now, this woman was a cat hater and everyone knew it, so he asked her, 'Why are you buying cat food when you hate cats so much?'

She replied, 'You won't believe this,' and told him how her little girl had been begging her for a cat, but she kept refusing. Then, a few days before, the child had begged again, so Mum finally told her little girl, 'Well, if God gives you a cat, I'll let you keep it.'

She told the minister, 'I watched my child go out in the yard, get on her knees and ask God for a cat. And really, Reverend, you won't believe this, but I saw it with my own eyes. A kitten suddenly came flying out of the blue sky, with its paws spread out, and landed right in front of her!'

A city couple was camping on the shores of a lake. The young wife, very pulchritudinous, decided to give the locals a thrill by sunbathing in the nuddy.

'That's fine with me,' said her husband. 'I'm going to try to catch some fish for lunch.' And he headed off looking for a good spot.

About 30 minutes later he returned and found his wife in tears. One of her breasts had been painted green, the other red and her bottom was blue.

'What on earth!?'

'Some rednecks from town came and told me they don't allow any nudity around these parts. And they painted me!'

'Those bastards! I'll fix them!' And the husband headed for town and found the rednecks in the pub. 'Who's the arsehole who painted my wife red, green and blue?' he shouted.

A huge bloke, about six foot six, stepped forward, flexing the muscles on his immense arms so that his tattoos danced. 'I did!' he boomed. 'What have you got to say about it?'

And the husband said, 'I just wanted you to know that the first coat of paint is dry.'

**B**eryl went to the doctor for an examination. She got the lot, top to toe. He tested her blood pressure, her heartbeat. He looked down her throat, into her ears, up her nose, rubber-gloved her backside. Etc. etc. But he couldn't do her blood sugar because his little Glucometer wasn't working.

So he asked her to return in a couple of weeks 'and bring a specimen'. By then, he explained, his little gadget would be back from the repair shop.

She looked confused but agreed. On returning home her husband, Fred, asked how things went. Beryl said fine, but she had to go back in a couple of weeks 'with a specimen'.

Fred said, 'What's a specimen, Beryl?'

'I don't know, Fred. I was too embarrassed to ask.'

'Why don't you go next door and ask Shirley? Shirley knows everything,' said Fred.

So Beryl went next door and when she returned, about half an hour later, her clothing was torn and she had scratches and bruises all over. She'd even lost a few handfuls of hair.

'Jesus Christ! What happened to you?' asked Fred.

'Well, I went next door like you said to ask Shirley what a specimen was. She told me to piss in a bottle.

I told her to shit in her handbag. And one thing led to another.'

**A** woman meets a bloke in a bar. They talk, they connect, they end up leaving together.

They get to his place and, as he shows her around his flat, she notices that his bedroom is completely packed with teddy bears. Hundreds of small bears on a shelf all the way along the floor, medium-sized ones on a shelf a little higher, and huge bears on the top shelf along the wall.

The woman is very surprised that this guy would have a collection of teddy bears, especially one that's so extensive. But she decides not to mention this to him.

She turns to him . . . They kiss . . . And then they rip each other's clothes off and bonk like mad.

After an intense night of passion they are lying together in the afterglow. The woman rolls over and asks, smiling, 'Well, how was it?'

The bloke says, 'You can have any prize from the bottom shelf.'

Conscience is what hurts when everything else feels so good.

Talk is cheap because supply exceeds demand.

Even if you are on the right track, you'll get run over if you just sit there.

Love is grand; divorce is a hundred grand.

I am in shape. Round is a shape.

**T**ime may be a great healer, but it's a lousy beautician.

**N**ever be afraid to try something new. Remember, amateurs built the ark. Professionals built the *Titanic*.

**T**wo men are in a doctor's office. Each of them is to get a vasectomy. The nurse comes into the room and tells both men, 'Strip and put on these gowns before going in to see the doctor.'

A few minutes later she returns and reaches into one man's gown. She proceeds to fondle and ultimately masturbate him. In shock, he asks, 'Why are you doing that?' To which she replies, 'We have to vacate the sperm from your system to have a clean procedure.'

The man, not wanting to be a problem and

enjoying it, allows her to complete her task. After she is through, she proceeds to the next man.

She starts to fondle the man as she had with the previous bloke, but then she drops to her knees and proceeds to give him oral sex.

The first man, seeing this, quickly responds, 'Hey! Why is it that I get a hand job and he gets a blow job?'

The nurse simply replies, 'That's the difference between bulk-billing and private insurance.'

A sky diver jumped from an aircraft but his parachute didn't open properly. Well, the pilot chute popped out but something was wrong with the main chute. So he fell to earth at a thousand miles an hour – straight into a garbage can. In a particularly embarrassing position, head down and arse up.

A couple of gays passed by. One of them looked at the man head first in the garbage can: 'Who threw out this arse? It's still usable.'

**A** salesman rang the bell at a suburban home, and the door was opened by a nine-year-old boy puffing on a long black cigar.

Hiding his amazement, the salesman asked the young man, 'Is your mother home?'

The boy took the cigar out of his mouth, flicked ashes on the carpet, and asked, 'What do you think?'

**N**ow that I'm 'older', here's what I've discovered:

**1.** I started out with nothing, and I still have most of it.

**2.** My wild oats have turned into prunes and All-bran.

**3.** Now I've finally got my head together, my body is falling apart.

**4.** Funny, I don't remember being absentminded.

**5.** All reports are in; life is now officially unfair.

**6.** If all is not lost, where is it?

**7.** It is easier to get older than it is to get wiser.

**8.** Some days you're the dog; some days you're the hydrant.

**9.** I wish the buck stopped here; I sure could use a few ...

**10.** Kids in the back seat cause accidents.

**11.** Accidents in the back seat cause ... kids.

**12.** It's hard to make a comeback when you haven't been anywhere.

**13.** The only time the world beats a path to your door is when you are in the bathroom.

**14.** If God wanted me to touch my toes, he would have put them on my knees.

**15.** When I'm finally holding all the cards, why does everyone decide to play chess?

**16.** It's not hard to meet expenses. They're everywhere.

**17.** These days I spend a lot of time thinking about the hereafter . . . I go somewhere to get something and then wonder what I'm here after.

The old priest was sick of all the people in his parish who kept confessing to adultery. One Sunday in the pulpit, he said, 'If I hear one more person confess to adultery, I'll quit!'

Well, everyone liked him, so they came up with a code word. Someone who had committed adultery would say they had 'fallen'.

This seemed to satisfy the old priest and things went well, until the priest died at a ripe old age. About a week after the new priest arrived, he visited the mayor of the town and seemed very concerned.

The priest said, 'You have to do something about the sidewalks in town. When people come into the confessional, they keep talking about having fallen.'

The mayor started to laugh, realising that no-one had told the new priest about the code word.

Before the mayor could explain, the priest shook an accusing finger at the mayor and said, 'I don't know what you're laughing about. Your wife fell three times this week!'

**P**oliticians and nappies have one thing in common. They should both be changed regularly and for the same reason.

**T**he scene is a cocktail party. The setting is stylish. The guests are glamorous. All except for a very, very unattractive woman who is desperately working the crowd, trying to find an unattached bloke.

She sees someone standing apart and zeros in. Seeing her coming he prepares for flight, but is too late.

'Hello,' she says.

'Hello,' he replies, cautiously.

'I haven't seen you around here before.'

'Well, I've been away.'

'Ooh, how exciting! Where were you? In Europe?'

'No,' says the bloke, trying to come up with a response that will get rid of her. 'As a matter of fact I've been in jail.'

'Really! And why were you in jail?'

'Well, 15 years ago I hacked my wife into pieces with a meat cleaver.' And he looks at her with cold, implacable eyes, trying to do a Hannibal Lecter impersonation.

'Then,' she says with a hopeful smile, 'that means you're single, right?'

A British man, a Frenchman and an American man are on a safari in Africa when they are taken prisoner by a savage group of villagers. As they're being brought to the village, they are told that death is their only option. However, they can choose how to kill themselves.

The British man requests a pistol and, crying out 'Long live the Queen!', he blows his brains out.

The other two watch in horror as the savages flay the man and make his skin into a canoe.

The Frenchman is next, and he requests a sabre. 'Vive la France!' he cries out as he disembowels himself.

The American guy watches again as they make his skin into a canoe.

The American requests a fork with which to kill himself. As soon as it is handed to him, he starts stabbing himself violently, screaming, 'So much for your fucking canoe!'

Two Irishmen walk into a pet shop and head straight to the bird section. Gerry says to Paddy, 'Dat's dem.' The salesman comes over and asks if he can help.

'Yeah, we'll have four of dem dere birds in dat cage op dere,' says Gerry. 'Put dem in a peeper bag.' The salesman does and they pay for the birds and leave the shop.

They get into Gerry's van and drive high up into the hills and stop at the top of a cliff with a 500-foot drop. 'Dis looks loike a grand place, eh?' says Gerry. 'Oh, yeh, dis looks good,' replies Paddy.

They flip a coin and Gerry wins the toss. 'I guess I git to go first, eh Paddy?' says Gerry. He then takes two of the birds out of the bag, places them on his shoulders and jumps off the cliff.

Paddy watches his mate drop off the edge and go straight down for a few seconds, which is followed by a SPLAT! As Paddy looks over the edge of the cliff, he shakes his head and says, 'Fock dat, dis budgie jumpin' is too fockin' dangerous for me.'

A moment later, Seamus arrives. He, too, has been to the pet shop, and walks up carrying the familiar 'peeper bag'. He pulls a parrot out of the bag, and then Paddy notices that, in his other hand, Seamus is carrying a gun.

'Hi Paddy. Watch this,' Seamus says, and launches himself over the edge of the cliff. Paddy watches as halfway down, Seamus takes the gun and blows the parrot's head off. Seamus continues to plummet until there is a SPLAT!, as he joins Gerry's remains at the bottom. Paddy shakes his head and says, 'An' oim never troyin' dat parrot shooting nider.'

A few minutes after Seamus splats himself, Sean strolls up. He, too, has been to the pet shop and walks up carrying a 'peeper bag'. Instead of a parrot he pulls a chicken out of the bag, and launches himself off the cliff with the usual result. Once more Paddy shakes his head – 'Fock me, Sean. First dere was Gerry wit his budgie jumpin'. Den Seamus parrot shooting and now you blimmin' hen glidin'.'

**A**fter a long night of making love the young bloke rolled over, pulled out a cigarette from his jeans and searched for his lighter. Unable to find it, he asked the girl if she had one at hand.

'There might be some matches in the top drawer,' she replied.

He opened the drawer of the bedside table and found a box of matches set neatly on top of a framed picture of another man. Naturally, the bloke began to worry.

'Is this your husband?' he inquired nervously.
'No, silly,' she replied, snuggling up to him.
'Your boyfriend, then?' he asked.
'No, not at all,' she said, nibbling away at his ear.
'Well, who is he then,' demanded the bewildered bloke.

Calmly, the girl replied, 'That's me before the operation.'

**A** blind bloke goes into a bar and announces that he's got a new blonde joke.

The woman next to him, built like a brick dunny, leans over and whispers into his ear, 'Look, you're blind. So you probably don't realise you're in a lesbian bar. Let me warn you. The bartender is blonde. The girls playing billiards are blonde. And you're sitting next to me, and I'm a 100kg blonde. Now, do you still want to tell that blonde joke?'

'No,' said the blind man, 'not if I have to explain it five times.'

**The Penguin Bumper Book of Australian Jokes**

## TEN BEST THINGS TO SAY IF YOU GET CAUGHT SLEEPING AT YOUR DESK

**10.** They told me at the blood bank this might happen.

**9.** This is just a 15-minute power nap like they raved about at that time-management course you sent me to.

**8.** Whew! Must have left the top off the Tipp-Ex. You got here just in time!

**7.** I wasn't sleeping. I was meditating on the mission statement and envisioning a new paradigm.

**6.** I was testing my keyboard for drool resistance.

**5.** I was doing a highly specific yoga exercise to relieve work-related stress. Are you discriminating against people who practise yoga?

**4.** Why did you interrupt me? I had almost figured out a solution to our biggest problem.

**3.** There is a little voice coming from the keyboard saying, 'I wish I was connected to a Mac.'

**2.** Someone must have put decaff in the wrong cup.

**1.** 'In Jesus' name, Amen.'

**God** grant me the senility to forget the people I never liked anyway, the good fortune to run into the ones that I do, and the eyesight to tell the difference.

**T**wo elephants walk off a cliff . . . boom boom!

**Q:** What should you do if you see your ex-husband rolling around in pain on the ground?

**A:** Shoot him again.

**Q:** How can you tell when a man is well hung?

**A:** When you can just barely slip your finger in between his neck and the noose.

**Q:** Why do little boys whine?

**A:** Because they're practising to be men.

**Q:** How many men does it take to screw in a light bulb?

**A:** Three – one to screw the bulb, and two to listen to him brag about the screwing part.

**Q:** What do you call a handcuffed man?

**A:** Trustworthy.

**Q:** What does it mean when a man is in your bed gasping for breath and calling your name?

**A:** You didn't hold the pillow down long enough.

**Q:** Why do doctors slap babies' butts right after they're born?

**A:** To knock the penises off the smart ones.

**Q:** Why do men name their penises?

**A:** Because they don't like the idea of having a stranger make 90% of their decisions.

**Q:** Why does it take 100 000 000 sperm to fertilise one egg?

**A:** Because not one will stop and ask directions.

**Q:** Why do female black widow spiders kill their males after mating?

**A:** To stop the snoring before it starts.

**Q:** What's the best way to kill a man?

**A:** Put a naked woman and a six-pack in front of him. Then tell him to pick only one.

**Q:** What do men and pantyhose have in common?

**A:** They either cling, run or don't fit right in the crotch!

**Q:** Why do men whistle when they're sitting on the toilet?

**A:** Because it helps them remember which end they need to wipe.

### The Penguin Bumper Book of Australian Jokes

**Q:** What is the difference between men and women . . .?

**A:** A woman wants one man to satisfy her every need. A man wants every woman to satisfy his one need.

**Q:** How does a man keep his youth?

**A:** By giving her money, furs and diamonds.

**Q:** How do you keep your husband from reading your email?

**A:** Rename the mail folder 'instruction manuals'.

The woman's husband had been slipping in and out of a coma for several months, yet she had stayed by his bedside every single day.

One day, when he came to, he motioned for her to come nearer.

As she sat by him, he whispered, eyes full of tears, 'You know what? You have been with me through all the bad times. When I got fired, you were there to support me. When my business failed, you were there. When I got shot, you were by my side. When we lost the house, you stayed right here. When my health started failing, you were still by my side ... You know what?'

'What dear?' she gently asked, smiling as her heart began to fill with warmth.

'I think you're bad luck.'

**B**loke goes to the doctor's.

'Doctor, I've got a cricket ball stuck up my backside.'

'How's that?'

'Don't you start!"

**The Penguin Bumper Book of Australian Jokes**

### RULES FOR INDOOR GOLF

**1.** Each player will furnish his own equipment for play; normally one club and two balls.

**2.** Course to be played must be approved by the owner of the hole.

**3.** Unlike outdoor golf, the object is to get the club in the hole and keep the balls out of the hole.

**4.** For the most effective play, the club should have a firm shaft. Course owners are permitted to check the stiffness of the shaft before play begins.

**5.** Course owners reserve the right to restrict the length of the club to avoid damage to the hole.

# The Penguin Bumper Book of Australian Jokes

**6.** The object of the game is to take as many strokes as necessary until the course owner is satisfied. Failure to do so may result in being denied permission to play the course again.

**7.** It is usually considered bad form to begin playing the hole immediately upon arriving at the course. The experienced player will normally admire the entire course with special attention paid to well-formed bunkers.

**8.** Players are cautioned not to mention any other courses that they have played or currently are playing to the owner of the course being played. Upset owners have been known to damage players' equipment for this reason.

**9.** Players should assure themselves that their match has been properly scheduled, especially on a different course being played for the first time. Previous players have been known to get irate if they find someone else playing what they considered to be their own private course.

**10.** Players should not assume a course is in shape for play at all times. Some owners may be embarrassed if their course is temporarily under repair and the player is advised to use tact in the determination. More advanced players will find alternative means of play when this is the case.

**11.** It is considered outstanding performance, time permitting, to play the same hole several times in one match.

**12.** Course owners shall be the sole judge of who is the best player.

**13.** It is considered bad form for a player to reveal his score to other players or that he has even played the course. Players who have contracted for exclusive rights to play a private course are cautioned that information reaching the owner that he has played some other courses may result in the contract being cancelled and a suit for damages instituted.

### A PRAYER FOR THE STRESSED

Grant me the serenity to accept the things I cannot change, the courage to change the things I cannot accept, and the wisdom to hide the bodies of those I had to kill today because they got on my nerves.

Help me also to be careful of the toes that I step on today as they may be connected to the feet that I have to kiss tomorrow.

Help me always give 100% at work . . .
12% on Monday
23% on Tuesday
40% on Wednesday
20% on Thursday
5% on Friday.

Help me to remember . . .

When I am having a bad day and it seems that people are trying to wind me up, it takes 42 muscles to frown, 28 muscles to smile but only four to extend my arm and smack someone in the mouth.

Ben and Becky, each five years old, decided to get married. So Ben went to Becky's dad to ask for her hand in marriage.

'Where will you live?' asked Becky's dad, thinking this was cute.

'Well,' said Ben, 'I figured I could just move into Becky's room. It's plenty big for both of us.'

'And how will you live?'

'I get $5 a week allowance and Becky gets $5 a week allowance. That should be enough.'

Getting exasperated since Ben seemed to know all the answers, Becky's dad asked, 'And what if little ones come along?'

'Well,' said Ben, 'we've been lucky so far.'

A boss is determined not to hire an Irishman, so he decides to set a test for Murphy, hoping Murphy won't be able to answer the questions, allowing the boss to refuse him the job without getting into an argument:

'The first question is: without using numbers, represent the number nine.'

So Murphy says, 'Dat's easy,' and proceeds to draw three trees.

The boss says, 'What the hell's that?'

Murphy says, 'Tree 'n tree 'n tree makes nine.'

'Fair enough,' says the boss.

'The second question, same rules, but represent 99.'

Murphy stares into space for awhile, then makes a smudge on each tree. 'Der yar go, sir,' he says.

The boss scratches his head and says, 'How on earth do you get that to represent 99?'

Murphy says, 'Each tree's dirty now! So it's dirty tree 'n dirty tree 'n dirty tree. Dat's 99.'

The boss is getting worried he's going to have to hire him, so says, 'All right. Question three, same rules, but represent the number 100.'

Murphy stares into space again, then he shouts, 'Got it!' He makes a little mark at the base of each tree, and says, 'Der yar go, sir! One hundred!'

The boss looks at Murphy's attempt and thinks, 'Ha! Got him this time.'

'Go on Murphy, you must be mad if you think that represents 100.'

Murphy leans forward and points to the marks at the tree bases, and says, 'A little dog comes along and craps on each tree, so now you've got dirty tree an' a turd, dirty tree an' a turd, an' dirty tree an' a turd. Which makes 100. When do I start me job?'

**A** Qantas jumbo lifted off the tarmac at Sydney and headed for LA. Long after the safety demo and the warning about Deep Vein Thrombosis, and just before the cabin crew started offering drinks, the captain made an announcement on the intercom. 'Ladies and gentlemen, this is your captain speaking. Welcome to flight QF3, nonstop from Sydney to Los Angeles. The weather ahead is good and we should have a smooth and uneventful flight. Now sit back, relax and . . . Oh, Jesus Christ! Ah, fuck!'

A profound silence followed.

Finally the captain came back on the intercom. 'Ladies and gentlemen, I'm sorry if I caused you any concern earlier but, while I was talking to you, one of the flight attendants brought me a cup of hot coffee and spilt it in my lap.'

He then chuckled and said, 'You should see the front of my pants.'

Whereupon a passenger in Economy yelled loudly, 'That's nothing, you bastard! You should see the *back* of mine!'

A bloke, on his way home from work, comes to a dead halt in traffic. And he's there for ages. 'This traffic is even worse than usual,' he thinks. 'Not a sign of movement.'

He notices a policeman walking back and forth between the lines of cars, so rolls down his window to ask, 'Officer, what's the hold up?'

The policeman replies, 'John Howard's so depressed about the thought of moving with Janette back to his old house that he's stopped his motorcade in the middle of the freeway and is threatening to douse himself in petrol and set himself on fire. He says his family hates him and he doesn't have the money to pay for the house renovations. So we're taking up a collection for him.'

'Oh really? How much have you got so far?'

'Well, despite the price of petrol, around three hundred litres. But a lot of people are still siphoning.'

The scene is the high school at Eltham, one of Melbourne's most attractive outer suburbs. The teacher is reminding her class of tomorrow's big exam.

'Now, students, I cannot accept any excuses for you not being here tomorrow. The exam is far, far too important. Wagging it will not be acceptable.'

'But what if it's a really, really good excuse?' asks a girl.

'Well, I might consider a nuclear attack or serious

personal injury or critical illness. Or a death in your immediate family. But that's it. No other excuses whatsoever!'

Whereupon the class smart-arse raises his hand and says, 'What would you say tomorrow if I said I was suffering from complete and utter sexual exhaustion?'

The class begins snickering. When silence is restored, the teacher smiles sympathetically at the boy, shakes her head, and says, 'Well, I guess you'll have to write the exam with your other hand.'

When I'm not in my right mind, my left mind gets pretty crowded.

Everyone has a photographic memory. Some don't have film.

# The Penguin Bumper Book of Australian Jokes

**B**oycott shampoo! Demand the REAL poo!

**I**f you choke a smurf, what colour does it turn?

**W**ho is General Failure and why is he reading my hard disk?

**W**hat happens if you get scared half to death twice?

**T**hree blokes die together and go to heaven.
St Peter says, 'We only have one rule. Don't step on the ducks.'
The blokes enter heaven and see ducks everywhere, it's almost impossible not to step on a duck.

The first bloke accidentally steps on one, and soon St Peter comes along with the ugliest woman he's ever seen. St Peter chains them together and says, 'Your punishment is to be chained to this ugly woman forever.'

The next day the second bloke steps on a duck. And sure enough, St Peter arrives with another ugly woman and chains them together.

The third bloke is more careful. He goes for months without stepping on any ducks.

One day St Peter appears with a gorgeous woman, blonde, blue-eyed and very sexy. He chains them together and leaves without a word. The bloke remarks, 'I wonder what I did to deserve this?'

She replies, 'I don't know about you, but I stepped on a duck.'

### AND GOD CREATED MAN

It was the sixth day of Genesis and God was in the creating mood. He had just created the mule and told

# The Penguin Bumper Book of Australian Jokes

him, 'You will be mule, working constantly from dusk to dawn, carrying heavy loads on your back. You will eat grass and you will lack intelligence. You will live for 50 years.'

The mule answered, 'To live like this for 50 years is too much. Please, give me no more than 20.' And so it was.

Then God created the dog and told him, 'You will hold vigilance over the dwellings of Man, to whom you will be his greatest companion. You will eat his table scraps and live for 30 years.'

And the dog responded, 'Lord, to live 30 years as a dog is too much. Please, no more than 15 years.' And so it was.

God then created the monkey and told him, 'You are the monkey. You will swing from tree to tree, acting like an idiot. You will be funny, and you shall live for 40 years.'

And the monkey responded, 'Lord, to live 40 years as the clown of the world is too much. Please, Lord, give me no more than 30 years.' And so it was.

Finally, God created Man and told him, 'You are Man, the only rational being that walks the earth. You will use your intelligence to have mastery over the creatures of the world. You will dominate the earth and live for 20 years.'

And Man responded, 'Lord, to be Man for only 20 years is too little. Please, Lord, give me the 30 years the mule refused, the 15 years the dog refused, and the ten years the monkey rejected.' And so it was.

And God made Man to live 20 years as a man, then marry and live 30 years like a mule working and carrying heavy loads on his back. Then, his children will become teenagers and he will live 15 years as a dog, guarding his house and eating leftovers after they empty the pantry; and, in his old age, he will live ten years as a monkey, acting like a fool to amuse his grandchildren. And it was so.

Mick is appearing on the Irish version of the television mega-hit 'Who Wants to be a Millionaire?'

The compere says, 'Mick, you've done fine so far. Five hundred thousand pounds and the next question will give you the first ever million pounds. But if you get it wrong you'll be out of the game. Are you ready?'

Mick says, 'Sure, I'll have a go.'

The compere says, 'Which of the following birds does not build its own nest? Is it (a) a robin, (b) a sparrow, (c) a cuckoo or (d) a thrush? Remember, Mick, it's worth a million.'

'I think I know what it is, but I'm not 100 per cent sure. No, I haven't got a clue. Can I phone a friend, please?'

'Yes, Mick. Who do you want to phone?'

'I'll phone Paddy back home in the village.'

So the compere phones Paddy.

'Hello?'

'Hello Paddy. It's "Who Wants to be a Millionaire" here. I've your friend Mick with us and he's doing very, very well. He's on five hundred thousand but needs your help to get the million. Now, the next voice you hear will be Mick's. He'll explain the question. There are four possible answers and just one correct answer. And you have 30 seconds to answer. So I'll now hand over to Mick.'

'Paddy,' says Mick, 'which of the following birds doesn't build its own nest? Is it (a) a robin, (b) a sparrow, (c) a cuckoo or (d) a thrush?'

'Jesus, Mick, that's simple,' says Paddy. 'It's a cuckoo.'

### The Penguin Bumper Book of Australian Jokes

'You think?'
'I'm sure.'
'Thanks Paddy.'
'Well, do you want to stick on five hundred thousand or play on for the first ever million, Mick?'
'I want to play. I'll go with cuckoo.'
'And that's your final answer?'
'It is.'
'Are you confident?'
'Yes, fairly. Paddy sounded sure.'
'Mick you had five hundred thousand and you said cuckoo. Well, you've just won one million pounds. Here's your cheque. You've been a great contestant. Audience, please put your hands together for Mick.'

And there is thunderous applause.

Next night, Mick is back in the village and takes Paddy down the local to fill him full of Guinness. Sitting at the bar Mick says, 'Tell me, Paddy. How in God's name did you know that it was the cuckoo that doesn't build its own nest?'

'Listen Mick,' says Paddy, 'everybody knows the fucken' cuckoo lives in a clock.'

**A** Jewish man, a Catholic and Morman were having drinks at the bar following a business meeting.

The Jewish man, bragging about his virility, proclaimed, 'I have four sons. One more and I'll have a basketball team.'

The Catholic man pooh-poohed this accomplishment, stating, 'That's nothing. I have ten sons. One more and I'll have a football team.'

To which the Morman replied, 'You fellas ain't got a clue. I have 17 wives. One more and I'll have a golf course.'

**T**wo builders, Fred and Bill, are seated either side of a table in a rough pub, when a well-dressed man enters, orders a beer and sits on a stool at the bar.

The two builders start to speculate about the occupation of the 'suit'.

Fred: 'I reckon he's an accountant.'

Bill: 'No way! He's a stockbroker.'

Fred: 'He's no stockbroker! A stockbroker wouldn't come in here!'

# The Penguin Bumper Book of Australian Jokes

The argument repeats itself for some time until the volume of beer gets the better of Fred and he makes for the toilet. On entering the toilet he sees that the 'suit' is standing at a urinal. Curiosity and several jugs get the better of the builder.

Fred: 'Scuse me . . . no offence meant, but me and me mate were wondering what you do for a living?'

Suit: 'No offence taken! I'm a logical scientist by profession.'

Fred: 'Oh! What's that then?'

Suit: 'I'll try to explain by example . . . do you have a goldfish at home?'

Fred: 'Well, yeah, I do as it happens!'

Suit: 'Well, it's logical to follow that you keep it in a bowl or in a pond. Which is it?'

Fred: 'It's in a pond.'

Suit: 'Well, then it's reasonable to suppose that you have a large garden.'

Fred: 'As it happens, yes I have got a big garden.'

Suit: 'Well, then it's logical to assume in this town that if you have a large garden then you have a large house.'

Fred: 'As it happens I've got a five-bedroom house . . . built it myself.'

Suit: 'Well, given that you've built a five-bedroom

house it is logical to assume that you haven't built it just for yourself and that you are quite probably married.'

Fred: 'Yes, I am married, I live with my wife and three children!'

Suit: 'Well, then it's logical to assume that you are sexually active with your wife.'

Fred: 'Yep! Four nights a week!'

Suit: 'Well, then it's logical to suggest that you do not masturbate very often.'

Fred: 'Me? Never!'

Suit: 'Well, there you are, that's logical science at work!'

Fred: 'How's that then?'

Suit: 'Well, from finding out that you had a goldfish, I've told you about the size of your garden, your house, your family and about your sex life.'

Fred: 'I see. That's pretty impressive. Thanks, mate!'

They both leave the toilet and Fred returns to his mate.

Bill: 'I see the suit was in there. Did you ask him what he did?'

Fred: 'Yep! He's a logical scientist!'

Bill: 'What's that then?'

Fred: 'I'll try to explain. Do you have a goldfish?'
Bill: 'Nope.'
Fred: 'Then you're a wanker.'

**H**usband and wife go off to bed. As soon as they settle down, the man leans over and whispers softly, 'Hey snuggle boopy boops, your lickle hubby wubby isn't quite ready for bye-byes yet.'

The wife takes the hint and says, 'OK, but I have to use the bathroom first.'

So off she goes, but on her way back she trips over a piece of carpet and lands flat on her face.

Her husband jumps up concerned, 'Oh my little honey bunny. Is your nosey-wosey all right?'

No harm is done, so she jumps into bed and they have sex for two hours.

Afterwards, the wife goes off to the bathroom again, but on her way she trips over the piece of carpet and again lands flat on her face on the floor.

Her husband looks over and grunts, 'Clumsy bitch!'

**The Penguin Bumper Book of Australian Jokes**

## SIGNS SPOTTED AROUND THE WORLD

In a Bangkok drycleaner:
DROP YOUR TROUSERS HERE FOR THE BEST RESULTS.

In a mens rest room in Japan:
TO STOP LEAK TURN COCK TO THE RIGHT.

In a Nairobi restaurant:
CUSTOMERS WHO FIND OUR WAITRESSES RUDE OUGHT TO SEE THE MANAGER.

On the grounds of a private school:
NO TRESPASSING WITHOUT PERMISSION.

On an Athi River highway:
TAKE NOTICE: WHEN THIS SIGN IS UNDER WATER, THIS ROAD IS IMPASSABLE.

On a poster at Kencom:
ARE YOU AN ADULT THAT CANNOT READ? IF SO, WE CAN HELP.

In a city restaurant:
OPEN SEVEN DAYS A WEEK AND WEEKENDS.

### The Penguin Bumper Book of Australian Jokes

On an automatic rest-room hand dryer:
DO NOT ACTIVATE WITH WET HANDS.

In a Pumwani maternity ward:
NO CHILDREN ALLOWED.

In a cemetery:
PERSONS ARE PROHIBITED FROM PICKING FLOWERS FROM ANY BUT THEIR OWN GRAVES.

In a Japanese public bath:
FOREIGN GUESTS ARE REQUESTED NOT TO PULL COCK IN TUB.

A Tokyo hotel's rules and regulations:
GUESTS ARE REQUESTED NOT TO SMOKE OR DO OTHER DISGUSTING BEHAVIOURS IN BED.

Hotel notice, Tokyo:
IS FORBIDDEN TO STEAL HOTEL TOWELS PLEASE. IF YOU ARE NOT A PERSON TO DO SUCH A THING IS PLEASE NOT TO HAD NOTIS.

On the menu of a Swiss restaurant:
OUR WINES LEAVE YOU NOTHING TO HOPE FOR.

**The Penguin Bumper Book of Australian Jokes**

In a Tokyo bar:
SPECIAL COCKTAILS FOR THE LADIES WITH NUTS.

In a Bangkok temple:
IT IS FORBIDDEN TO ENTER A WOMAN EVEN A FOREIGNER IF DRESSED AS A MAN.

Hotel room notice, Chiang-Mai, Thailand:
PLEASE DO NOT BRING SOLICITORS INTO YOUR ROOM.

Hotel brochure, Italy:
THIS HOTEL IS RENOWNED FOR ITS PEACE AND SOLITUDE. IN FACT, CROWDS FROM ALL OVER THE WORLD FLOCK HERE TO ENJOY ITS SOLITUDE.

Hotel lobby, Bucharest:
THE LIFT IS BEING FIXED FOR THE NEXT DAY. DURING THAT TIME WE REGRET THAT YOU WILL BE UNBEARABLE.

Hotel elevator, Paris:
PLEASE LEAVE YOUR VALUES AT THE FRONT DESK.

Hotel, Yugoslavia:
THE FLATTENING OF UNDERWEAR WITH PLEASURE IS THE JOB OF THE CHAMBERMAID.

Hotel, Japan:
YOU ARE INVITED TO TAKE ADVANTAGE OF THE CHAMBERMAID.

In the lobby of a Moscow hotel across from a Russian Orthodox monastery:
YOU ARE WELCOME TO VISIT THE CEMETERY WHERE FAMOUS RUSSIAN AND SOVIET COMPOSERS, ARTISTS, AND WRITERS ARE BURIED DAILY EXCEPT THURSDAY.

Hotel catering to skiers, Austria:
NOT TO PERAMBULATE THE CORRIDORS IN THE HOURS OF REPOSE IN THE BOOTS OF ASCENSION.

From a restaurant menu, Poland:
SALAD A FIRM'S OWN MAKE; LIMPID RED BEET SOUP WITH CHEESY DUMPLINGS IN THE FORM OF A FINGER; ROASTED DUCK LET LOOSE; BEEF RASHERS BEATEN IN THE COUNTRY PEOPLE'S FASHION.

# The Penguin Bumper Book of Australian Jokes

Supermarket, Hong Kong:
FOR YOUR CONVENIENCE, WE RECOMMEND COURTEOUS, EFFICIENT SELF-SERVICE.

From a Russian newspaper:
THERE WILL BE A MOSCOW EXHIBITION OF ARTS BY 15 000 SOVIET REPUBLIC PAINTERS AND SCULPTORS. THESE WERE EXECUTED OVER THE PAST TWO YEARS.

In an East African newspaper:
A NEW SWIMMING POOL IS RAPIDLY TAKING SHAPE SINCE THE CONTRACTORS HAVE THROWN IN THE BULK OF THEIR WORKERS.

Hotel, Vienna:
IN CASE OF FIRE, DO YOUR UTMOST TO ALARM THE HOTEL PORTER.

A sign posted in Germany's Black Forest:
IT IS STRICTLY FORBIDDEN ON OUR BLACK FOREST CAMPING SITE THAT PEOPLE OF DIFFERENT SEX, FOR INSTANCE, MEN AND WOMEN, LIVE TOGETHER IN ONE TENT UNLESS THEY ARE MARRIED WITH EACH OTHER FOR THIS PURPOSE.

Hotel, Zurich:

BECAUSE OF THE IMPROPRIETY OF ENTERTAINING GUESTS OF THE OPPOSITE SEX IN THE BEDROOM, IT IS SUGGESTED THAT THE LOBBY BE USED FOR THIS PURPOSE.

An advertisement by a Hong Kong dentist:
TEETH EXTRACTED BY THE LATEST METHODISTS.

From a Russian book on chess:
A LOT OF WATER HAS BEEN PASSED UNDER THE BRIDGE SINCE THIS VARIATION HAS BEEN PLAYED.

A laundry in Rome:
LADIES, LEAVE YOUR CLOTHES HERE AND SPEND THE AFTERNOON HAVING A GOOD TIME.

Tourist agency, Czechoslovakia:
TAKE ONE OF OUR HORSE-DRIVEN CITY TOURS. WE GUARANTEE NO MISCARRIAGES.

Advertisement for donkey rides, Thailand:
WOULD YOU LIKE TO RIDE ON YOUR OWN ASS?

In the window of a Swedish furrier:
FUR COATS MADE FOR LADIES FROM THEIR OWN SKIN.

### The Penguin Bumper Book of Australian Jokes

The box of a clockwork toy made in Hong Kong:
GUARANTEED TO WORK THROUGHOUT ITS USEFUL LIFE.

In a Swiss mountain inn:
SPECIAL TODAY – NO ICE-CREAM.

Airline ticket office, Copenhagen:
WE TAKE YOUR BAGS AND SEND THEM IN ALL DIRECTIONS.

On the door of a Moscow hotel room:
IF THIS IS YOUR FIRST VISIT TO RUSSIA, YOU ARE WELCOME TO IT.

Cocktail lounge, Norway:
LADIES ARE REQUESTED NOT TO HAVE CHILDREN IN THE BAR.

At a Budapest zoo:
PLEASE DO NOT FEED THE ANIMALS. IF YOU HAVE ANY SUITABLE FOOD, GIVE IT TO THE GUARD ON DUTY.

Doctors office, Rome:
SPECIALIST IN WOMEN AND OTHER DISEASES.

Hotel, Acapulco:
THE MANAGER HAS PERSONALLY PASSED ALL THE WATER SERVED HERE.

Information booklet about using a hotel airconditioner, Japan:
COOLES AND HEATES: IF YOU WANT JUST CONDITION OF WARM AIR IN YOUR ROOM, PLEASE CONTROL YOURSELF.

Car rental brochure, Tokyo:
WHEN PASSENGER OF FOOT HEAVE IN SIGHT, TOOTLE THE HORN. TRUMPET HIM MELODIOUSLY AT FIRST, BUT IF HE STILL OBSTACLES YOUR PASSAGE THEN TOOTLE HIM WITH VIGOUR.

Laughing stock: cattle with a sense of humour.

Why do psychics have to ask you for your name?

**W**ear short sleeves! Support your right to bare arms.

**F**or Sale: Parachute. Only used once, never opened, small stain.

**A** man walking along a California beach was deep in prayer. All of a sudden he said out loud, 'Lord grant me one wish.'

Suddenly the sky clouded above his head and in a booming voice the Lord said, 'Because you have been faithful to me in all ways, I will grant you one wish.'

The man said, 'Build a bridge to Hawaii, so I can drive over any time I want to.'

The Lord said, 'Your request is very materialistic. Think of the logistics of that kind of undertaking. The supports required to reach the bottom of the Pacific! The concrete and steel it would take! I can do it, but it is hard for me to justify your desire for worldly things. Take a little more time and think of another wish, a wish you think would honour and glorify me.'

The man thought about it for a long time. Finally he said, 'Lord, I have been married and divorced four times. All of my wives said that I am uncaring and insensitive. I wish that I could understand women. I want to know how they feel inside, what they are thinking when they give me the silent treatment, why they cry, what they mean when they say "nothing" and how I can make a woman truly happy.'

After a few minutes, God said, 'You want two lanes or four on that bridge?'

**T**wo women are having lunch together and discussing the merits of cosmetic surgery.

The first woman says, 'I need to be honest with you. I'm getting a boob job.'

The second woman says, 'Oh that's nothing. I'm thinking of having my arsehole bleached!'

To which the first replies, 'I just can't picture your husband as a blond!'

# The Penguin Bumper Book of Australian Jokes

**A** young couple have been married for just over a month, and the young bride isn't getting any sex. Every night her husband arrives home from work, then has a quick shower and heads down to the pub. Afterwards, he stumbles home completely intoxicated and unfit for any sexual activity.

On this night, though, the young bride decides to surprise her husband. When he stumbles home from the bar, his wife is seated provocatively on the sofa, wearing nothing but suspenders, stockings and a pair of sexy lacy panties.

The drunken husband remarks, 'Let's go upstairs into the bedroom.'

As the young bride runs upstairs, she says under her breath, 'Yes! Finally I'm gonna get some action!'

When she enters the bedroom, she removes her remaining garments and sits on the edge of the bed in her lace panties.

The husband stumbles into the bedroom and says, 'Take off your panties and do a handstand in front of the mirror.'

'Great,' she thinks to herself.

She proceeds to do a handstand in front of the mirror. Then, he walks over to her, parts her legs, and places his chin in her crotch . . .

'The guys at the bar were right,' he said, 'a beard would suit me!'

An artist asked the gallery owner if there had been any interest in his paintings on display at that time.

'I have good news and bad news,' the owner replied. 'The good news is that a gentleman inquired about your work and wondered if it would appreciate in value after your death. When I told him it would, he bought all 15 of your paintings.'

'That's wonderful,' the artist exclaimed. 'What's the bad news?'

'The guy was your doctor.'

### LIES THAT AUSTRALIAN TV ADVERTS WOULD HAVE US BELIEVE

DISPOSABLE RAZORS WORTH $1 EACH ARE MADE USING SPACE-AGE TECHNOLOGY.

### The Penguin Bumper Book of Australian Jokes

PEOPLE WHO USE BRAND X ARE MENTALLY RETARDED.

REALLY SEXY GIRLS WITH BIG TITS ARE WAITING FOR YOU TO CALL THEM NOW.

EVERY AUSTRALIAN DREAMS OF BUYING A HOUSE.

WHEN YOU GET THAT HOUSE, YOUR WIFE WILL SMILE AND HUG YOU ON THE FRONT LAWN WHILE A HAPPY REAL ESTATE AGENT REPLACES THE 'FOR SALE' SIGN WITH ONE THAT SAYS 'SOLD!'

A BLOKE WILL ALWAYS WIPE HIS BROW WITH HIS FOREARM AFTER DRINKING BEER FROM A CAN.

BANK TELLERS ARE HAPPY.

BUTCHERS ARE FAT.

WOMEN DON'T DRINK BEER.

ABORIGINES DON'T EXIST. UNLESS THEY'RE ERNIE DINGO.

SKATEBOARD RIDING LEADS TO COKE DRINKING.

### The Penguin Bumper Book of Australian Jokes

Milk pours in slow motion.

People close their eyes after drinking coffee.

Tony Lockett wouldn't punch out Greg Matthews for telling him he needed a hair transplant.

The opinions of morons emerging from cinemas are of great value.

Toilet paper and your arse have nothing to do with each other.

Stocks are limited.

Madness and insanity are desirable qualities in some retailers.

All Mexicans wear sombreros, have moustaches, are quite stupid and eat nothing but corn chips.

John Laws still isn't sure that people know what he means when he says 'Valvoline'.

WHEN A PACKET OR CONTAINER IS EMPTY, SOME SAD-FACED DICKHEAD HAS TO TURN IT UPSIDE DOWN AND SHAKE IT TO BE SURE.

WHEN MEN WEAR BRAND-NEW CLOTHES THEY HAVE TO PUT THEIR HANDS IN THEIR POCKETS.

MODELS HAVE ORGASMS WHEN THEY EAT CHOCOLATE OR ICE-CREAM.

GIRLS PLAY TENNIS, WATER SKI AND LAUGH A LOT WHEN HAVING THEIR PERIODS.

**A** first-grade teacher collected well-known proverbs, gave each child in her class the first half of a proverb and asked them to come up with the remainder.

Better to be safe than ... punch a fifth-grader.

Strike while the ... bug is close.

# The Penguin Bumper Book of Australian Jokes

It's always darkest before . . . Daylight Savings Time.

Never underestimate the power of . . . termites.

You can lead a horse to water but . . . how?

Don't bite the hand that . . . looks dirty.

No news is . . . impossible.

A miss is as good as a . . . mister.

You can't teach an old dog new . . . maths.

If you lie down with dogs, you'll . . . stink in the morning.

Love all, trust . . . me.

The pen is mightier than the . . . pigs.

An idle mind is . . . the best way to relax.

Where there's smoke there's . . . pollution.

Happy the bride who . . . gets all the presents.

# The Penguin Bumper Book of Australian Jokes

A penny saved is . . . not much.

Two's company, three's . . . the Musketeers.

Don't put off till tomorrow what . . . you put on to go to bed.

Laugh and the whole world laughs with you, cry and . . . you have to blow your nose.

None are so blind as . . . Stevie Wonder.

Children should be seen and not . . . spanked or grounded.

If at first you don't succeed . . . get new batteries.

You get out of something what you . . . see pictured on the box.

When the blind lead the blind . . . get out of the way.

Better late than . . . pregnant.

'Doctor, I can't stop singing "The Green Green Grass of Home".'

'That sounds like Tom Jones Syndrome.'

'Is it common?'

'It's not unusual.'

The Rev. Fred Nile was making a speech about X-rated videos. 'I disguised myself and went into a video store at King's Cross and rented one of these cassettes – and was horrified to find, by my count, five acts of oral sex, three of sodomy, a transsexual making love to a dog and a woman accommodating five men at once. And as a member of the Legislative Council here in NSW, I vow that such tapes as this will no longer befoul our fair community.'

Concluding his fiery denunciation, he asked, 'Are there any questions?'

And five people chorused, 'Which video store at the Cross?'

**D**id you hear the one about the blonde fox?

It got caught in a trap, chewed its leg off and was still stuck.

**A**n island in the South Pacific. In the middle, a volcano that's been dormant for decades. Suddenly the ground begins to shake and, from the previously cold crater, there's a trickle of lava. As the smell of sulphur grows ever stronger the witchdoctor says to the chief, 'We must sacrifice a virgin to appease the volcano.'

'Sorry,' says the chief, 'I've used up all the virgins. So I guess we'll just have to get used to the noise.'

**Teaching Maths in 1950:** A logger sells a truckload of lumber for $100. His cost of production is four-fifths of the price. What is his profit?

**The Penguin Bumper Book of Australian Jokes**

**Teaching Maths in 1960:** A logger sells a truckload of lumber for $100. His cost of production is four-fifths of the price, or $80. What is his profit?

**Teaching Maths in 1970:** A logger exchanges a set 'L' of lumber for a set 'M' of money. The cardinality of set 'M' is 100. Each element is worth one dollar. Make 100 dots representing the elements of the set 'M'. The set 'C', the cost of production, contains 20 fewer points than set 'M'. Represent the set 'C' as a subset of set 'M' and answer the following question: What is the cardinality of the set 'P' for profits?

**Teaching Maths in 1980:** A logger sells a truckload of lumber for $100. Her cost of production is $80 and her profit is $20. Your assignment: Underline the number 20.

**The Penguin Bumper Book of Australian Jokes**

**Teaching Maths in 1990:** By cutting down beautiful forest trees, the logger makes $20. What do you think of this way of making a living? How did the forest birds and squirrels feel as the logger cut down the trees? There are no wrong answers.

**Teaching Maths in 1995:** By laying off 40% of its loggers, a company improves its stock price from $80 to $100. How much capital gain per share does the CEO make by exercising his stock options at $80? Assume capital gains are no longer taxed, because this encourages investment.

**Teaching Maths in 2001:** A company outsources all of its loggers. The firm saves on benefits, and when demand for its product is down, the logging work force can easily be cut back. The average logger employed by the company earned $50 000, had three weeks vacation, a nice retirement plan and medical insurance. The contracted logger charges $30 an hour. Was outsourcing a good move?

### ELEMENT NAME: WOMAN

Symbol: WO
Atomic Weight: (don't ask)

Physical Properties: Generally round in form. Boils at nothing and may freeze any time. Melts whenever treated properly. Very bitter if not used well.

Chemical Properties: Very active. Highly unstable. Possesses strong affinity with gold, silver, platinum and precious stones. Violent when left alone. Able to absorb great amounts of exotic food. Turns slightly green when placed next to a better specimen.

Usage: Highly ornamental. An extremely good catalyst for dispersion of wealth. Probably the most powerful income-reducing agent known.

Caution: Highly explosive in inexperienced hands.

### ELEMENT NAME: MAN

Symbol: XY
Atomic Weight: (180 +/- 50)

### The Penguin Bumper Book of Australian Jokes

Physical Properties: Solid at room temperature, but gets bent out of shape easily. Fairly dense and sometimes flaky. Difficult to find a pure sample. Due to rust, aging samples are unable to conduct electricity as easily as young samples.

Chemical Properties: Attempts to bond with WO any chance it can get. Also tends to form strong bonds with itself. Becomes explosive when mixed with Kd (Element: Child) for prolonged periods of time. Neutralise by saturating with alcohol.

Usage: None known. Possibly good methane source. Good samples are able to produce large quantities on command.

Caution: In the absence of WO, this element rapidly decomposes and begins to smell.

### CHURCH BULLETIN BLUNDERS

- Bertha Belch, a missionary from Africa, will be speaking tonight at the Anglican Church. Come tonight and hear Bertha Belch all the way from Africa.

- Announcement in the church bulletin for a National PRAYER AND FASTING Conference. 'The cost for attending the Prayer and Fasting conference includes meals.'

- Miss Charlene Mason sang, 'I will! not pass this way again!' giving obvious pleasure to the congregation.

- The peacemaking meeting scheduled for today has been cancelled due to conflict.

- The sermon this morning: 'Jesus Walks on the Water'. The sermon tonight: 'Searching for Jesus'.

- Next Thursday there will be tryouts for the choir. They need all the help they can get.

- Barbara remains in the hospital and needs blood donors for more transfusions. She is also having trouble sleeping and requests tapes of the reverend's sermons.

- The rector will preach his farewell message after which the choir will sing 'Break Forth into Joy'.

- Remember in prayer the many who are sick of our community.

- Smile at someone who is hard to love. Say 'hell' to someone who doesn't care much about you.

# The Penguin Bumper Book of Australian Jokes

- Don't let worry kill you off – let the Church help.

- Irving Benson and Jessie Carter were married on 24 October in the church. So ends a friendship that began in their school days.

- At the evening service tonight, the sermon topic will be 'What the hell?' Come early and listen to our choir practice.

- Eight new choir robes are needed due to the addition of several new members and to the deterioration of some older ones.

- The senior choir invites any member of the congregation who enjoys sinning to join the choir.

- Scouts are saving aluminium cans, bottles and other items to be recycled. Proceeds will be used to cripple children.

- The Lutheran men's group will meet at 6 p.m. Steak, mashed potatoes, green beans, bread and dessert will be served for a nominal feel.

- For those of you who have children and don't know it, we have a nursery downstairs.

- Please place your donation in the envelope along with the deceased person(s) you want remembered.

# The Penguin Bumper Book of Australian Jokes

- Attend and you will hear an excellent speaker and heave a healthy lunch.

- The church will host an evening of fine dining, superb entertainment and gracious hostility.

- Potluck supper Sunday at 5 p.m. – prayer and medication to follow.

- The ladies of the Church have cast off clothing of every kind. They may be seen in the basement on Friday afternoon.

- This evening at 7 p.m. there will be a hymn sung in the park across from the Church. Bring a blanket and come prepared to sin.

- Ladies Bible Study will be held Thursday morning at 10. All ladies are invited to lunch in the Fellowship Hall after the B.S. is done.

- The pastor would appreciate it if the ladies of the congregation would lend him their electric girdles for the pancake breakfast next Sunday morning.

- The eighth-graders will be presenting Shakespeare's Hamlet in the Church basement Friday at 7 p.m. The congregation is invited to attend this tragedy.

- Weight Watchers will meet at 7 p.m at the First Presbyterian Church. Please use large double door at the side entrance.

- Low Self-Esteem Support Group will meet Thursday at 7 p.m. Please use the back door.

### THE FIVE STAGES OF DRUNKENNESS

Stage 1 – SMART

This is when you suddenly become an expert on every subject in the known Universe. You know everything and want to pass on your knowledge to anyone who will listen. At this stage you are always RIGHT. And, of course, the person you are talking to is very WRONG. This makes for an interesting argument when both parties are SMART.

## Stage 2 – GOOD LOOKING

This is when you realise that you are the BEST LOOKING person in the entire bar and that people fancy you. You can go up to a perfect stranger, knowing they fancy you and really want to talk to you. Bear in mind that you are still SMART, so you can talk to this person about any subject under the sun.

## Stage 3 – RICH

This is when you suddenly become the richest person in the world. You can buy drinks for the entire bar because you have an armoured truck full of money parked behind the bar. You can also make bets at this stage, because, of course, you are still SMART. So naturally you will win all your bets. It doesn't matter how much you bet because you are RICH. You will also buy drinks for everyone that you fancy, because now you are the BEST LOOKING person in the world.

## Stage 4 – BULLETPROOF

You are now ready to pick fights with anyone and everyone, especially those with whom you have been betting or arguing. This is because nothing can hurt you. At this point you can also go up to the partners of the people who you fancy and challenge them to a battle of wits or money. You have no fear of losing this battle because you are SMART, you are RICH and hell, you're BETTER LOOKING than they are!

Stage 5 – INVISIBLE

This is the Final Stage of Drunkenness. At this point you can do anything because NO-ONE CAN SEE YOU. You can stand on a table to impress the people who you fancy because the rest of the people in the room cannot see you. You are also invisible to the person who wants to fight you. You can walk through the street singing at the top of your lungs because no-one can see or hear you and, because you're still SMART, you know all the words.

**W**hen I was 14, I hoped that one day I would have a boyfriend.

When I was 16, I got a boyfriend, but there was no passion. So I decided I needed a passionate guy, with a zest for life.

# The Penguin Bumper Book of Australian Jokes

In college, I dated a passionate bloke, but he was too emotional. Everything was an emergency, he was a drama queen, cried all the time and threatened suicide. So I decided I needed a boy with stability.

When I was 25 I found a very stable bloke but he was boring. He was totally predictable and never got excited about anything. Life became so dull that I decided I needed a boy with some excitement.

When I was 28 I found an exciting boy, but I couldn't keep up with him. He rushed from one party to another, never settling on anything. He did mad, impetuous things and flirted with everyone he met. He made me miserable as often as happy. He was great fun initially and very energetic, but directionless. So I decided to find a boy with some ambition.

When I turned 31, I found a smart, ambitious boy with his feet planted firmly on the ground, so I moved in with him. He was so ambitious that he dumped me and took everything I owned.

I am older now and am looking for a guy with a very big dick.

**The Penguin Bumper Book of Australian Jokes**

Little Johnny ran into the house and asked, 'Mummy, can little girls have babies?'

'No,' said his mum, 'of course not.'

Little Johnny then ran back outside and his mum heard him yell to his friends, 'It's okay, we can play that game again!'

A blonde was playing Trivial Pursuit one night. It was her turn. She rolled the dice and landed on 'Science & Nature'. Her question was, 'If you are in a vacuum and someone calls your name, can you hear it?'

She thought for a time and then asked, 'Is it on or off?'

A woman in a hot-air balloon realised she was lost. She reduced altitude and spotted a man below. She descended a bit more and shouted, 'Excuse me, can you help me? I promised a friend I would meet him an hour ago, but I don't know where I am.'

The man below replied, 'You are in a hot-air balloon hovering approximately 30 feet above the ground. You are between 40 and 41 degrees north latitude and between 59 and 60 degrees west longitude.'

'You must be a Mac operator,' said the balloonist.

'I am,' replied the man. 'How did you know?'

'Well,' answered the balloonist, 'everything you told me is technically correct, but I have no idea what to make of your information, and the fact is I am still lost. Frankly, you've not been much help so far.'

The man below responded, 'You must be an account manager.'

'I am,' replied the balloonist, 'but how did you know?'

'Well,' said the man, 'you don't know where you are or where you are going. You have risen to where you are due to a large quantity of hot air. You made a promise which you have no idea how to keep, and you expect me to solve your problem. The fact is, you are in exactly the same position you were in before we met. But now, somehow, it's my fault.'

**The Penguin Bumper Book of Australian Jokes**

**W**hose cruel idea was it for the word 'lisp' to have an 's' in it?

**S**ince light travels faster than sound, isn't that why some people appear bright until you hear them speak?

**H**ow come abbreviated is such a long word?

**W**hy do you press harder on a remote-control when you know the battery is dead?

**S**ince Americans throw rice at weddings, do Asians throw hamburgers?

A blonde decides one day that she is sick and tired of all these blonde jokes and how all blondes are perceived as stupid, so she decides to show her husband that blondes really are smart.

While her husband is at work, she decides that she'll paint a couple of rooms in the house.

The next day, after her husband leaves for work, she gets down to the task at hand. Her husband arrives home at 5.30 and smells the distinctive smell of fresh paint. He walks into the living room and finds his wife lying on the floor in a pool of sweat. He notices that she's wearing a ski jacket and a fur coat at the same time, so he goes over and asks her if she is OK. She says yes.

So he asks what she's doing. She replies that she wanted to prove to him that not all blonde women are dumb and that she wanted to do this by painting the house. He then asks her why she has on a ski jacket and a fur coat.

She said that the directions on the paint can said, 'FOR BEST RESULTS, PUT ON TWO COATS.'

**A** little kid gets on a city bus and sits right behind the driver. The kid starts yelling, 'If my dad was a bull and my mum a cow, I'd be a little bull.'

The driver starts getting mad at the noisy kid, who continues with, 'If my dad was an elephant and my mum a girl elephant, I'd be a little elephant.'

The kid went on with several animals until the bus driver got angry and yelled at the kid, 'What if your dad was a serial killer and your mum a prostitute?'

The kid smiled and said, 'I'd be a bus driver!'

**U**naware that Indianapolis is on Eastern Standard Time and Chicago on Central Standard Time, Keith inquired at the Indianapolis airport about a plane to Chicago.

'The next flight leaves at 1 p.m.,' a ticket agent said, 'and arrives in Chicago at 1.01 p.m.'

'Would you repeat that please,' Keith asked. The agent did so and then inquired, 'Do you want a reservation?'

'No,' said Keith, 'but I think I'll hang around and watch that thing take off!'

Three blokes are out having a relaxing day of fishing. Out of the blue they catch a mermaid. She begs to be set free in return for granting each of them a wish.

Now, one of the blokes just doesn't believe it and says, 'OK, if you can really grant wishes, then double my IQ.'

The mermaid says, 'Done.' Suddenly he starts reciting Shakespeare flawlessly – and analyses it with extreme insight.

The second bloke is so amazed he says to the mermaid, 'Triple my IQ.'

The mermaid says, 'Done!' He then starts to spout the solutions to mathematical problems that have stymied chemists, physicists and mathematicians since the beginning of time.

The last bloke is so impressed he says to the mermaid, 'Quintuple my IQ.'

The mermaid looks at him and says, 'I don't normally try to change people's minds when they make a wish, but I really wish you'd reconsider.'

He says, 'No way. I want you to quintuple my IQ, and if you don't, I won't set you free.'

'Please,' says the mermaid. 'You don't know what you're asking . . . it will change your entire view of the universe . . . Won't you ask for something else – ten million dollars . . . anything?'

No matter how hard the mermaid pleads, he remains steadfast. He insists on having his IQ increased fivefold. The mermaid sighs and says, 'Done!'

And he becomes a woman.

Little Johnny was sitting in class one day. All of a sudden he needed to go to the toilet. He yelled out, 'Miss Jones. I need to take a piss!'

The teacher replied, 'Now Johnny, that is NOT the proper word to use in this situation. The correct word to use is urinate. Please use the word "urinate" in a sentence correctly, and I will allow you to go.'

Little Johnny thinks for a bit, then says, 'You're an eight, but if you had bigger tits, you'd be a ten!!'

**The Penguin Bumper Book of Australian Jokes**

### LETTER FROM MY DEAR SWEET GRANDMA

The other day I went up to a local Christian bookstore and saw a 'Honk If You Love Jesus' bumper sticker. I was feeling particularly devout that day after coming from an exhilarating choir performance, so I bought the sticker and put it on my bumper. Boy, am I glad I did!

What an uplifting experience that followed! I was stopped at a red light at a busy intersection, just thinking about how wonderful the Lord is and I didn't notice that the light had changed. It's a good thing someone else loves Jesus because if he hadn't honked, I'd never have noticed the light!

I found that LOTS of people love Jesus! While I was sitting there, the guy behind started honking like crazy, and then he leaned out of his window and screamed, 'For the love of GOD! GO! GO! Jesus Christ, GO!' What an exuberant cheerleader he was for Jesus! Everyone started honking! I just leaned out of my window and started waving and smiling at all those lovely people.

I saw another gentleman waving in a funny way with only his middle finger stuck up in the air. I asked my teenage grandson in the back seat what that meant. He said that it was probably a Chinese good luck sign or something.

Well, I've never met anyone from China, so I leaned out the window and gave him the good luck sign back.

My grandson burst out laughing . . . why, even he was enjoying this religious experience! A couple of the people were so caught up in the joy of the moment that they got out of their cars and started walking towards me.

I bet they wanted to ask me what church I attended, but this was when I noticed the light had changed. So, I waved to all my sisters and brothers and drove on through the intersection. I noticed I was the only car that got through before the light changed again and I felt kind of sad that I had to leave them after all the love we had shared. So I slowed the car down, leaned out of the window and gave them all the Chinese good luck sign one last time as I drove away. Praise the Lord for such wonderful folks! – Love, Grandma.

**A** hungry lion was roaming through the jungle looking for something to eat. He came across two men. One was sitting under a tree reading a book, the other was typing away on his typewriter. The lion quickly pounced on the man reading the book and devoured him. Even the king of the jungle knows that readers digest and writers cramp.

**T**wo blondes were driving in a soft-top Saab. As they cruised along, enjoying the feeling of the wind blowing through their pale tresses, they came to an intersection. And though the light was red, they just kept going.

The blonde in the passenger seat found herself wondering, 'Didn't we just go through a red light?'

A few minutes later, another intersection. Another red light. And once again, the Saab sailed right through.

This time the blonde in the passenger seat was almost certain the light was red. But perhaps she was wrong.

Getting somewhat nervous she decided to pay very close attention to the road. At the next intersection, she did her best to concentrate.

Yes, the light was definitely red. And, yes, they drove right through. She turned to the blonde driving and said, 'Do you know we just went through three red lights in a row? You could have killed us!'

The blonde turned to her and said, 'Oh, am I driving?'

**F**irst bloke: My wife's an angel.
*Second bloke: You're in luck. Mine's still alive.*

**A** bloke went to the police station wishing to speak to the burglar who, having broken into his house the night before, had been arrested a few blocks away.

'You'll get your chance in court,' said the policeman at the desk.

'But all I want to know,' said the bloke, 'is how he got into the house without waking my wife. I've been trying to do that for years.'

### The Penguin Bumper Book of Australian Jokes

'I can let you have this top-of-the-line stereo for $900, minus six per cent, for cash,' the salesman said.

The customer, not able to figure out the calculation, said he would think about the deal and return the next day.

That evening, the fellow asked his blonde female friend: 'If you were offered $900 minus six per cent, how much would you take off?'

She replied, 'Everything but my earrings.'

Dear Dad,

$chool i$ $uper. I'm making lot$ of friend$ and playing lot$ of $port and $tudying very hard and getting lot$ of $leep. And I $imply can't think of anything I need. $o if you'd like, you could just $end me a card a$ it would be beaut to hear from you.

Love, your $on.

The reply:

Dear Son,

I kNOw that astroNOmy, ecoNOmics and oceaNOgraphy aren't eNOugh to keep an hoNOur student busy. Do NOt forget that the pursuit of kNOwledge is a NOble task and you can never study eNOugh.

Love, Dad.

A young bloke and a very beautiful woman meet on holidays and fall in love. And being in love, they decide to tell each other the truth.

'I must warn you, darling,' says the bloke, 'that I'm a golf fanatic. I live golf. I eat golf. I sleep and breathe golf.'

'Well, I'll be honest, too,' she says. 'I'm a hooker.'

The man looks crestfallen for a moment. And then asks: 'Are you keeping your wrists straight?'

The blonde reports for her university final examination. The exam consists of 'yes/no' type questions. She takes her seat in the examination hall, stares at the question paper for five minutes and then, in a fit of inspiration, takes her purse out, removes a coin and starts tossing the coin and marking the answer sheet – Yes for heads and No for tails.

Within half an hour she is all done, whereas the rest of the class is sweating it out. During the last few minutes, she is seen desperately throwing the coin, muttering and sweating. The moderator, alarmed, approaches her and asks what is going on.

'I finished the exam in half an hour. But I'm rechecking my answers.'

An Anglican minister dies and is waiting in line at the Pearly Gates. Ahead of him is a bloke in a loud shirt, leather jacket, jeans and sunglasses.

St Peter opens his great big book and asks the bloke, 'Who are you? I need your name and profession so that I can decide whether or not to admit you to the Kingdom of Heaven.'

And he replies, 'I'm Barry Cohen, taxidriver, New York City.'

St Peter turns a few pages of the book, smiles and says to the cab driver, 'Takest thou this silken robe and golden staff and enter the Kingdom of Heaven where you will be very, very happy for all eternity.'

So the cab driver gets into heaven with his robe and staff and it's the Anglican minister's turn. 'I, St Peter, am the Reverend Arthur Briggs, pastor of the North Balwyn Anglican Church for the last 43 years.'

Once again, St Peter consults the book. And he says to the minister, 'Take this cotton robe and wooden staff and enter the Kingdom of Heaven.'

'Hang on!' says the Anglican minister. 'That bloke was just a taxidriver and he got a silken robe and golden staff. It just doesn't seem fair.'

'Up here, everything is based on results,' says St Peter. 'When you preached, people slept. When he drove, people prayed.'

### The Penguin Bumper Book of Australian Jokes

**A** drover who'd spent his whole life in Cape York came to the city. He'd never seen a train or the tracks they run on. So he was walking along the tracks, studying the rails and the sleepers, when he heard a whistle – wooooo! – but had no idea what it was. Inevitably he was hit by a giant steam engine but, miraculously, suffered just a glancing blow. He was thrown to the side of the tracks and suffered some minor internal injuries and a few broken bones.

After a few weeks in the hospital recuperating, he wandered down the hall to where some nurses were boiling a kettle for a cup of tea. Taking his aluminium walking stick, he battered and bashed the kettle into an unrecognisable lump of metal. The nurses were aghast. 'Why did you ruin our kettle?'

And the drover replied, 'It's best to deal with these things while they're small.'

**THE FOLLOWING ARE TAKEN FROM REAL RESUMES AND COVER LETTERS – BY PEOPLE SEEKING EXECUTIVE EMPLOYMENT**

I DEMAND A SALARY COMMISERATE WITH MY EXTENSIVE EXPERIENCE.

## The Penguin Bumper Book of Australian Jokes

I have lurnt Wordperfect 6.0 computer and spreadsheet progroms.

Received a plague for Sales Person of the Year.

Wholly responsible for two (2) failed financial institutions.

Failed bar exam with relatively high grades.

It's best for employers that I not work with people.

You will want me to Head Honcho in no time.

Am a perfectionist and rarely if ever forget details.

I have an excellent track record, although I am not a horse.

My goal is to be a meteorologist, but since I possess no training in meteorology, I suppose I should try stock brokerage.

## The Penguin Bumper Book of Australian Jokes

As indicted, I have over five years of analysing investments.

Personal interests: Donating blood. Fourteen gallons so far.

Instrumental in ruining entire operation for a chainstore.

Note: Please don't misconstrue my fourteen jobs as job-hopping. I have never quit a job.

Reason for leaving last job: They insisted that all employees get to work by 8.45 a.m. every morning. Could not work under those conditions.

The company made me a scapegoat, just like my three previous employers.

References: None. I've left a path of destruction behind me.

A dedicated shop steward was checking out Melbourne brothels, hoping to sign sex workers up for the Miscellaneous Workers Union whilst, at the same time, giving each premises an appropriate rating.

At the first brothel he asked the madam, 'Is this a union house?'

'Sorry, it isn't,' she said.

'So if I pay you $100, what cut do the girls get?'

'The house gets $80 and the girls get $20,' the madam replied.

Outraged at this exploitation of the working class, he went to the brothel next door. 'Is this a union house?' he asked the madam.

'Yes, it is.'

'And if I pay you $100 what cut do the girls get?'

'The girls get $80 and the house gets $20.'

'Fine, fine,' the bloke said. And he looked around the room and pointed to a very attractive girl. 'I'd like her.'

'I'm sure you would,' said the madam, gesturing to an unattractive old dear in the corner, 'but Beryl has seniority.'

**S**he'd been working at an investment bank but decided it was time to go out on her own. Being shrewd and diligent, she did pretty well – and decided it was time to hire an in-house lawyer. So she began interviewing candidates.

'As you'll understand,' she said to one of the first applicants, 'in a business like this, our personal integrity must be beyond question. So let me ask you this question. Are you an honest lawyer?'

'Honest?' replied the candidate. 'Let me tell you something about honesty. I'm so honest that my father lent me $15 000 for my education and I paid back every penny as soon as I'd tried my first case.'

'And what sort of case was that?'

He squirmed in his seat. 'Well, Dad sued me for the money.'

**W**hy do banks charge you a 'non-sufficient funds fee' on money they already know you don't have?

**The Penguin Bumper Book of Australian Jokes**

If a tree falls in the forest and no-one is around to see it, do the other trees make fun of it?

Why are there five syllables in the word 'monosyllabic'?

A kid from the western district, working on his dad's wheat farm, accidentally overturned a truckload of grain. The farmer next door came to sympathise. 'Don't worry, son. Forget your troubles for a while and come and have a cup of tea with me and the missus. Then I'll help you get the truck back on its wheels.'

'That's very nice of you,' the kid answered, 'but I don't think Dad would like me to.'

But the farmer insisted. 'Come on, son.'

'Well, OK,' said the kid, 'but Dad won't like it.'

After a cup of tea and a slice of bread and jam, the boy thanked the farmer. 'I feel a lot better now but I still reckon Dad's going to be very, very cranky.'

'Don't be silly,' said the farmer. 'By the way, where is your dad?'

'Under the truck,' said the kid.

**A** ventriloquist is touring the clubs and stops to entertain in a small town. He's going through his usual run of off-colour and 'dumb blonde' jokes when a blonde woman in the fourth row stands on her chair and shouts: 'I've heard just about enough of your stupid blonde jokes, DICKHEAD! What makes you think you can stereotype women that way? What connection can a person's hair colour possibly have with their fundamental worth as a human being?

'It's morons like you that prevent women like myself from being respected at work and in our communities and from reaching our full potential, because you and your anachronistic kind continue to perpetuate negative images of not only blondes, but women in general, for the sake of cheap laughs. You are a pathetic relic of the past, and what you do is not only contrary to discrimination laws in every civilised country, it is deeply offensive to people with modern sensibilities and basic respect for their fellow citizens. You should hang your head in shame, you pusillanimous little maggot.'

Flustered, the ventriloquist begins to apologise, when the blonde yells, 'You stay out of this, Mister! I'm talking to the git on your knee!'

### THREE PROOFS THAT JESUS WAS MEXICAN

**1.** His first name was Jesus.

**2.** He was bilingual.

**3.** He was always being harassed by the authorities.

But then there are equally good arguments that . . .

## JESUS WAS BLACK

**1.** He called everybody 'brother'.

**2.** He liked Gospel.

**3.** He couldn't get a fair trial.

But then there are equally good arguments that . . .

## JESUS WAS JEWISH

**1.** He went into his father's business.

**2.** He lived at home until he was 33.

# The Penguin Bumper Book of Australian Jokes

**3.** He was sure his mother was a virgin, and his mother was sure he was God.

But then there are good arguments that . . .

## JESUS WAS ITALIAN

**1.** He talked with his hands.

**2.** He had wine with every meal.

**3.** He used olive oil.

But there are good arguments that . . .

# The Penguin Bumper Book of Australian Jokes

## JESUS WAS CALIFORNIAN

**1.** He never cut his hair.

**2.** He walked around barefoot.

**3.** He started a new religion.

But then there are equally good arguments that . . .

## JESUS WAS IRISH

**1.** He never got married.

**2.** He was always telling stories.

**3.** He loved green pastures.

But perhaps the most compelling evidence...

### THREE PROOFS THAT JESUS WAS A WOMAN...

**1.** He had to feed a crowd at a moment's notice when there was no food.

**2.** He kept trying to get the message across to a bunch of men who JUST DIDN'T GET IT.

**3.** Even when he was dead, he had to get up because there was more work for him to do.

**A** bloke with a black eye boards a plane bound for Pittsburgh and sits down in his seat. He notices immediately that the bloke next to him has a black eye too. He says to him, 'Hey this is a coincidence. We both have black eyes. Mind if I ask how you got yours?'

The other bloke says, 'Well, it just happened. It was a tongue twister accident. See, I was at the ticket counter and this gorgeous blonde with the most massive breasts in the world was there. So, instead of saying I'd like two tickets to Pittsburgh, I accidentally said I'd like two pickets to Tittsburgh. So she socked me a good one.'

'Wow!' said the first bloke, 'this is unbelievable. Mine was a tongue twister too! I was at the breakfast table and I wanted to say to my wife, ' "Please pour me a bowl of Frosties, honey," but I accidentally said, "You've ruined my life, you evil, self-centred, fat-arse bitch." '

**T**he executive was interviewing a young blonde for a position in his company. He wanted to find out something about her personality so he asked, 'If you could have a conversation with someone, living or dead, who would it be?'

The blonde quickly responded, 'The living one.'

**W**hat do you call nine blondes standing in a circle?
*A dope ring.*

**W**hy can't blondes take coffee breaks?
*They're too hard to retrain.*

### MEDICAL TERMS EXPLAINED

| | |
|---|---|
| Artery | The study of paintings. |
| Bacteria | Back door to cafeteria. |
| Barium | What doctors do when patients die. |
| Benign | What you be after you be eight. |

# The Penguin Bumper Book of Australian Jokes

| | |
|---|---|
| Catscan | Searching for kitty. |
| Colic | A sheep dog. |
| D & C | Where Washington is. |
| Dilate | To live long. |
| Enema | Not a friend. |
| Fester | Quicker than someone else. |
| Fibula | A small lie. |
| Genital | Non-Jewish person. |
| Impotent | Distinguished, well-known. |
| Labour Pain | Getting hurt at work. |
| Morbid | A higher offer than I bid. |
| Nitrates | Cheaper than day rates. |
| Node | Was aware of. |
| Tablet | A small table. |
| Terminal Illness | Getting sick at the bus station. |
| Tumour | More than one. |
| Urine | Opposite of you're out. |
| Varicose | Nearby, close by. |

**A** police officer stops a blonde for speeding and asks her very nicely if he can see her licence. She replies in a huff, 'I wish you guys would get your act together. Just yesterday you take away my licence and then today you expect me to show it to you!'

## A SELECTION OF ACTUAL LABELS

On a blanket from Taiwan:
NOT TO BE USED AS PROTECTION FROM A TORNADO.

On a helmet mounted-mirror used by US cyclists:
REMEMBER, OBJECTS IN THE MIRROR ARE ACTUALLY BEHIND YOU.

On a Taiwanese shampoo bottle:
USE REPEATEDLY FOR SEVERE DAMAGE.

On the bottle-top of a UK flavoured-milk drink:
AFTER OPENING, KEEP UPRIGHT.

On an NZ insect spray:
THIS PRODUCT NOT TESTED ON ANIMALS.

In a US guide to setting up a new computer:
TO AVOID CONDENSATION FORMING, ALLOW THE BOXES TO WARM UP TO ROOM TEMPERATURE BEFORE OPENING.
(Sensible, but the instructions were on the INSIDE of the box.)

On a Japanese product used to relieve painful haemorrhoids:
LIE DOWN ON BED AND INSERT POSCOOL SLOWLY UP TO THE PROJECTED PORTION LIKE A SWORD-GUARD INTO ANAL DUCT. WHILE INSERTING POSCOOL FOR APPROXIMATELY FIVE MINUTES, KEEP QUIET.

In some country, on the bottom of Coke bottles:
OPEN OTHER END.

On a packet of Sunmaid raisins:
WHY NOT TRY TOSSING OVER YOUR FAVOURITE BREAKFAST CEREAL?

On a Sears hairdryer:
DO NOT USE WHILE SLEEPING.

On a bag of Fritos:
YOU COULD BE A WINNER! NO PURCHASE NECESSARY. DETAILS INSIDE.
(The shoplifter special.)

On a bar of Dial soap:
DIRECTIONS – USE LIKE REGULAR SOAP.

## The Penguin Bumper Book of Australian Jokes

On Tesco's Tiramisu dessert (printed on the bottom of the box):
DO NOT TURN UPSIDE DOWN.

On Marks & Spencer Bread Pudding:
PRODUCT WILL BE HOT AFTER HEATING.

On a Korean kitchen knife:
WARNING: KEEP OUT OF CHILDREN.

On a string of Chinese-made Christmas lights:
FOR INDOOR OR OUTDOOR USE ONLY.

On a Japanese food processor:
NOT TO BE USED FOR THE OTHER USE.

On Sainsbury's peanuts:
WARNING – CONTAINS NUTS.

On an American Airlines packet of nuts:
INSTRUCTIONS – OPEN PACKET, EAT NUTS.

On a Swedish chainsaw:
DO NOT ATTEMPT TO STOP CHAIN WITH YOUR HANDS OR GENITALS.

# The Penguin Bumper Book of Australian Jokes

On a child's Superman costume:
WEARING OF THIS GARMENT DOES NOT ENABLE YOU TO FLY.

On some frozen dinners:
SERVING SUGGESTION: DEFROST.

On a hotel-provided shower cap in a box:
FITS ONE HEAD.

On packaging for a Rowenta iron:
DO NOT IRON CLOTHES ON BODY.

On Boot's 'Children's' cough medicine:
DO NOT DRIVE CAR OR OPERATE MACHINERY.

On Nytol sleep aid:
WARNING: MAY CAUSE DROWSINESS.

A little boy about 12 years old was walking down the footpath dragging a flattened frog on a string behind him. He came up to the doorstep of a house of ill repute and knocked on the door. When the madam answered it, she saw the little boy and asked what he wanted.

He said, 'I want to have sex with one of the women inside. I have the money to buy it, and I'm not leaving until I get it.'

The madam figured, why not. So she told him to come in. Once in, she told him to pick any of the girls he liked.

He asked, 'Do any of the girls have any diseases?'

Of course the madam said no.

He said, 'I heard all the men talking about having to get a shot after making love with Amber. THAT's the girl I want.'

Since the little boy was so adamant and had the money to pay for it, the madam told him to go to the first room on the right. He headed down the hall dragging the squashed frog behind him.

Ten minutes later he came back, still dragging the frog, paid the madam, and headed out the door.

The madam stopped him and asked, 'Why did you pick the only girl in the place with a disease, instead of one of the others?'

He said, 'Well, if you must know, tonight when I

get home, my parents are going out to a restaurant to eat, leaving me at home with a babysitter. After they leave, my babysitter will have sex with me because she just happens to be very fond of cute little boys. She will then get the disease that I just caught. When Mum and Dad get back, Dad will take the babysitter home. On the way, he'll jump the babysitter's bones, and he'll catch the disease. Then when Dad gets home from the babysitter's, he and Mum will go to bed and have sex, and Mum will catch it. In the morning, when Dad goes to work, the milkman will deliver the milk, have a quickie with Mum and catch the disease. And HE's the bastard who ran over my fucking FROG!'

**W**hy do they call it the Department of Interior when they are in charge of everything outdoors?

**I**f vegetarians eat vegetables, what do humanitarians eat?

**T**ell a man that there are 400 billion stars and he'll believe you. Tell him a bench has wet paint and he has to touch it.

**A** blonde and a brunette are in a lift, heading up. It stops at the third floor and a bloke gets in. He is very, very good looking. Wearing a three-piece Armani suit, he's got a great build and a good bum. The only problem? The girls notice that he has a bad case of dandruff.

When he gets off on the fifth, the brunette turns to the blonde, 'Someone should give him Head and Shoulders.'

To which the blonde replies, 'How do you give "shoulders"?'

**A** bloke picked up a girl in a bar and took her home. After some preliminary drinks, they got undressed, climbed into bed and started going at it. After a few minutes, the girl started laughing. The bloke asked her what she found so amusing.

'Your organ,' she replied, 'it's a bit on the small side.'

'Well,' he replied, 'it's not used to playing in cathedrals.'

**T**wo men were on a hunting trip. While one stayed in the log cabin, the other went out looking for a bear. He soon found a huge grizzly but only wounded it. The enraged bear charged towards him. He dropped his rifle and started running for the cabin.

He ran pretty fast but the bear was just a little faster and gained on him with every step. Just as he reached the open cabin door, he tripped and fell flat. Too close behind to stop, the bear tripped over him and went rolling into the cabin.

The man jumped up, closed the cabin door and yelled to his friend inside, 'You skin this one while I go and get another!'

**The Penguin Bumper Book of Australian Jokes**

Dear Subscriber:

Telecommunications has never been easier!

Welcome to REITHCard, an exciting new development in telecommunications.

REITHCard is proudly brought to you in co-operation with our venture partners who have joined us in the vanguard of community service throughout the world.

REITHCard (Responsibility Excused In The House) is an unprecedented offer guaranteed to keep you in touch with loved ones, friends and business colleagues at any time NO MATTER WHERE YOU ARE. But the best feature of REITHCard is the ENORMOUS SAVINGS it offers subscribers.

Here's how it works:

Each REITHCard has a personal, special four-digit PTPT (Pity The Poor Taxpayer) number. By dialling the PTPT number as a prefix to any number you wish to dial throughout the world, you can talk as long and as often as you like – entirely FREE of charge! This incredible deal is made possible through our high volume of Telecoms business which enables us to allocate the cost of the service to a CFPM (Contempt For Public Money) account.

## The Penguin Bumper Book of Australian Jokes

Accounting is easy. There is absolutely NO PAPERWORK! REITHCard takes care of everything – it's all so easy.

As a special bonus, if you accept this offer within ten days, we will upgrade your REITHCard to UTT category (Up The Taxpayer) enabling you to freely pass the PTPT number on to members of your family, staff, hotel receptionists and even passing taxidrivers. And unlike any other card, REITHCard allows you to make calls on the same PTPT simultaneously from up to twelve different locations around the globe!

To qualify for this special offer you must agree to follow the Prime Minister's parliamentary Code of Practice. To register for this FREE service, visit our website at www.polliesperks.gov.au and enter your username. Go to <Code of Practice> and click 'Accept'. There is no need to read the entire document because it is never enforced.

PLUS! If you apply for this outstanding offer within ten days you also receive at NO COST your choice of one of the following bestsellers:

*Altruism in Public Service* by Mal Colston.

*Don't Blame Me, It's Dad's Idea* by Sophie Gosper.

*Developing a Better Memory* by Carmen Lawrence.

**The Penguin Bumper Book of Australian Jokes**

*Overcoming Memory Lapses* by Alan Bond.
*Sad but Never Sorry* by John Howard.
*How to Retire Wealthy* by Bob Hawke.
*Bringing Home the Bacon: Recollections of life on the farm* by Paul Keating.
*Going for Gold* by Michael Knight.
And there's more! The first 250 subscribers receive 5000 bonus FREQUENTLIAR points with the airline of their choice.
SIGN UP NOW AT www.reithcard.com.au

---

If 'con' is the opposite of 'pro', then what is the opposite of progress?

Why is it lemon juice contains mostly artificial ingredients, but dishwashing liquid contains real lemons?

**W**hy doesn't glue stick to the inside of the bottle?

**W**hat do little birdies see when they get knocked unconscious?

**T**om is walking along a beach when he comes across a lamp partially buried in the sand. He picks up the lamp and rubs it, and two genies appear.

The genies tell him he has been granted three wishes. Tom makes his three wishes and the genies disappear.

The next thing Tom knows, he's in a bedroom in a mansion surrounded by 50 beautiful women. He makes love to all of them and begins to explore the house.

Suddenly he feels something soft beneath his feet and looks down. The floor is covered in $100 bills. Then there's a knock at the door. Tom answers the door and standing there are two people dressed in Ku

### The Penguin Bumper Book of Australian Jokes

Klux Klan outfits. They drag him outside to the nearest tree, throw a rope over a limb and hang him by the neck until he is dead. As the two Klansmen are walking away, they remove their hoods and it's the two genies.

One genie says to the other, 'Hey, I can understand the first wish – having all those beautiful women in a big mansion to make love to, that makes a lot of sense. I can also understand wanting to be a millionaire. But why he would want to be hung like a black man is beyond me!'

**A** man entered a local paper's pun contest. He sent in ten different puns in the hope that at least one of the puns would win.

Unfortunately, no pun in ten did.

**B**ill Gates died in a car accident. He found himself in Purgatory being sized up by God.

'Well, Bill, I'm really confused. I'm not sure whether to send you to Heaven or Hell. After all, you enormously helped society by putting a computer in almost every home in the world and yet you created that ghastly Windows 95. I'm going to do something I've never done before. In your case, I'm going to let you decide where you want to go!'

Bill replied, 'Well, thanks God. What's the difference between the two?'

God said, 'I'm willing to let you visit both places briefly if it will help you make a decision.'

'Fine. But where should I go first?' Bill asked.

God said, 'I'm going to leave that up to you.'

Bill said, 'OK then, let's try Hell first.' So Bill went to Hell. It was a beautiful, clean, sandy beach with clear waters. There were thousands of beautiful women running around, playing in the water, laughing and frolicking about. The sun was shining and the temperature was perfect.

Bill was very pleased. 'This is great!' he told God. 'If this is Hell, I REALLY want to see Heaven!'

'Fine,' said God, and off they went.

Heaven was a high place in the clouds, with angels drifting about playing harps and singing. It was nice but not as enticing as Hell. Bill thought for a moment and made his decision. 'Hmmm, I think I prefer Hell,' he told God.

'Fine,' replied God, 'as you desire.' So Bill Gates went to Hell.

Two weeks later, God decided to check up on the late billionaire to see how he was going in Hell. When God arrived in Hell, he found Bill shackled to a wall, screaming amongst the hot flames in a dark cave. He was being burned and tortured by demons.

'How's everything going, Bill?' God asked.

Bill responded – his voice full of anguish and disappointment. 'This is awful. This is not what I expected. I can't believe this happened. What happened to that other place with the beaches and the beautiful women playing in the water?'

God said, 'That was the screen saver.'

### WHAT MY MOTHER TAUGHT ME!

My mother taught me TO APPRECIATE A JOB WELL DONE:
'If you're going to kill each other, do it outside – I just finished cleaning!'

### The Penguin Bumper Book of Australian Jokes

My mother taught me RELIGION:
'You better pray that will come out of the carpet.'

My mother taught me about TIME TRAVEL:
'If you don't behave, I'm going to knock you into the middle of next week!'

My mother taught me LOGIC:
'Because I said so, that's why.'

My mother taught me FORESIGHT:
'Make sure you wear clean underwear, in case you're in an accident.'

My mother taught me IRONY:
'Keep laughing and I'll "give" you something to cry about.'

My mother taught me about CONTORTIONISM:
'Will you "look" at the dirt on the back of your neck!'

My mother taught me about the science of OSMOSIS:
'Shut your mouth and eat your supper!'

**The Penguin Bumper Book of Australian Jokes**

My mother taught me about STAMINA:
'You'll sit there 'til you've eaten all your vegies.'

My mother taught me about WEATHER:
'It looks as if a tornado swept through your room.'

My mother taught me about HYPOCRISY:
'If I've told you once, I've told you a million times – don't exaggerate!'

My mother taught me about BEHAVIOUR MODIFICATION:
'Stop acting like your father!'

My mother taught me about ENVY:
'There are millions of less fortunate children in this world who don't have wonderful parents like you do.'

**A** husband and wife are travelling by car from Melbourne to Sydney. After many hours on the road they're too tired to continue and decide to stay overnight at a motel. They drive past a few shabby-looking examples – rooms at $60 to $80 a night – and then take a room at the one that looks best of all.

They explain that they just want to use the room for four hours and then get back on the road, expecting a substantial discount.

But when they check out, four hours later, they're handed a bill for $350. The husband is outraged. 'Why is the charge so high? OK, this is a good motel. But the rooms aren't worth $350. Christ, you don't have to pay that for a five-star hotel in a capital city.'

He's informed the $350 is a standard rate. So the husband insists on speaking to the owner.

The owner listens to the complaint and explains that his motel has an Olympic-size pool. And out the back there's a huge conference centre available for guests to use. And had they stayed overnight, 'we have entertainment in the little cafe . . . some of the best performers from Melbourne and Sydney have appeared here.'

But no matter what the owner says, no matter what facility he mentions, the husband replies, 'But we didn't use it.'

The owner won't budge. So, finally, the husband pays up.

He writes a cheque and hands it over. But the owner is astonished when he looks at the amount. 'Hang on, you've made this cheque out for $100.'

'That's right,' says the husband. 'I charged you $250 for sleeping with my missus.'

'But I didn't!' says the owner.

'Well,' the husband replies, 'she was here, and you could have.'

## Random thoughts

A careful study of economics usually reveals that the best time to buy anything is last year.

A perfectionist is one who takes great pains, and gives them to everyone else.

A picture may be worth a thousand words but it uses up a thousand times more memory.

## The Penguin Bumper Book of Australian Jokes

Accomplishing the impossible means only that the boss will add it to your regular duties.

Character is like a fence – it cannot be strengthened by whitewash.

In the 60s people took acid to make the world weird. Now the world is weird and people take Prozac to make it normal.

Just when I was getting used to yesterday, along came today.

My mind not only wanders, it sometimes leaves completely.

The measure of a man's intelligence is inversely proportional to the amount of time he keeps his mouth open.

When trouble arises and things look bad, there is always one individual who perceives a solution and is willing to take command. Usually that individual is crazy.

WHEN I WAS LITTLE, MY GRANDFATHER USED TO MAKE ME STAND IN A CLOSET FOR FIVE MINUTES WITHOUT MOVING. HE SAID IT WAS ELEVATOR PRACTICE.

The Pope and Bill Clinton died on the same day. A computer glitch caused the Pope to be sent to Hell and Clinton to Heaven. Strong representations were made by the Pope, and he was told it WAS a computer glitch, and it would be sorted out. But he would have to spend overnight in Hell, which he did.

The authorities were as good as their word and the next day the Pope met Clinton on the stairway as they were on their way up/down.

'I'm very sorry about this, Bill. But all my life I've been looking forward to the day I would arrive in Heaven and meet the Virgin Mary.'

'If only I'd known,' says Clinton, 'you're just 24 hours too late.'

## The Penguin Bumper Book of Australian Jokes

### WHY IT'S GREAT TO BE A BLOKE

A five-day holiday requires one overnight bag.

Phone conversations are over in 30 seconds flat.

Queues for the bathroom don't exist.

All your orgasms are real.

You don't have to lug a handbag full of useless stuff around.

You get brownie points for the slightest act of thoughtfulness or consideration.

You never have to clean a toilet.

You can be showered and ready to go in ten minutes.

You save time by washing every third week.

# The Penguin Bumper Book of Australian Jokes

IF SOMEONE FORGETS TO INVITE YOU TO SOMETHING, IT MEANS THAT THEY FORGOT TO INVITE YOU. IT DOESN'T MEAN THAT THEY HATE YOU. HE OR SHE CAN STILL BE YOUR FRIEND.

YOU DON'T HAVE TO SHAVE BELOW YOUR NECK.

NONE OF YOUR COWORKERS HAVE THE POWER TO MAKE YOU CRY.

YOU DON'T HAVE TO CURL UP NEXT TO A HAIRY BACKSIDE EVERY NIGHT.

IF YOU'RE 34 AND SINGLE, NOBODY EVEN NOTICES.

YOU CAN WRITE YOUR NAME IN THE SNOW.

BIOLOGICAL CLOCK?
FLOWERS FIX EVERYTHING.

YOU NEVER HAVE TO WORRY ABOUT OTHER PEOPLE'S FEELINGS.

YOU GET TO THINK ABOUT SEX 90% OF YOUR WAKING HOURS.

## The Penguin Bumper Book of Australian Jokes

Reverse parking is easy.

Foreplay is optional.

Window shopping is what you do when you buy windows.

You never feel compelled to stop a friend from getting laid. In fact, you encourage them.

Mechanics tell you the truth.

You don't give a rat's arse if no-one notices your new haircut.

You never look at the size of a baby's head and cringe.

The whole world is your urinal.

Hot wax never comes near your pubic area.

One mood all the time.

Same work, more pay!

### The Penguin Bumper Book of Australian Jokes

GREY HAIR AND WRINKLES ADD CHARACTER.

THE REMOTE CONTROL IS YOURS AND YOURS ALONE.

PEOPLE NEVER GLANCE AT YOUR CHEST WHEN YOU'RE TALKING TO THEM.

YOU HAVE A NORMAL AND HEALTHY RELATIONSHIP WITH YOUR MOTHER.

YOU CAN BUY CONDOMS WITHOUT THE SHOPKEEPER IMAGINING YOU NAKED.

IF YOU DON'T CALL YOUR MATE WHEN YOU SAY YOU WILL, HE WON'T TELL YOUR OTHER FRIENDS AND THEY WON'T TRY TO WORK OUT WHAT THE PROBLEM IS.

SOME DAY YOU'LL BE A DIRTY OLD MAN. AND YOU'RE LOOKING FORWARD TO IT.

YOU NEVER HAVE TO MISS A SEXUAL OPPORTUNITY BECAUSE YOU'RE NOT IN THE MOOD.

DIETING INVOLVES GETTING REGULAR-SIZED FRIES WITH YOUR BURGER.

## The Penguin Bumper Book of Australian Jokes

Porn movies are designed specifically with you in mind.

You don't have to remember everyone's birthdays and anniversaries.

Not liking a person doesn't exclude having great sex with them.

Life will go on if the bedsheets don't get changed once in a while.

Having a beer belly is a perfect reason for wearing a T-shirt.

Your mates can be trusted never to trap you with 'So . . . notice anything different?'

Your mates never say, 'Well, if you don't know what you did wrong, I'm certainly not telling you.'

Your mates never say, 'Talk to me.'

In the Year 3 classroom in an upper London school, the kids were coming in from lunch. The teacher, Miss Elliot, said to the first boy who walked in the door, 'What did you do during lunch today, Chris?' Chris said, 'I played in the sandpit miss.'

Miss Elliot said, 'Isn't that interesting. If you can spell sand on the blackboard, you can have a sweet.' Chris got up and, after a lot of struggling, wrote S-A-N-D on the blackboard. He got a sweet.

Next to walk through the door was little Frankie. Miss Elliot said, 'What did you do during lunch today, Frankie?' He said, 'I played in the sandpit with Chris, Miss.'

She said, 'Isn't that nice. If you can spell pit on the blackboard, then you can have a sweet.' He writes P-I-T on the blackboard, and gets a sweet.

Next to come in from lunch is little Ahmed. Miss Elliot said, 'What did you do during lunch, Ahmed?' And Ahmed replied, 'I went to play in the sandpit, Miss, but Chris and Frankie, they threw rocks at me!'

'Why, that's blatant racial discrimination! If you can spell "blatant racial discrimination" on the blackboard, then you can have a sweet.'

## The Penguin Bumper Book of Australian Jokes

Three hang-glider pilots – one from New Zealand, one from South Africa and the other from Australia – were sitting around a campfire near Ayers Rock, each embroiled in the bravado for which they were famous.

A night of tall tales began . . . Kenyon the Kiwi said, 'I must be the meanest, toughest hang-glider dude there is. Why, just the other day, I landed in a field, scared a crocodile loose from a nearby swamp and it ate six men before I wrestled it to the ground . . . and killed it with my bare hands.'

Jerry from South Africa couldn't stand to be bettered. 'Well you guys, I lended ifter a 200-mile flight on a tiny trail ind a 15-foot Namibian desert snike slid out from under a rock and made a move for me. I grebbed thet bugger with my bare hinds and beet its head off ind sucked the poison down in one gulp. Ind I'm still here today.'

Kevin, the Australian, remained silent, slowly poking the fire with his penis.

**The Penguin Bumper Book of Australian Jokes**

I went into a bookstore and asked the saleswoman, 'Where's the self-help section?' She said if she told me, it would defeat the purpose.

Isn't the best way to save face to keep the lower part shut?

War doesn't determine who's right, just who's left.

At the 1999 World Women's Conference the first speaker from Canada stood up: 'At last year's conference we spoke about being more assertive with our husbands. Well, after the conference I went home and told my husband that I would no longer cook for him and that he would have to do it himself. After the first day I saw nothing. After the second day I saw nothing. But after the third day I saw that he had cooked a wonderful roast lamb.'

The crowd cheered.

The second speaker from France stood up: 'After last year's conference I went home and told my husband that I would no longer do his laundry and that he would have to do it himself. After the first day I saw nothing. After the second day I saw nothing. But after the third day I saw that he had done not only his own washing but my washing as well.'

The crowd cheered.

The third speaker from Italy stood up: 'After last year's conference I went home and told my husband that I would no longer do his cooking, cleaning or shopping and that he would have to do it himself. After the first day I saw nothing. After the second day I saw nothing. But after the third day I could see a little bit out of my left eye.'

A shearer breasts the bar at a favourite country pub and sees four very attractive young women sitting at a table. He thinks to himself, 'I might be in here,' orders a schooner of VB and casually saunters over to the ladies.

And in his best effort at a classy accent he inquires, 'Any of you sheilas want a root?'

The ladies whisper amongst themselves before the tallest one – the one with the blondest hair and the biggest, bluest eyes – stands up and says, 'I didn't at first, but I do *now*, you smooth-talking bastard!'

### THREE CORPORATE LESSONS

Lesson Number One:

A crow was sitting on a tree, doing nothing all day. A small rabbit saw the crow, and asked him, 'Can I also sit like you and do nothing all day?' The crow answered, 'Sure, why not.' So the rabbit sat on the ground below the crow and rested. All of a sudden, a fox appeared, jumped on the rabbit and ate it.

Moral of the story: To be sitting and doing nothing, you must be sitting very, very high up.

Lesson Number Two:

A turkey was chatting with a bull. 'I would love to be able to get to the top of that tree,' sighed the turkey, 'but I haven't got the energy.' 'Well, why don't you nibble on some of my droppings?' replied the bull. 'They're packed with nutrients.' The turkey pecked at a lump of dung and found that it actually gave him enough strength to reach the first branch of the tree. The next day, after eating some more dung, he reached the second branch. Finally, after a fortnight, there he was, proudly perched at the top of the tree. He was promptly spotted by a farmer, who shot the turkey out of the tree.

Moral of the story: Bullshit might get you to the top, but it won't keep you there.

Lesson Number Three:

A little bird was flying south for the winter. It was so cold that the bird froze and fell to the ground in a large field. While it was lying there, a cow came by and dropped some dung on it. As the frozen bird lay there in the pile of cow dung, it began to realise how warm it was. The dung was actually thawing him out! He lay there all warm and happy, and soon began to sing for joy. A passing cat heard the bird singing and came to investigate. Following the sound, the cat discovered the bird under the pile of cow dung, and promptly dug him out and ate him!

The morals of the story are:

**1.** Not everyone who drops shit on you is your enemy.

**2.** Not everyone who gets you out of shit is your friend.

**3.** When you're in deep shit, keep your mouth shut.

In Summary:

An organisation is like a tree full of monkeys, all on different limbs at different levels, some climbing up, some fooling around and some simply just idling ... The monkeys on top look down and see a tree full of smiling faces. The monkeys on the bottom look up and see nothing but arseholes.

# The Penguin Bumper Book of Australian Jokes

## THE WISDOM OF CHILDREN

'NEVER TRUST A DOG TO WATCH YOUR FOOD.'
RICHARD, AGED 10.

'WHEN YOUR DAD IS MAD AND ASKS YOU, "DO I LOOK STUPID?", DON'T ANSWER.' JESSICA, AGED 9.

'NEVER TELL YOUR MUM HER DIET'S NOT WORKING.'
JOHN, AGED 14.

'STAY AWAY FROM PRUNES.' ANDY, AGED 9.

'WHEN YOUR MUM IS MAD AT YOUR DAD, DON'T LET HER BRUSH YOUR HAIR.' EMILY, AGED 11.

'NEVER LET YOUR THREE-YEAR-OLD BROTHER IN THE SAME ROOM AS YOUR SCHOOL HOMEWORK.' REBECCA, AGED 14.

'A PUPPY ALWAYS HAS BAD BREATH – EVEN AFTER EATING A TIC-TAC.' AARON, AGED 9.

'NEVER HOLD A DUSTBUSTER AND A CAT AT THE SAME TIME.' SAMANTHA, AGED 9.

'YOU CAN'T HIDE A PIECE OF BROCCOLI IN A GLASS OF MILK.' DIANNE, AGED 9.

'DON'T WEAR POLKA-DOT UNDERWEAR UNDER WHITE SHORTS.' KRISTY, AGED 11.

'IF YOU WANT A KITTEN, START OUT BY ASKING FOR A HORSE.' KYLIE, AGED 15.

'FELT-TIP MARKERS ARE NOT GOOD TO USE AS LIP-STICK.' MOLLY, AGED 9.

'DON'T PICK ON YOUR SISTER WHEN SHE'S HOLDING A CRICKET BAT.' JOEL, AGED 10.

'WHEN YOU GET A BAD MARK IN SCHOOL, SHOW YOUR MUM WHEN SHE'S ON THE PHONE.' ALICIA, AGED 13.

'NEVER TRY TO BAPTISE A CAT.' RORY, AGED 8.

**A** man takes his Rottweiler to the vet.

'My dog's cross-eyed, is there anything you can do for him?'

'Well,' says the vet, 'let's have a look at him.' So he picks the dog up and examines his eyes, then checks his teeth. Finally, he says, 'I'm going to have to put him down.'

'Why? Because he's cross-eyed?'

'No, because he's really heavy.'


**O**ne fine day Mr Rabbit goes running through the forest and he sees a giraffe rolling a big fat joint and says, 'Giraffe! Giraffe! Why do you smoke puff? Come run with me and get fit instead.'

So the giraffe stops rolling his reefer and runs with the rabbit.

They come across an elephant doing lines of cocaine on a mirror. The rabbit says, 'Elephant! Elephant! Why do you do drugs? Come run with us instead and get fit.' So the elephant stops and goes running with them.

They come across a lion preparing a syringe of smack. 'Lion! Lion!' cries the rabbit, 'why do you do drugs? Come run with us instead.'

The lion, with a mighty roar, squashes the little rabbit to smithereens.

'No!' the giraffe and elephant cry, 'Why did you do that? All he was trying to do was help you out!'

The lion says, 'Fucking rabbit, always makes me run around this wanky forest when he's done a few pills.'

**A** local man was found murdered in his home in Perth over the weekend. Detectives at the scene found the man face down in his bathtub. The tub had been filled with milk and Cornflakes, and the deceased had a banana protruding from his rear. Police suspect it's the work of a cereal killer.

**A** preacher wanted to raise money for his church and, being told there was a fortune in horseracing, he decided to purchase a horse and enter it in the races.

However, at the local auction, the going price for horses was so high that the preacher settled on a donkey instead. The preacher figured that, since he bought the animal, he might as well race it. To his great surprise, the donkey did quite well and came in third place.

The next day, the racing sheets carried this headline:

PREACHER SHOWS ASS.

The preacher was so pleased with the donkey that he entered it in the races again, and this time the animal won first place. The paper said:

PREACHER'S ASS OUT IN FRONT

The bishop was so upset with this kind of publicity that he ordered the preacher not to enter the donkey in any more races. The newspaper printed this headline:

BISHOP SCRATCHES PREACHER'S ASS

This was too much for the bishop and he ordered the preacher to get rid of the donkey. The preacher decided to give the animal to a nun in a local convent. The next day, the headline read:

NUN HAS BEST ASS IN TOWN

The bishop fainted. When he came round, he informed the nun that she would have to dispose of the donkey. The nun searched, finally finding a farmer willing to buy the animal for ten dollars. The paper reported this event too:

NUN PEDDLES ASS FOR TEN BUCKS

They buried the bishop the next day.

**B**ack in the olden days, a man was travelling through Switzerland. Nightfall was rapidly approaching and the man had nowhere to sleep. He went to a farmhouse and asked the farmer if he could spend the night.

The farmer told him that it would be alright and that he could sleep in the barn.

The man went into the barn to bed down and the farmer went back to the house. The farmer's daughter came downstairs and asked the farmer, 'Who was that man going into the barn?'

'That's some fellow travelling through. He needs a place to stay for the night, so I said he could sleep in the barn.'

The daughter then asked the farmer, 'Did you offer him anything to eat?'

'Gee, no, I didn't,' the farmer answered. His daughter replied, 'Well, I'm going to take him some food.'

She went into the kitchen, prepared a plate of food and then took it out to the barn. The daughter was in the barn for an hour before returning to the house. When she returned, her clothes were all dishevelled and buttoned up wrong and she had several strands of straw tangled up in her long blonde hair. She immediately went upstairs to her bedroom and went to sleep.

A little later the farmer's wife came down and asked the farmer why their daughter went to bed so early. 'I don't know,' he said, 'I told a man that he could sleep in the barn and our daughter took him some food.'

'Oh,' replied the wife. 'Did you offer the man anything to drink?'

'Umm, no I didn't.'

'I'm going to take something out there for him to drink.'

The wife went to the cellar, got a bottle of wine, then went to the barn. She did not return for over an hour. When she did return, her clothes were also messed up and she had straw twisted into her blonde hair. She went straight upstairs to bed.

Next morning at sunrise, the man in the barn got

up and continued on his journey, waving to the farmer as he left the farm. A few hours later, the daughter woke up and came rushing downstairs. She went out to the barn, only to find it empty. She ran back to the house. 'Where's the man from the barn?' she eagerly asked her father.

Her father answered, 'He left several hours ago.'

'What?' she cried. 'He left without saying goodbye? After all we had together! I mean, last night he made such passionate love to me.'

'What?' shouted the farmer and ran out into the front yard looking for the man.

By now the man was halfway up the side of the mountain. The farmer screamed at him, 'I'm gonna get you! You had sex with my daughter!'

The man looked back down from the mountainside, cupped his hands next to his mouth, and yelled out: 'I LAID DE OLADEE TOO!'

And that's how yodelling began.


A man who lives in a street in Mount Waverley is down at the pub getting shit-faced with a mate of his who lives in the same street.

When he gets home he says to his wife that his

mate said he had made love to every woman in the street, except one.

The wife responded, 'That'll be that stuck-up bitch Mrs Smith in number three.'

**A**fter the Sydney Olympics there was a big auction of unsold souvenirs and memorabilia. People paid big money for volunteer uniforms, for giant kewpie dolls used in the closing ceremony, for Olympic T-shirts and even demountable homes that had been used in the Olympic village. On and on the auction went – you could bid for the giant shark that had carried Greg Norman around the arena, or for the giant camera that Elle Macpherson had straddled. Then there were the Victa mowers used in that gala opening – and a wide variety of flags and bunting.

A bloke went along to see if he could buy a bargain – but all he could afford was one box of Sydney Olympic frangers. As issued to Olympic athletes. He worried that they might be too big for him but, after all, they were very cheap.

So he took them home and showed his wife. 'Sydney Olympic condoms?' she said.

'Yep, and they come in three colours. Gold, Silver and Bronze.'

'What colour are you going to wear tonight,' she asked.

'Gold, of course,' said the man proudly.

The wife looked at him for a long moment. 'Why don't you wear silver?'

'Why silver?'

'Well, it would be nice if you came second for a change.'

A bloke meets a beautiful girl in a bar and she agrees to spend the afternoon with him for $500.

So they go to a motel and bonk furiously, and expensively, for hours.

When they're finished, he confesses that he doesn't have any cash with him – but he'll have his secretary write a cheque and mail it to her. He'll call the payment 'Rent for Apartment'.

On the way to the office he decides he's been extravagant – that $500 was far too much. So he has his secretary send a cheque for $250, along with the following note:

'Dear Madam,

Enclosed find cheque in the amount of $250 for rent of your apartment. I am not sending the amount agreed upon, because when I rented the apartment I was under the impression that:

**1.** It had only had a couple of previous occupants.

**2.** That there was plenty of heat.

**3.** That it was small enough to make me feel cosy and at home.

However, on close inspection, it was obvious that it had had many previous occupants, that there wasn't much heat and that it was entirely too large.'

On receiving the note, the young woman returned the cheque with the following note:

'Dear Sir,
First of all, I cannot understand how you expect a beautiful apartment to remain unoccupied indefinitely. As for the heat, there was plenty of it, if you knew how to turn it on. Regarding the space, the apartment is of regular size, but if you don't have enough furniture to fill it, please do not blame the landlady.'

Saddam Hussein is sitting in his office wondering who to invade when his phone rings. 'Mr Hussein,' a heavily accented voice says. 'This is Paddy in County Cavan, Ireland. I am ringing to inform you that I am officially declaring war on you!'

'Well, Paddy,' Saddam replies. 'This indeed is important news! Tell me, how big is your army?'

'At this moment in time,' says Paddy, after a moment's calculation, 'there is myself, my cousin Sean, my next-door neighbour Gerry and the entire dominoes team from the pub. That makes eight!'

Saddam sighs and says, 'I must tell you, Paddy, that I have one million men in my army waiting to move on my word.'

'Oh crap,' says Paddy, 'I'll have to ring you back!' Sure enough, the next day Paddy rings back. 'Right, Mr Hussein, the war is still on! We have managed to acquire some equipment!'

'What equipment would that be, Paddy?' Saddam asks.

'Well, we have two combine harvesters, a bulldozer and Murphy's tractor from the farm.'

Once more Saddam signs and says, 'Paddy, I have 16 000 tanks, 2000 mine layers, 14 000 armoured cars and my army has increased to one and a half million since we last spoke.'

'Fuck me!' says Paddy. 'I'll have to ring you back!'

Sure enough, Paddy rings again the next day. 'Right, Mr Hussein, the war is still on! We have managed to get ourselves airborne! We've kitted out old Ted's crop-sprayer with a couple of rifles in the cockpit and the bridge team has joined us as well!'

Once more Saddam sighs and says, 'I must tell you, Paddy, that I have 1000 bombers and 2000 MiG attack planes and my military complex is surrounded by laser-guided surface-to-air missile sites and since we last spoke my army has increased to two million.'

'Oh bollocks,' says Paddy, 'I'll have to ring you back.'

Sure enough, Paddy calls again the next day. 'Right, Mr Hussein. I am sorry to tell you that we have had to call off the war.'

'I'm sorry to hear that,' says Saddam. 'Why the sudden change of heart?'

'Well, we've given it careful consideration and decided there's no way we can cope with two million prisoners!'

**A** man staggers into an emergency room with concussion, multiple bruises, two black eyes and a five-iron wrapped tightly around his throat. Naturally, the doctor asks him what happened.

'Well, it was like this,' said the man. 'I was having a quiet round of golf with my wife, when at a difficult hole we both sliced our balls into a pasture of cows.

We went to look for them and while I was rooting around I noticed one of the cows had something white at its rear end. I walked over and lifted up the tail and, sure enough, there was the golf ball with my wife's monogram on it . . . stuck right in the middle of the cow's bum. That's when I made my mistake.'

'What did you do?' asks the doctor.

'Well, I lifted the tail and yelled to my wife, 'Hey, this looks like yours!".'

**L**ast night I played a blank tape at full blast. The mime next door went nuts.

**J**ust think how much deeper the ocean would be if sponges didn't live there.

**I**f olive oil comes from olives, where does baby oil come from?

When I went to lunch today I noticed this elderly lady sitting on a bench near the shops and she was sobbing her eyes out. I stopped and asked her what was wrong. She said, 'I have a 22-year-old husband at home. He makes love to me every morning and then gets up and makes me pancakes, sausages, fresh fruit and freshly ground, brewed coffee.'

I said, 'Well then, why are you crying?'

She said, 'He makes me homemade soup for lunch and my favourite brownies and then makes love to me half the afternoon.'

'I said, 'Well then, why are you crying?'

She said, 'For dinner he makes me a gourmet meal with wine and my favourite dessert and then makes love to me until 2 a.m.'

I said, 'Well, why in the world would you be crying?'

She said, 'I CAN'T REMEMBER WHERE I LIVE!!!'

## NEW REMOTE CONTROL CAN BE OPERATED BY REMOTE

No more leaning forward to get remote from coffee table means greater convenience for TV viewers.

TOKYO – Television watching became even more convenient this week with Sony's introduction of a new remote-controlled remote control.

The new device, which can be controlled via remote control through the use of a second remote control unit, will replace older models that needed to be held in the hand to be operable.

'Constantly leaning forward to pick up the remote control from the coffee table is a tiresome, cumbersome chore that will soon be a thing of the past,' Sony director of product development, Dan Ninomiya, said. 'These new remotes, should they be left on the coffee table or in some other hard-to-reach place, will not need to be picked up and actually pointed at the screen in order to work.'

The new remote control – along with the additional remote it is designed to control – will soon come standard with all Sony televisions, allowing viewers to remain 'more immobile, more stationary, and more physically inert than ever before'.

'Imagine a remote control capable of switching channels on your television right from its spot on the table, one that requires no clumsy fumbling about the hands to operate,' Ninomiya said. 'Well, that bold, inactive future is here.'

The Sony remote-controlled remote control, or RCRC, also puts an end to worries about losing the remote in the couch.

'The RCRC works from anywhere in the room, even deep inside a hide-a-bed sofa,' a Sony press release read. 'This puts an end to distracting remote searches, frustrating lifting and stacking of cushions, as well as eventual cushion replacement after retrieval, an annoying task that can sometimes result in missed programming and, in some cases, serious waste of valuable television-viewing time.'

As an added convenience, in the event that the RCRC itself is accidentally placed in a less-than-immediately-accessible spot, it will come with an additional third remote control.

'Should the second remote end up under a magazine or newspaper, the third remote will still be capable of controlling the second remote, enabling the second remote to change channels on the first one, and ultimately the television itself, with just the touch of a button,' Sony spokesperson Rich Hervey explained. 'Regardless of the location of the remote control unit, the ease and comfort of remote-control television viewing will be assured.'

To ensure that the third remote is not lost as well, it will come with a handy adhesive pad affixing it to the owner's forehead at all times. Or, in the case of more expensive models, it will be implanted directly within the sinus passages of the user.

'This,' Hervey said, 'will make the loss of the third remote control a possibility that is, at most, remote.'

Home entertainment industry insiders predict that the new RCRCs will be hugely successful.

'These things are fantastic,' said *Seated Viewing Magazine* editor Ted Kohrs at a recent Las Vegas trade show demonstrating the new product. 'I've been here all morning and my heart's only beaten six times!'

It is believed that the new Sony remote may prove even more popular than competitor Toshiba's new Pepsinjection intravenous soda-drip televisions as the hot home-entertainment item for 2002.

Little Johnny sees his daddy's car pass the playground and go into the woods. Curious, he follows the car and sees Daddy and Aunt Jane in a passionate embrace. Little Johnny finds this so exciting and can barely contain himself as he runs home and starts to tell his mother.

'Mummy, Mummy, I WAS AT THE PLAYGROUND AND DADDY AND . . .'

Mummy tells him to slow down. She wants to hear the story. So Little Johnny tells her. 'I was at the playground and I saw Daddy's car go into the woods with Aunt Jane. I went back to look and he was giving Aunt Jane a big kiss, then he helped her take off her shirt. Then Aunt Jane helped Daddy take his pants off. Then Aunt Jane lay down on the seat, then Daddy . . .'

At this point, Mummy cut him off and said, 'Johnny, this is such an interesting story, suppose you save the rest of it for suppertime. I want to see the look on Daddy's face when you tell it tonight.'

At the dinner table, Mummy asks Little Johnny to tell his story. Johnny starts his story, describing the car going into the woods, the undressing, lying down on the seat and, '. . . then Daddy and Aunt Jane did that same thing Mummy and Uncle Bill used to do when Daddy was in the Navy!!'

**L**ittle Johnny returns from school and says he got an F in arithmetic.

'Why?' asks the father.

'The teacher asked, "How much is 2x3?" I said "six".'

'But that's right!'

'Then she asked me, "How much is 3x2?"'

'What's the fucking difference?' asks the father.

'That's what I said!'

**L**ittle Johnny goes to school, and the teacher says, 'Today we are going to learn multi-syllable words, class. Does anybody have an example of a multi-syllable word?'

Little Johnny waves his hand, 'Me, Miss Rogers, me me!!'

Miss Rogers: 'All right, little Johnny, what is your multi-syllable word?'

Little Johnny says, 'Mas-tur-bate.'

Miss Rogers smiles and says, 'Wow, little Johnny, that's a mouthful.'

Little Johnny says, 'No, Miss Rogers, you're thinking of a blow job.'

One day, during a lesson on proper grammar, the teacher asked for a show of hands from those who could use the word 'beautiful' in the same sentence twice.

First, she called on little Suzie, who responded with, 'My father bought my mother a beautiful dress and she looked beautiful in it.'

'Very good, Suzie,' replied the teacher. She then called on little Michael.

'My mummy planned a beautiful banquet and it turned out beautifully,' he said.

'Excellent, Michael.' Then the teacher called on little Johnny.

'Last night, at the dinner table, my sister told my father that she was pregnant, and he said, "Beautiful, just fucking beautiful!".'

Imagine if major companies from all around the world started producing or sponsoring condoms. They would become fashionable and companies would probably advertise more openly. Imagine the trademarks:

Nike Condoms: Just do it.

Toyota Condoms: Oh . . . what a feeling!

Ford Condoms: The ride of your life.

Microsoft Condoms: Where do you want to go today?

KFC Condoms: Finger Lickin' Good.

M&Ms Condoms: Melt in your mouth, not in your hands.

Coca-Cola Condoms: It's the Real Thing.

Eveready Condoms: Keep going and going . . .

Macintosh Condoms: It does more, it costs less, it's that simple.

Pringles Condoms: Once you pop, you can't stop.

### The Penguin Bumper Book of Australian Jokes

**A** bloke walked into a bar in New Zealand and ordered a Foster's. The barman looked up and said, 'You're not from around here. Where are you from?'

The bloke said, 'I'm from Australia.'

The barman asked, 'What do you do in Australia?'

The bloke responded, 'I'm a taxidermist.'

The barman said, 'What the hell is a taxidermist?'

The bloke said nervously, 'I mount animals.'

The barman grinned and shouted to the whole bar, 'It's okay! He's one of us!'

**A** train hits a bus load of nuns and they all perish. They are in Heaven trying to enter the pearly gates past St Peter.

He asks the first nun: 'Sister Karen, have you ever had any contact with a penis?' The nun giggles and shyly replies, 'Well once I touched the head of one with the tip of my finger.'

St Peter says, 'OK, dip the tip of your finger in the holy water and pass through the gate.'

St Peter asks the next nun the same question,

'Sister Elizabeth have you ever had any contact with a penis?'

The nun is a little reluctant but replies, 'Well, once I fondled and stroked one.'

St Peter says, 'OK, dip your whole hand in the holy water and pass through the gate.'

All of a sudden there is a lot of commotion in the line of nuns, one nun is pushing her way to the front of the line. When she reaches the front St Peter says, 'Sister, Sister, what seems to be the rush?'

The nun replies, 'If I'm going to have to gargle that holy water, I want to go before Sister Mary sticks her arse in it!!'

**A** highway patrolman pulled alongside a speeding Nissan on the freeway. Glancing at the car, he was astounded to see that the blonde behind the wheel was knitting! Realising that she was oblivious to his flashing lights and siren, the officer cranked down his window, turned on his bullhorn and yelled, 'PULL OVER!'

'No,' the blonde yelled back, 'it's a scarf!'

An airline captain was breaking in a very pretty new blonde stewardess. The route they were flying had a stay-over in another city, so upon their arrival, the captain showed the stewardess the best place for airline personnel to eat, shop and stay. The next morning, as the pilot was preparing the crew for the day's route, he noticed the new stewardess was missing. He called her hotel and asked what had happened.

She answered the telephone, sobbing, and said she couldn't get out of her room.

'You can't get out of your room?' queried the captain. 'Why not?'

The stewardess replied, 'There are only three doors in here,' she cried, 'one is the bathroom, one is the closet, and one has a sign that says "DO NOT DISTURB".'

### Advice to single men

What follows is a guide to making your girlfriend happy. Do something she likes and you get points. Do something she dislikes and points are subtracted.

## Simple Duties

| | |
|---|---:|
| You make the bed | +1 |
| You make the bed but forget to add the decorative pillows | 0 |
| You throw the bedspread over rumpled sheets | -1 |
| You leave the toilet seat up | -5 |
| You replace the toilet paper roll when it's empty | 0 |
| When the toilet paper roll is barren, you resort to Kleenex | -1 |
| You check out a suspicious noise at night | 0 |
| You check out a suspicious noise and it's nothing | 0 |
| You check out a suspicious noise and it's something | +5 |
| You pummel it with a six iron | +10 |
| It's her father | -10 |

## Social Engagements

| | |
|---|---:|
| You stay by her side the entire party | 0 |
| You stay by her side for a while, then leave to chat with a friend | -2 |
| Named Tiffany | -4 |
| Tiffany is a dancer | -6 |
| Tiffany has implants | -8 |

## Her Birthday

| | |
|---|---|
| You take her out to dinner | 0 |
| You take her out to dinner and it's not a sports bar | +1 |
| Okay, it is a sports bar | -2 |
| And it's an all-you-can-eat night | -3 |
| It's a sport bar and it's an all-you-can-eat night and your face is painted the colours of your favourite team | -10 |

## Thoughtfulness

| | |
|---|---|
| You forget her birthday completely | -20 |
| You forget your anniversary | -30 |
| You forget to pick her up at the bus stop | -45 |
| And the pouring rain dissolves her leg cast | -60 |

## A Night Out

| | |
|---|---|
| You take her to a movie | +2 |
| You take her to a movie she likes | +4 |
| You take her to a movie you hate | +6 |
| You take her to a movie you like | -2 |
| It's called *Deathcop 3* | -3 |
| You lied and said it was a foreign film about orphans | -15 |

## Flowers

| | |
|---|---|
| You buy her flowers only when it's expected | 0 |
| You buy her flowers as a surprise just for the heck of it | +20 |
| You give her wildflowers you've actually picked yourself | +30 |
| And she contracts Lyme disease | -25 |

## Your Physique

| | |
|---|---|
| You develop a noticeable potbelly | -15 |
| You develop a noticeable potbelly and exercise to get rid of it | +10 |
| You develop a noticeable potbelly and resort to loose jeans and baggy Hawaiian shirts | -30 |
| You say, 'I don't care because you have one too' | -800 |

## Finances

| | |
|---|---|
| You spend a lot of money on something impractical | -5 |
| Something she can't use | -10 |
| Such as a motorised model aeroplane | -20 |
| And she got a small appliance for her birthday | -40 |

# The Penguin Bumper Book of Australian Jokes

## Driving
| | |
|---|---|
| You lose the directions on a trip | -4 |
| You lose the directions and end up getting lost | -10 |
| You end up getting lost in a bad part of town | -15 |
| You get lost in a bad part of town and meet the locals up close and personal | -25 |
| You know them | -60 |

## The Big Question
| | |
|---|---|
| She asks, 'Do I look fat?' | -5 |
| (Sensitive questions always start with a deficit) | |
| You hesitate in responding | -10 |
| You reply, 'Where?' | -35 |

## Communication
| | |
|---|---|
| When she wants to talk about a problem, you listen, displaying what looks like a concerned expression | 0 |
| When she wants to talk, you listen, for over 30 minutes | +5 |
| You listen for more than 30 minutes without looking at the TV | +10 |
| She realises this is because you've fallen asleep | -20 |

## The Penguin Bumper Book of Australian Jokes

A big bloke from the bush is trying out for a Sydney Rugby team.

'Can you tackle?' asks the coach.

'Watch this!' says the boy from the bush – and proceeds to run full-speed into a telephone pole. He shatters it into splinters.

'Pretty good,' says the coach. 'I'm impressed. But can you run?'

'Of course I can run,' says the boy from the bush. And he's off like a shot. And, in just over nine seconds, he'd done a 100-yard dash.

'Bewdy,' said the coach. 'But can you pass a football?'

The young bloke hesitated for a few seconds.

'Well,' he said, 'if I can swallow it, I can probably pass it.'

A man was eating in a fancy restaurant, and there was a gorgeous blonde eating at the next table. He had been checking her out all night, but lacked the nerve to go talk to her.

# The Penguin Bumper Book of Australian Jokes

Suddenly she sneezed and her glass eye went flying out of her socket towards the man. With his quick reflexes, he caught it in mid-air.

'Oh, my God, I'm soooo sorry,' the woman said as she popped her eye back in the socket. 'Let me buy you dinner to make it up to you.'

They enjoyed a wonderful dinner together and afterwards the woman invited him back to her place for a drink. After a bit she took him into the bedroom and began undressing him. The couple had wild, passionate sex many times during the night.

The next morning when he awoke, she was already up and brought him breakfast in bed.

The guy was amazed. 'You know, you are the perfect woman. Are you this nice with every guy you meet?'

'No,' she replied. 'You just happened to catch my eye!'

**Q:** What do you call two guys hanging on a wall by a window?

**A:** Kurt and Rod.

**A** woman walked up to a little old man rocking in a chair on his porch.

'I couldn't help noticing how happy you look,' she said. 'What's your secret for a long, happy life?'

'I smoke three packets of cigarettes a day,' he said. 'I also drink a case of whisky a week, eat fatty foods and never exercise.'

'That's amazing,' said the woman. 'How old are you?'

'Twenty-six,' he said.


'**D**octor,' the embarrassed man said, 'I have a sexual problem. I can't get it up for my wife any more.'

'Mr Thomas, bring her back with you tomorrow and let me see what I can do.'

So, the worried fellow returned with his wife the following day. The doctor greeted the couple and then said, 'Please remove your clothes, Mrs Thomas.'

The woman obliged and removed her clothing.

'OK, now turn all the way around. Now lie down

please ... Uh-huh, I see. Alright, you can put your clothes back on.'

While the woman was busy dressing herself again, the doctor took the husband aside. 'You're in perfect health,' he said to the man. 'Your wife didn't give me an erection either.'

Steve is shopping for a new motorcycle. He finally finds one for a great price. The motorcycle is missing a seal though, so whenever it rains Steve has to smear Vaseline over the spot where the seal should be.

Steve's girlfriend is having him over for dinner to meet her parents one evening. He drives his new motorcycle to his girlfriend's house. She is waiting outside for him when he arrives. 'No matter what happens at dinner tonight, don't say a word. Our family had a fight a while ago about doing the dinner dishes. We haven't done any since ... and the first person to speak at dinner has to do them.'

Steve sits down for dinner and soon notices that his girlfriend wasn't exaggerating. It is just how she described it. Dishes are piled up to the ceiling in the kitchen and nobody is saying a word. Steve decides to have a little fun. He grabs his girlfriend, throws her onto the table and has sex with her in front of her parents. His girlfriend is a little flustered, her father is obviously livid, and her mother is horrified. Yet, when Steve and his girlfriend resume their places at the dinner table, nobody says a word.

A few minutes later, Steve grabs his girlfriend's mum, throws her onto the table and does a repeat performance. Now his girlfriend is furious, her father is boiling, and her mother is a little more pleased. But still, there is complete silence at the table.

Suddenly, there is a loud clap of thunder and it starts to rain. Steve remembers his motorcycle outside and so he jumps up and grabs his jar of Vaseline.

With a look of terror in his eyes, the girlfriend's father backs away from the table and exclaims, 'OK, enough already. I'll do the damn dishes!'

An attorney was sitting in his office late one night when the Devil appeared before him. The Devil told the lawyer, 'I have a proposition for you. You can win every case you try, for the rest of your life. Your clients will adore you, your colleagues will stand in awe of you, and you will make embarrassing sums of money. All I want in exchange is your soul, your wife's soul, your children's souls, the souls of your parents, grandparents and parents-in-law, and the souls of all your friends and law partners.'

The lawyer thought about this for a moment, then asked, 'So, what's the catch?'

**A** bloke loses his dog. 'Put an ad in the paper,' says a friend.

So he does. A little classified reading, 'HERE BOY!'

**C.**1500 AD. God looks down from his heavenly throne at his mendicant orders to see which of them is doing well. And they are all doing fine. So He decides to reward each of them with a wish.

First God speaketh to the leader of the Dominicans and says, 'Verily I say unto you, you can have a wish.'

And the leader of the Dominicans replies, 'Lord, Lord, would you please help us to understand more clearly the distinction between essence and existence.'

With a snap of the divine fingers and a flash of lightning, it is done.

Then God speaketh to the head of the Franciscans and sayeth, 'I will grant you one wish.'

The leader of the Franciscans replies, 'Lord, Lord, will you please help us to understand more deeply the mystery of life.'

And with a snap of the divine fingers and a flash of lightning, it is done.

Finally God visits the head of the Jesuits and sayeth to the black Pope, 'I will grant you one wish.'

And the Jesuit replies, 'Actually, Lord, we're doing fine. Could you please just leave us alone?'

**A** blonde decided she wanted a new hobby. So she went to the bookstore and looked at all the titles. Stamp Collecting. Ikebana. Gardening. Quilt-making. And then she saw a book on Ice Fishing. Ice fishing? She was fascinated, and studied and studied and studied the topic until she finally decided she was ready. Then she booked a trip to Canada and, arriving at a tourist destination famed for its ice fishing, started buying all the gear she'd need.

Finally she got to the ice, found a quiet little area, placed her padded stool in position and carefully laid out her tools.

Just as she was about to start sawing her little frozen porthole, a booming voice from the sky bellowed, 'There are no fish under the ice!'

Startled, she repacked her belongings, folded her stool and moved further along the ice.

There she poured some hot chocolate from a thermos and started to cut a new hole. Again the voice from above bellowed, 'There are no fish under the ice!'

She wasn't sure what to do. This wasn't covered in any of the reference books. So she packed up her gear and moved to the far side of the ice. Once there, she stopped for a few moments to regain her calm and was particularly careful in the way she set everything up. She arranged her tools from left to right. Positioned her stool just so. And just as she was about to cut the hole, the voice again boomed, 'There are no fish under the ice!'

By now the blonde was terrified and, looking skyward, said, 'Is that you, Lord?'

And the voice boomed back, 'No, this is the manager of the skating rink.'

### THINGS YOU DON'T WANT TO OVERHEAR ON AN AIRLINE PA SYSTEM:

- Hello, this is Captain O'Riley. I wanted to take this time to remind you that your seat cushions can be used as flotation devices.
- This is the captain speaking. We're going to play a little game of Geography Trivia. Look out the window and if you can recognise where we are, tell your flight attendant and receive an extra packet of nuts.
- This sudden loss of altitude allows a unique view of the local terrain. Just part of our airline's commitment to make your flight a memorable experience.
- Ummmm ... sorry ...
- Aaaah, look, we're going to have to return to Sydney. We forgot something.

- You may have noticed the loss of an engine. However the reduction in weight and drag will allow us to fly much more efficiently.
- This is your Captain speaking. Look, it would be a good idea right now if everyone closed their shades and watched the in-flight movie.
- We've now reached our cruising altitude of 30 000 feet and . . . bugger it!
- Thank you for choosing Ansett.

A farmer was disturbed when he found out his son was masturbating several times a day in the shearing shed.

'Son, you've got to stop that! Go out and get yourself a girl.'

So the boy went out and found himself a farmer's daughter to whom he got married.

But a week or so after the wedding, the farmer again found his son masturbating in the shearing shed.

'Stop that!' he yelled. 'Your wife's a fine young girl.'

'I know dad,' the boy replied, 'but her arm gets tired.'

## WHAT MEN REALLY MEAN WHEN THEY SAY . . .

'I can't find it.'
REALLY MEANS 'It didn't fall into my outstretched hands, so I'm completely clueless.'

'That's women's work.'
REALLY MEANS 'It's dirty, difficult and thankless.'

'Will you marry me?'
REALLY MEANS 'Both my roommates have moved out, I can't find the washer, and there is no more peanut butter.'

'It's a guy thing.'
REALLY MEANS 'There is no rational thought pattern connected with it, and you have no chance at all of making it logical.'

'Can I help with dinner?
REALLY MEANS 'Why isn't it already on the table?'

'It would take too long to explain.'
REALLY MEANS 'I have no idea how it works.'

'I'm getting more exercise lately.
REALLY MEANS 'The batteries in the remote are dead.'

'We're going to be late.'
REALLY MEANS 'Now I have a legitimate excuse to drive like a maniac.'

'Take a break, honey, you're working too hard.'
REALLY MEANS 'I can't hear the game over the vacuum cleaner.'

'That's interesting, dear.'
REALLY MEANS 'Are you still talking?'

'Honey, we don't need material things to prove our love.'
REALLY MEANS 'I forgot our anniversary again.'

'It's a really good movie.'
REALLY MEANS 'It's got guns, knives, fast cars and naked women.'

'You know how bad my memory is.'
REALLY MEANS 'I remember the words to the theme song of "F Troop", the address of the first girl I kissed, the Vehicle Identification Number of every car I've ever owned, but I forgot your birthday.'

'I was just thinking about you, and got you these roses.'
REALLY MEANS 'The girl selling them on the corner was a real babe, wearing a thong.'

'Oh, don't fuss. I just cut myself. It's no big deal.'
REALLY MEANS 'I have actually severed a limb, but will bleed to death before I admit I'm hurt.'

'I do help around the house.'
REALLY MEANS 'I once threw a dirty towel near the laundry basket.'

'Hey, I've got reasons for what I'm doing.'
REALLY MEANS 'And I sure hope I think of some pretty soon.'

'What did I do this time?'
REALLY MEANS 'What did you catch me at?'

'I heard you.'
REALLY MEANS 'I haven't the foggiest clue what you just said, and am hoping desperately that I can fake it well enough so that you don't spend the next three days yelling at me.'

'You really look terrific in that outfit.'
REALLY MEANS 'Please don't try on one more outfit. I'm starving.'

'I missed you.'
REALLY MEANS 'I can't find my sock drawer, the kids are hungry and we are out of toilet paper.'

'I'm not lost. I know exactly where we are.'
REALLY MEANS 'No-one will ever see us alive again.'

'This relationship is getting too serious.'
REALLY MEANS 'I like you as much as I like my truck.'

'I don't need to read the instructions.'
REALLY MEANS 'I am perfectly capable of screwing it up without printed help.'

'Dad, I have to do a project for school. Can I ask you a question?'

'Yes, my boy. What's the question?'

'What's this word "politics" mean?'

'Well, let's take our home for example. I'm the wage-earner, so let's call me capitalism. Your mother administrates the money, so we'll call her the government. We take care of your needs, so let's call you the people. We'll call the maid the working class and your baby brother the future. Do you understand?'

'I'm not entirely sure, Dad. I'll have to think about it.'

That night, awakened by his baby brother's crying, the boy went to see what was wrong. He found that the baby had a shitty nappy and went to his parents' room to tell his mum, who was sound asleep. This necessitated passing the maid's room where, peeking through the keyhole, he saw his father in bed with her.

So the lad went back to his bedroom and fell asleep.

'Dad,' he said next morning, 'I think I understand politics now.'

'Good, son. Explain it to me in your own words.'

'Well, while capitalism is screwing the working class, the government is sound asleep, the people are being ignored and the future is full of shit.'

Once upon a time there was a bloke who loved baked beans. He loved them despite the fact that they had a rather embarrassing consequence.

One day he met a young woman and fell in love – but before he proposed marriage he decided it was time to confront his addiction to baked beans, given the social embarrassments they tended to produce.

So he saw a therapist who helped him deal with his addiction. And, at last, he gave up beans.

The couple were soon married and started to live happily ever after.

But one evening, on his way home from work, he had car trouble. And while waiting for the RACV, he couldn't resist going into a nearby cafe and having, yes, a plate of baked beans. So he walked up and down the road for ten or 15 minutes, farting like a trooper.

When he arrived home, his wife was very concerned. 'Darling, darling, I've been worried as worried. But thank heavens you're here as I've got the most wonderful surprise for dinner.'

And she blindfolded him, led him to a chair at the end of the dining table. But just as she was about to remove the blindfold, the phone rang – and she went to answer it.

Taking the opportunity he shifted his weight from one buttock to the other and let go. The result was loud and lethal.

He took the napkin from his lap and vigorously fanned the air about him and was confident that things had returned to normal when, all of a sudden, he felt another urge. So he shifted his weight to the other buttock and let go again.

This was a real prize-winner. Something for the Guinness Book of Records.

Whereupon his wife returned from the telephone,

asked him if he'd peeked, and then removed the blindfold. And there was his surprise. Twelve dinner guests seated around the table for his 35th birthday.

She woke in the middle of the night and found her husband missing from the bed. She listened carefully and could hear what sounded like sobbing from downstairs. Putting on her robe and slippers, she descended the stairs and found her husband curled up in a little ball, crying his heart out.

'Darling, what's the matter?' she asked. 'Did you fall down the stairs?'

'No, no. It's not that.'

'Then what is it?'

'Remember, 20 years ago, I got you pregnant?'

'Yes, and my father said if you didn't marry me you'd go to jail.'

'Well, I would have been released tonight.'

A priest was walking through the cemetery when he came upon a young boy who was energetically masturbating.

'My son, you shouldn't be doing that,' said the priest. 'You should be saving that for when you get married.'

The boy hung his head, pulled up his trousers, and said, 'Yes, Father.'

About ten years later, the priest was in the confessional when the same young man, now in his early 20s, came in.

'Yes, my son?'

'Father, I don't know if you'll remember me, but about ten years ago you caught me masturbating in the cemetery. And I'll never forget the advice you gave.'

'And what was that, my son?'

'Well, you told me that I was doing wrong and should be saving it for when I get married.'

'Yes, that was good advice,' said the priest. 'Did you take it?'

'Yes, Father, I did. But there's only one problem.'

'What's that, my son?'

'Well, I have a 55-gallon drum of the stuff in the back of my Holden ute. Now that I'm getting married, what am I supposed to do with it?'

## THE PERFECT DAY FOR HER:

| | |
|---|---|
| 08.15 | Wake up to hugs and kisses |
| 08.30 | Weigh in five pounds lighter than yesterday |
| 08.45 | Breakfast in bed, freshly squeezed orange juice and croissants |
| 09.15 | Soothing hot bath with fragrant lilac bath oil |
| 10.00 | Light workout at club with handsome, funny personal trainer |
| 10.30 | Facial, manicure, shampoo and comb out |
| 12.00 | Lunch with best friend at outdoor cafe |
| 12.45 | Notice ex-boyfriend's wife, she's gained 30 pounds |
| 13.00 | Shopping with friends, unlimited credit |
| 15.00 | Nap |

| | |
|---|---|
| 16.00 | Three dozen roses delivered by florist, card is from secret admirer |
| 16.15 | Light workout at club, followed by gentle massage |
| 17.30 | Pick out outfit for dinner, primp before the mirror |
| 19.30 | Candlelight dinner for two followed by dancing |
| 22.00 | Hot shower (alone) |
| 22.30 | Make love |
| 23.00 | Pillow talk, light touching and cuddling |
| 23.15 | Fall asleep in his big strong arms |

## THE PERFECT DAY FOR HIM:

| | |
|---|---|
| 06.00 | Alarm |
| 06.15 | Blow job |
| 06.30 | Excellent bowel motion while reading sporting pages |
| 07.00 | Breakfast. Pancakes with maple syrup |
| 07.30 | Limo arrives |
| 07.45 | Have a few drinks en route to Tullamarine |
| 08.15 | Private plane to Sydney |

# The Penguin Bumper Book of Australian Jokes

| | |
|---|---|
| 09.30 | Pick up by another limo, taken to Royal Sydney Golf Club |
| 09.45 | Front nine (two under) |
| 11.45 | Lunch, two dozen oysters on the half shell, three Heinekens |
| 12.15 | Blow job |
| 12.30 | Back nine (four under) |
| 14.15 | Limo back to airport |
| 15.15 | Arrive FNQ, go marlin fishing with all-female crew |
| 16.30 | Land World Record light tackle Marlin |
| 18.45 | Shit, shower and shave |
| 19.00 | Watch ABC news. Stock market booms. Investments go up in value. |
| 19.30 | Dinner at five-star restaurant |
| 21.00 | Remy Martin and Cuban Partagas cigar |
| 21.30 | Sex with three women |
| 23.00 | Massage and jacuzzi |
| 23.45 | Bed (alone) |
| 23.55 | Sleep |

**The Penguin Bumper Book of Australian Jokes**

**A** tourist walks into an antique shop in Melbourne's Chinatown. Picking through the objects on display he discovers a detailed, life-sized bronze sculpture of a rat. The sculpture is so interesting and unique that he picks it up and asks the shop owner what it costs.

'Twelve dollars for the rat, sir,' says the shop owner, 'and $1000 more for the story behind it.'

'You can keep the story, old man,' he replies, 'but I'll take the rat.'

The transaction complete, the tourist leaves the store with the bronze rat under his arm. As he crosses the street in front of the store, two live rats emerge from a sewer drain and fall into step behind him.

Nervously looking over his shoulder, he begins to walk faster, but every time he passes another sewer, more rats come out and follow him. By the time he's walked two blocks, at least a hundred rats are at his heels, and people begin to point and shout. He walks even faster, and soon breaks into a trot as multitudes of rats swarm from sewers, basements, vacant lots and abandoned cars.

Rats by the thousands are at his heels, and as he sees the waterfront at the bottom of the hill, he panics and starts to run flat out. No matter how fast he runs, the rats keep up, squealing hideously, now not just thousands but millions, so that by the time he comes rushing up to the water's edge a trail of rats twelve city blocks long is behind him.

Making a mighty leap, he jumps up onto a light post, grasping it with one arm while he hurls the bronze rat into the Yarra River with the other as far as he can heave it. Pulling his legs up and clinging to the light post, he watches in amazement as the seething tide of rats surges into the river, where they drown.

Shaken and mumbling, he makes his way back to the antique shop.

'Ah, so you've come back for the rest of the story,' says the owner.

'No,' says the tourist thoughtfully. 'I was just wondering if you have a bronze lawyer.'

Two engineering students were walking across the RMIT campus when one said, 'Where did you get your mountain bike?'

And the second engineer replied, 'Well, I was walking through the Treasury Gardens yesterday when a beautiful woman rode up on this bike. She threw it to the ground, took off all her clothes and said "Take what you want".'

The other engineer nodded approvingly. 'Good choice. The clothes probably wouldn't have fit.'

**I**f at first you don't succeed, destroy all evidence that you tried.

**E**xperience is something you don't get until just after you need it.

**S**uccess always occurs in private, and failure in full view.

**The Penguin Bumper Book of Australian Jokes**

The problem with the gene pool is that there is no lifeguard.

A clear conscience is usually the sign of a bad memory.

A fool and his money are soon partying.

I'd kill for a Nobel Peace Prize.

Borrow money from pessimists; they don't expect it back.

99 per cent of lawyers give the rest a bad name.

# The Penguin Bumper Book of Australian Jokes

## TRANSCRIPTION OF A GUEST MAKING A ROOM-SERVICE ORDER IN AN ASIAN HOTEL

Room
Service
(RS):         'Morny. Ruin sorbees.'
Guest (G): 'Sorry, I thought I'd dialled room service.'
RS:           'Rhy ... Ruin sorbees. Morny! Djewish to odor sunteen?'
G:            'Uh, yes ... I'd like some bacon and eggs.'
RS:           'Ow July den?'
G:            'What?'
RS:           'Ow July den? Pry, boy, pooch?'
G:            'Oh, the eggs! How do I like them? Sorry, scrambled please.'
RS:           'Ow July dee bayhcem ... crease?'
G:            'Crisp will be fine.'
RS:           'Hokay. An san tos?'
G:            'What?'
RS:           'San tos. July san tos?'
G:            'I don't think so.'
RS:           'No? Judo one toes?'
G:            'I feel really bad about this, but I don't know what "judo one toes" means.'

RS: 'Toes! Toes! Why djew Don one toes? Ow bow singlish mopping we bother?'

G: 'English muffin! I've got it! You were saying "toast". Fine. Yes, an English muffin will be fine.'

RS: 'We bother?'

G: 'No . . . just put the bother on the side.'

RS: 'Wad?'

G: 'I mean butter . . . just put it on the side.'

RS: 'Copy?'

G: 'Sorry?'

RS: 'Copy . . . tea . . . mill?'

G: 'Yes, coffee please. And that's all.'

RS: 'One minnie. Ass ruin torino fee, strangle ache, crease baychem, tossy singlish mopping we bother honey sigh, and copy . . . rye?'

G: 'Whatever you say.'

RS: 'Tendjewberrymud.'

G: 'You're welcome.'

## The Penguin Bumper Book of Australian Jokes

**A** man was driving home one evening when he realised that it was his daughter's birthday and he hadn't bought her a present. He drove to the mall and ran to the toy store and asked the store manager, 'How much is that new Barbie in the window?'

The manager replied, 'Which one? We have "Barbie goes to the Gym" for $19.95. "Barbie goes to the Ball" for $19.95. "Barbie goes Shopping" for $19.95. "Barbie goes to the Beach" for $19.95. "Barbie goes to the Nightclub" for $19.95. And "Divorced Barbie" for $375.'

'Why is "Divorced Barbie" $375, when all the others are $19.95?' the man asked, surprised.

' "Divorced Barbie" comes with Ken's car, Ken's house, Ken's boat, Ken's dog, Ken's cat and Ken's furniture.'

**T**wo blondes are walking through a shopping mall when one almost trips over a compact. She picks it up, opens it up, looks in the mirror and says, 'Hmmm, this person looks familiar.'

The second blonde says, 'Let me have a look.'

She looks in the mirror and says, 'Silly you, that's me!'

## Entries from patients' medical records, as dictated by GPs and specialists

- Patient has chest pain if she lies on her left side for over a year.
- On the second day the knee was better and on the third day it had completely disappeared.
- She has no rigours or shaking chills, but her husband states she was very hot in bed last night.
- The patient has been depressed ever since she began seeing me in 1992.
- The patient is tearful and cries constantly. She also seems to be depressed.
- Discharge status: Alive but without permission.
- Healthy-appearing, decrepit 69-year-old male, mentally alert but forgetful.
- The patient refused an autopsy.
- The patient has no past history of suicides.
- She is numb from her toes down.
- While in the ER, she was examined, X-rated and sent home.
- Occasional, constant, infrequent headaches.
- Rectal exam revealed a normal-sized thyroid.

### The Penguin Bumper Book of Australian Jokes

- She stated that she had been constipated for most of her life until 1985 when she got a divorce.
- I saw your patient today, who is still under our car for physical therapy.
- Exam of genitalia reveals that he is circumcised.
- The lab test indicated abnormal lover function.
- The patient was seen in consultation by Dr blank, who felt we should sit on the abdomen and I agree.
- Patient has two teenage children but no other abnormalities.

#### AUTHENTIC RATINGS OF OFFICER EFFICIENCY FROM MILITARY REPORTS

NOT THE SHARPEST KNIFE IN THE DRAWER.

GOT INTO THE GENE POOL WHILE THE LIFEGUARD WASN'T WATCHING.

A ROOM TEMPERATURE IQ.

GOT A FULL SIX-PACK, BUT LOST THE PLASTIC THINGY TO HOLD IT ALL TOGETHER.

# The Penguin Bumper Book of Australian Jokes

A PRIME CANDIDATE FOR NATURAL DESELECTION.

GATES ARE DOWN, THE LIGHTS ARE FLASHING BUT THE TRAIN ISN'T COMING.

SO DENSE, LIGHT BENDS AROUND HIM.

IF HE WERE ANY MORE STUPID, HE'D HAVE TO BE WATERED TWICE A WEEK.

WHEEL IS TURNING, BUT THE HAMSTER IS DEAD.

HIS MEN WOULD FOLLOW HIM ANYWHERE, BUT ONLY OUT OF CURIOSITY.

I WOULD NOT BREED FROM THIS OFFICER.

HE HAS CARRIED OUT EACH AND EVERY ONE OF HIS DUTIES TO HIS ENTIRE SATISFACTION.

HE WOULD BE OUT OF HIS DEPTH IN A CAR-PARK PUDDLE.

SINCE MY LAST REPORT HE HAS REACHED ROCK BOTTOM, AND HAS STARTED TO DIG.

He sets low personal standards and consistently fails to achieve them.

He has the wisdom of youth and the energy of old age.

Works well when under constant supervision or cornered like a rat in a trap.

This man is depriving a village somewhere of an idiot.

On his first day at Australian Consolidated Press, the young executive shouted into the phone, 'Get me a fucking cup of coffee, quickly!'

Instead of the compliant voice of a secretary he heard a menacing growl. 'You idiot, you've dialled the wrong extension. Do you know who you're talking to?'

'No,' said the new employee.

'This is Kerry Packer. I own the joint, you idiot.'

### The Penguin Bumper Book of Australian Jokes

And the new employee shouted back, 'And do you know who *you* are talking to, you idiot?'

'No,' replied Mr Packer.

'Good,' said the employee, and slammed down the phone.

**T**wo nuns went out of the convent to seek donations. One of them was known as Sister Mathematical (SM) and the other was known as Sister Logical (SL). It was getting dark and they were still a long way from the convent.

SL: A bloke has been following us for the past half-hour.
SM: I noticed him. What could he want?
SL: It's logical. He wants to have his way with us.
SM: Oh my God! At this rate, walking 4kph, he will reach us in 15 minutes. What can we do?
SL: Logically, we have to walk faster.
SM: We're now walking at 6kph but he's still catching up.

### The Penguin Bumper Book of Australian Jokes

SL: That's because he did the logical thing. He started to walk faster too.
SM: So what shall we do?
SL: The only logical thing to do is go off in different directions. He can't follow both of us.

Sister Mathematical arrives at the convent and is concerned that Sister Logical hasn't been seen. Finally, at long last, she arrives.

SM: Sister Logical, thank God you're safe. What happened?
SL: The only logical thing happened. The man couldn't follow both of us. So he followed me.
SM: And what happened then?
SL: The only logical thing to happen. I started to run.
SM: And what happened?
SL: The only logical thing that could happen. He started to run.
SM: What then?
SL: The only logical thing to happen happened. He reached me.
SM: What did you do?

SL: The only logical thing to do. I lifted my habit up.
SM: Oh sister, sister. And what did he do?
SL: The only logical thing to do. He pulled down his pants.
SM: Oh, no! And then what happened?
SL: Isn't it logical, sister? A nun with her dress up can run far faster than a man with his pants down.

**A** woman approaches her priest and says, 'Father, I have a problem. I have two talking cockatoos, but they only know how to say one thing.'

'And what's that, my child?'

'All they say is, "Hello, we're prostitutes. Want to have some fun?"'

'Dear oh dearie me,' said the priest. 'But I've a solution. Bring your cockatoos to my house and I'll put them with my talking parrots whom I've taught to pray and read the Bible. My parrots will teach your cockatoos to stop saying those terrible things.

They'll be taught to praise and to worship.'

'Bless you,' said the woman to the priest.

The next day she brought her cockatoos to the priest's house where his parrots were holding rosary beads and murmuring prayers in their cage. The lady put her cockatoos, which were females, in with the parrots, which were male. Immediately the cockatoos said, 'Hi, we're prostitutes, want to have some fun?'

And one male parrot looked at the other male parrot and said, 'Toss away the rosaries. Our prayers have been answered.'

The scene is an Anglican church where a traditional wedding is taking place. A little girl asks her mum, 'Why is the bride dressed in white?'

'Because white is the colour of virtue, of virginity, of chastity. And it is the colour of happiness. And today is the happiest day of her life.'

The little girl thinks for a minute and says, 'So why is the groom wearing black?'

'My wife is a liar,' said the bloke at the bar to the stranger sitting beside him.

'How do you know?'

'Well, she didn't come home last night. And when I asked her where she'd been, she said that she'd spent the night with her sister Betty.'

'And that was a lie?'

'Bloody oath. I know, because I spent the night with Betty.'

Dad picked his little boy up from school to take him to the dentist. Knowing that the kid had been desperate for a part in the school play he asked how things had gone.

Although worried about going to the dentist, the little bloke was very happy. 'I got a part! I get to play a man who's been married for 20 years.'

'Well, that's pretty good. That's a start. Before you know it, they'll give you a speaking part.'

A bloke was standing on a street corner, watching an attractive girl approach. It was a windy day and she was having a bit of trouble with her dress. As she got close, a strong gust blew it above her waist.

'A bit airy,' he said.

'What the hell did you expect? Feathers?'

The new Europe has more than a common currency. It now has a common Heaven and Hell, organised on completely different lines from the afterlife of the Americans.

In Euroheaven, the police are British, the cooks are French, the mechanics German, the lovers Italian and everything is organised by the Swiss.

In Eurohell, the chefs are British, the mechanics French, the lovers Swiss, the police German . . . and it's all organised by the Italians.

## Bumper Stickers

ONE MILLION SPERM AND *YOU* WERE THE FASTEST!

JESUS LOVES YOU. THE REST OF US THINK YOU'RE AN IDIOT.

HANG UP AND DRIVE!

WHERE THERE'S A WILL . . . I WANT TO BE IN IT.

EVER STOP TO THINK AND FORGET TO START AGAIN?

THIS WOULD BE REALLY FUNNY IF IT WEREN'T HAPPENING TO ME.

IF WE QUIT VOTING WILL THEY ALL GO AWAY?

THIS BUMPER STICKER EXPLOITS ILLITERATES.

EAT RIGHT, EXERCISE, DIE ANYWAY.

HE WHO LAUGHS LAST THINKS SLOWEST.

He who hesitates is not only lost but miles from the next exit.

It was kindergarten and the teacher was reading the story of the Three Little Pigs. She was at that part of the tale where the first little pig is trying to get building materials. 'And so the little pig went to the man with a wheelbarrow full of straw,' she read, 'and said "Pardon me, sir, but might I have some of that straw to build my house with?"'

Then the teacher asked the kiddies, 'And what do you think the man said?'

And one little boy raised his hand and said, 'I know! SHIT! A fucking talking pig!'

A Sunday School teacher was discussing the Ten Commandments with the youngest group. She dealt with the commandment to 'Honour thy father and thy mother' and asked the kiddies, 'Is there a commandment that teaches us how to treat our brothers and sisters?'

In an instant, one little boy answered, 'Thou shalt not kill.'

**Q:** How many women with PMS does it take to change a light bulb?

**A:** One. Only ONE! And do you know WHY it takes only ONE. Because no-one else in this house knows HOW to change a light bulb. They don't even notice that the light bulb is BURNT OUT. They would sit in this house in the dark for DAYS before they bloody well noticed. And once they noticed they wouldn't be able to find the spare globes despite the fact that they've been in the same bloody cupboard for the past 15 YEARS!

And if they did, by some miracle, actually find the bloody globes, TWO DAYS LATER the chair that they dragged from two rooms over to stand on to change the STUPID bulb would STILL BE IN THE

SAME SPOT! And underneath it would be the CRUMPLED BLOODY WRAPPER THE STUPID BLOODY LIGHT BULBS came in! And why? Because no-one in this house ever carries out the BLOODY GARBAGE! It's a wonder we haven't all suffocated from the PILES OF CRAP that are 12-feet deep THROUGHOUT THE ENTIRE HOUSE! IT WOULD TAKE AN ARMY TO CLEAN IT UP!

I'm sorry, what did you ask me?

There are ten million lawyers in the US and one of them, an immensely rich lawyer from Los Angeles, went duck hunting in rural Texas. He shot a bird that fell into a farmer's field – on the other side of the fence. And as he was climbing over the fence, an elderly farmer drove up on his John Deere and asked him what the hell he was doing.

The litigator said, 'I shot a duck. And now I'm going to get it.'

'No you're not,' said the farmer, 'this is my property, and you're not coming in.'

### The Penguin Bumper Book of Australian Jokes

The lawyer said, 'Look, buddy, I'm one of the best trial attorneys in California. In fact, I'm one of the best trial attorneys in the entire USA. And if you don't let me get that duck, I'm going to sue your ass. And I'll take everything you own.'

The old farmer smiled sweetly and said, 'Apparently you don't know how we do things in Texas. Here we settle little disagreements with the Texas Three Kick Rule.'

Intrigued, the lawyer asked, 'And just what is the Texas Three Kick Rule?'

The farmer explained. 'Well, I get to kick you three times and you get to kick me three times. And so on, back and forth, until someone gives up.'

The attorney thought about the rules of engagement and decided that he could easily take the old codger. So, yes, he'd abide by local custom.

Whereupon the farmer slowly hauled himself down from the John Deere and walked up to the lawyer.

His first kick planted the toe of a heavy work boot in the lawyer's groin. This dropped him to his knees. The second kick nearly wiped the nose off his face. The barrister fell flat on his belly when the farmer's third kick, to a kidney, had him on the verge of passing out.

But he summoned up every bit of his will and managed to clamber to his feet and said, 'OK, you old coot! Now it's my turn.'

Whereupon the old farmer grinned and said, 'Nah, I give up. You can go and get the duck.'

**A**n architect, an artist and an engineer were discussing whether it was better to be with a wife or a mistress. The architect said he enjoyed time with his wife because he was building a solid foundation for a long-term relationship.

The artist preferred his mistress, because of the comparative novelty in the passion.

And the engineer said, 'I like both.'

'Both?' the others inquired.

'Yes,' said the engineer. 'If you have a wife and a mistress, they will each assume you are spending time with the other woman, so that you can go to the office and get some work done.'

**A** seven-year-old girl admitted to mum and dad that a little boy had kissed her at kinder.

'How did that happen?' asked her father, concerned that she was having sexual experiences, no matter how innocent, at such an early age.

'Well, it wasn't easy,' she said, 'three girls helped me catch him.'

**A** septuagenarian Italian went to his parish priest and asked him to hear his confession. And they took the customary positions on either side of the divider.

'Father, forgive me, for I have sinned,' began the old man. 'At the beginning of World War Two, a beautiful woman knocked on the door of my farm and asked me to hide her from the Germans. So I hid her in the cellar. And they never found her.'

'But that's a good thing that you've done,' said the priest. 'It's certainly nothing that you need to confess.'

'No, it gets worse, Father. I'm afraid that I was

weak and during one of my wife's many pregnancies I told her she had to repay me for hiding her in the attic by providing me with sexual favours.'

The priest was silent. He thought about the man's confession for a long time. Finally he said, 'Well, it was a difficult period. And you were taking a large risk. You would have suffered terribly at the hands of the Germans if they'd found you hiding her. And I believe that God in his wisdom and mercy would balance the good and evil of your acts and judge you accordingly.'

'Thank you, thank you, Father,' said the old man. 'That's a great load off my mind. Now, can I ask you another question?'

'Of course, my son,' said the priest.

'Do I have to tell her that the war is over?'

**W**hat do Eskimos get from sitting on the ice too long?
*Polaroids.*

**The Penguin Bumper Book of Australian Jokes**

**W**hat do you call Santa's helpers?
*Subordinant clauses.*


**W**hy don't blind people like to skydive?
*Because it scares the dog.*


**W**hat's the difference between a Harley and a Hoover?
*The location of the dirt bag.*


**W**hy did pilgrims' pants always fall down?
*Because they wore their belt buckle on their hat.*


**W**hat's the difference between a bad golfer and a bad skydiver?
*A bad golfer goes WHACK, DAMN! A bad skydiver goes DAMN! WHACK!*

**W**hat goes clop-clop-clop, bang-bang, clop-clop-clop?
*An Amish drive-by shooting.*


**H**ow are a Texas tornado and a Tennessee divorce the same?
*Somebody's gonna lose the trailer.*


**A** mother was tucking her little boy into bed when they heard the rumble of thunder. Just as she was about to turn off the light he asked, with a tremor in his voice, 'Mummy, will you sleep with me?'

Mummy smiled reassuringly and gave him a loving hug. 'I can't, my darling,' she replied, 'I have to sleep with Daddy.'

A long silence followed, broken at last by his shaky little voice. 'The big sissy!'

**The Penguin Bumper Book of Australian Jokes**

Two little blokes, aged six and eight, were hyperactive and mischievous. Always in trouble. Always causing their parents concern. And if any mischief occurred in the neighbourhood, the boys were always blamed for it.

At their wits end, the parents consulted all the child psychologists and therapists they could find. Everybody tried, but nobody could help.

Then the parents heard of a clergyman who'd been successful in disciplining children in the past. 'Perhaps we should ask him to speak to our boys,' the wife said to her husband.

'We might as well. Before things get even worse.'

The clergyman agreed to speak with the children but insisted on seeing them individually.

The oldest boy went in to meet him first. The minister sat the boy down and asked him, very sternly, 'Where is God?' The boy sat silently. So the minister asked the question again. 'Where is God?' Again, silence from the child. Whereupon the minister raised his voice and shook his finger in the boy's face. 'WHERE IS GOD??'

The little boy ran from the room, ran all the way home and grabbed his little brother. 'Listen, we're in BIG trouble this time. God has gone missing and they think we did it.'

Once upon a time, in the days of Camelot, young King Arthur was ambushed and imprisoned by the monarch of a neighbouring kingdom.

He was about to have him beheaded, but was touched by Arthur's youthful charm. So he offered him his freedom – on condition that he answered a particularly difficult question. Arthur would have one year to come up with an answer. If he failed, he would be executed.

The question: 'What do women really want?'

This question has worried the most knowledgeable of men over the millennia – and to young Arthur it seemed intractably difficult. But seeking to avoid the axeman he accepted the challenge. Yes, he would have an answer by year's end.

So he journeyed far and wide, hither and thither, and asked everybody he met for help. He talked to princesses, priests, prostitutes, wise men and even the court jester.

But nobody could begin to give him a satisfactory answer.

However, most people did suggest he consult the

old witch, as only she might know the answer. But her price would be high. She was famous throughout the realm for her exorbitant prices.

The last day of the year arrived and Arthur, now desperate, decided to talk to the witch. She listened to the question, nodded wisely and agreed to give him the answer – but he'd have to accept her price. She wanted to marry Lancelot, the most handsome of the knights of the round table.

Arthur was horrified. The witch was hunchbacked and hideous, had only one tooth, smelt like a duck pond full of sewage and kept making odd, gutteral noises. He refused to force Lancelot to marry her.

But on learning of the crisis, Lancelot spoke to Arthur and told him that nothing was too big a sacrifice. 'We must save your life and preserve the round table.'

Hence the wedding of Lancelot and the witch was proclaimed.

And now, at the last moment, the witch answered Arthur's question. 'What a woman really wants is to be able to be in charge of her own life.'

It was instantly obvious to all that the witch had uttered a great truth. So Arthur's life would be spared. And so it was. The neighbouring king, happy with the revelation, gave Arthur both his freedom and his blessing.

The wedding between Lancelot and the witch was a momentous event. King Arthur was torn between anguish and relief, but Lancelot, as proper as ever, remained gentle and courteous. But the old witch was on her worst behaviour – she ate with her hands, belched and farted and made everyone very, very uncomfortable.

As the wedding night approached, Lancelot steeled himself for a horrific encounter. But behold! What a sight awaited him! The most beautiful woman he'd ever seen lay naked on the bed. Lancelot was astonished.

The beauty replied that since he'd been so very, very kind to her when she'd been so hideous she would be different in future. Half the time she would be her horrible, hideous self. And the other half, she would be the beautiful maiden. It was up to him to decide what he wanted her to be doing during the day and during the night.

It was a cruel predicament. During the day he'd like a very beautiful woman to show off to his friends. But that would mean, in the privacy of the bedroom, the witch. Or would it be better to have her by day, in all her hideousness, and a beautiful woman to share his bed?

Noble Lancelot finally decided that he would let the witch choose for herself. On hearing this, she announced that she would be beautiful all the time, because he had respected her. Because he had let her be in charge of her own life.

The moral: It doesn't matter if your woman is pretty or ugly, dumb or smart. Beneath it all, she's still a witch.

**N**o, the old lady wasn't at all worried about her 78-year-old husband chasing young girls.

'I've got a dog that chases cars,' she said. 'But if it caught one, what would it do? It can't drive.'

**I**t was mid-winter, snowing and very cold. Marilyn was on a first date with a bloke who took her on a daytrip to the snowfields.

They had a good time and were driving back that evening when, winding their way down the mountainside in a 4WD, she realised that she shouldn't have had that extra latte. And they were a long, long way from the next rest room.

So she implored her new friend to stop and let her pee beside the road. Otherwise it would be in the front seat of his car.

They stopped. She positioned herself out of sight, by the back mudguard, yanked down her pants and started.

Unfortunately, a recent snowfall provided a poor footing. So she let her bum rest against the rear fender to steady herself. The bloke stood on the other side of the car, watching for traffic.

And despite the embarrassing nature of the situation, all Marilyn could think about was the relief she felt.

Until, upon finishing, she realised that her buttocks were firmly glued against the car's bumper. Thoughts of tongues frozen to pump handles came to mind as she attempted to disengage her flesh from the icy metal. But it was as if she'd been super-glued.

Disturbed by her plight yet aware of the absurdity, she answered the bloke's concern about 'what was taking so long' with the reply that she was 'freezing her bum off and needed some help'.

He came round the car as she tried to cover herself with a sweater. As she looked pleadingly up into his eyes, he burst out laughing. She, too, got the giggles. Finally they managed to compose themselves and assess the dilemma. Both agreed it would take something hot to free her chilly cheeks from the grip of the icy metal.

Thinking about what had gotten her into the predicament in the first place, both realised there was only one way to get her free. So while she looked the other way, her first-time-date unzipped his pants and peed her bum off the car.

Which gives a whole new definition to the phrase of being 'pissed off'.

The following poem is all the work of George W. Bush. It is composed, entirely of genuine Bush quotes.

**Make the Pie Higher**, by George W. Bush.
I think we all agree, the past is over.
This is still a dangerous world. It's a world of madmen and uncertainty and potential mental losses.
Rarely is the question asked: 'Is our children learning?'
Will the highways of the Internet become more few?
How many hands have I shaked?
They misunderestimate me. I'm a pitball on the pant leg of opportunity.
I know that the human being and the fish can coexist.
Families is where our nation finds hope, where our wings take dream.
Put food on your family! Knock down the toll booth!
Vulcanise Society!
Make the pie higher! Make the pie higher!

The young bloke invited his mum over for dinner. During the meal, Mum couldn't help but notice how very beautiful his room-mate was.

Reading Mum's thoughts, the son said, 'I know what you must be thinking but I assure you that Julie and I are just room-mates.'

A week later, the room-mates discovered that something was missing. 'Ever since your mother came to dinner, I haven't been able to find that beautiful silver gravy ladle. You don't suppose she took it, do you?'

'Of course not. Mum wouldn't do that.'

'Well, what's happened to it?'

'OK, OK, I'll write her a letter.'

So he did.

'Dear Mum,
I'm not saying you "did" take a gravy ladle and I'm not saying you "did not" take a gravy ladle. But the fact remains that one has been missing ever since you were here for dinner.
Love, your son.'

Several days later, he received a letter from his mum.

'Dear Son,
I'm not saying you "do" sleep with your room-mate, and I'm not saying "you don't". But the fact remains that if she was sleeping in her own bed, she would have found the gravy ladle by now.
Love, Mum.'

# The Penguin Bumper Book of Australian Jokes

On their way to get married, a young couple had a head-on collision on the F1 freeway. And they found themselves sitting outside the Pearly Gates. While they waited for St Peter they wondered if, under the circumstances, it would be possible to get married in Heaven. So when St Peter finally appeared, they asked him.

St Peter said, 'You know, this is the first time anyone has asked that question. I'll have to find out.' And he disappeared into the wisps of cloud.

During that time, the couple waited patiently at the Pearly Gates. Hours passed, then days. Then months. And they began to wonder if they really should get married in Heaven, given that everything moves so slowly – given the nature of eternal life.

'What if it doesn't work out?' they asked each other. 'Will we be stuck together forever?'

Finally St Peter returned and, looking somewhat bedraggled, said, 'Yes, I've got a special dispensation for the two of you. You can get married in heaven.'

'Terrific,' said the couple, 'but what if things don't work out. What's the chance of getting a divorce in Heaven?'

Outraged, St Peter slammed the Pearly Gates in their faces.

'What's wrong?' asked the frightened couple.

'It took me three months to find a bloody priest up here,' St Peter shouted, 'how long do you think it will take me to find a bloody lawyer?'

I'm tired. Because I'm overworked. I've just calculated that there are 20 million people in this country, of whom seven million are retired, three million unemployed and another four million in school. That leaves six million. Of those, two million are employed by the federal government, half a million are in the armed services and 1.5 million work for state or local government. That leaves around 200 000, of whom 188 000 are in hospital and 11 998 are in jail. Which leaves a total of just two to do all the work. Namely you and me. And you're sitting reading this. So no bloody wonder I'm tired.

## Bumper stickers

All men are animals. Some just make better pets.

I used to have a handle on life, but it broke.

Wanted: Meaningful overnight relationship.

Beer. It's not just for breakfast any more.

I need someone really bad. Are you really bad?

---

Two women were at the local hairdressers getting a couple of permanent waves. And they were bemoaning the misbehaviour of their husbands.

'He's a bastard,' one said. 'I never know where he is at night.'

'I know what you mean,' said the other. 'One second mine's in the house, and the next he's pissed off, God knows where.'

'Well,' said a woman eavesdropping nearby. 'I always know where my husband is.'

'Really? How?'

'It's easy. I'm a widow.'

**A** sloth was strolling, very slowly, through the jungle, when a gang of snails mugged him – and beat him up very badly. They left him at the bottom of a tree with cuts and abrasions.

It tooks hours for him to gather enough strength to go to the local police station.

'What the hell happened to you?' the sergeant asked.

'A gang of snails beat me up,' he replied.

'Can you give me a description of what they looked like?'

'I don't know,' said the sloth, 'it all happened so fast.'

# The Penguin Bumper Book of Australian Jokes

**A**t the police station, the redneck explained to the constable why his cousins had shot him.

'Well, we wuz havin' a good time drinkin' when my cousin Ray picked up his shotgun and said, "Hey, do you blokes want to go huntin'?"

'And what happened?' the policeman asked.

'The last thing I remember,' said the redneck, 'was me standin' up and sayin' "sure, I'm game".'

**H**ow many fleas does it take to screw in a light bulb?
*Two.*

### SHE WAS SO BLONDE THAT SHE . . .

TRIPPED OVER THE CORDLESS PHONE.

SENT ME A FAX WITH A STAMP ON IT.

### The Penguin Bumper Book of Australian Jokes

PUT LIPSTICK ON HER FOREHEAD BECAUSE SHE WANTED TO MAKE UP HER MIND.

TOOK A RULER TO BED TO SEE HOW LONG SHE SLEPT.

WHERE IT SAID ON THE APPLICATION 'SIGN HERE', WROTE 'SAGITTARIUS'.

TOLD SOMEONE TO MEET HER AT THE CORNER OF WALK AND DON'T WALK.

ON HEARING THAT 90% OF ALL CRIMES WERE COMMITTED AROUND THE HOME, MOVED.

THOUGHT THAT SHE COULDN'T USE AN AM RADIO AT NIGHT.

SAID, 'LOOK, THEY'VE SPELT MACY'S WRONG' WHEN SHE SAW THE SIGN IN FRONT OF THE YMCA.

STARED AT THE FROZEN ORANGE JUICE BECAUSE IT SAID, 'CONCENTRATE'.

A man walks into a bar and orders a beer. He sips it and sets it down. A monkey swings across the bar and pisses in the pint.

The man asks the barman who owns the monkey. The barman replies, 'The piano player.' The man walks over to the piano player and says, 'Do you know your monkey pissed in my beer?'

The pianist replies, 'No, but if you hum it I'll play it.'

### Random thoughts

Always remember you're unique, just like everyone else.

We are born naked, wet and hungry. Then things get worse.

It's always darkest before dawn. So when you're going to steal next-door's newspaper, that's the time to do it.

## The Penguin Bumper Book of Australian Jokes

It may be that your sole purpose in life is to serve as a warning to others.

When you think nobody cares whether you're alive or dead, try missing a couple of car payments.

If you lend someone $20 and never see that person again, it was probably worth it.

When someone says, 'Do you want my opinion?' – it's always a negative one.

Pain and suffering are inevitable but misery is optional.

The word listen contains the same letters as the word silent.

A blonde decides to try horseback riding even though she hasn't had a single lesson or any prior experience. So she mounts the horse unassisted and it springs into motion, galloping at a steady and rhythmic pace. Whereupon the blonde begins to slip from the saddle and in terror grabs the horse's mane. But she can't get a firm grip. So she throws her arms around its neck but slides down the side of the horse anyway. It gallops along, impervious to its slipping rider. Finally the blonde leaps from the horse and tries to roll to safety. But her foot gets entangled in the stirrup and she's now at the mercy of the horse's pounding hooves as her head is struck against the ground again and again. And she's just moments away from unconsciousness when ... the Kmart manager runs out and unplugs the horse.

At the time when *Crouching Tiger, Hidden Dragon* was enjoying a blaze of Oscar-related publicity, West Tiger player John Hopoate plunged Rugby League to new depths by thrusting his finger up the rectum of another player. This event was immediately celebrated, in calls to radio stations and letters to the editor as a case of ... CROUCHING TIGER, HIDDEN FINGER.

All her life she'd been the most devout of Catholics. She married young and had a dozen children. Just after the 12th was born her beloved husband had a heart attack.

A few weeks after his funeral she remarried and, as the years passed, had another dozen children with her second husband. Whereupon he also passed away.

Within a few weeks she was engaged to be married a third time but, suddenly, she was laid low. The 24 children joined her fiancé at the death bed. But despite their prayers she gave a little shudder and ... died.

At her funeral, the priest looked tenderly down on the woman in the open coffin. Then he looked up to the heavens and said, 'At last! They're finally together!'

The fiancé was standing near the priest. 'Excuse me, Father, but do you mean she's with her first husband? Or her second husband?'

And the priest said, 'I meant her legs!'

When the body was first made, all the parts wanted to be boss. The brain said, 'I should be boss because I control the whole body's responses and functions.' And the feet said, 'No, we should be boss as we carry the brain about, so that it gets to where it wants to be.' And the hands said, 'We should be the boss because we do all the work and earn all the money.'

The debate went on and on as the eyes, the ears, the mouth, the heart, the spine and the lungs each insisted on their all-importance.

Finally, the arsehole spoke up – and all the other body parts laughed at it.

Deeply offended, the arsehole went on strike, blocked itself up and refused to function. Within days the eyes became crossed, the hands clenched, the feet twitched and the heart and lungs began to panic whilst the brain fevered. And so it was agreed, by all of them, that the arsehole should be the boss. So they passed the motion, and seconded it, and the arsehole passed a motion of its own.

And for quite a long time, the arse just sat there and crapped on.

The lesson for management? You don't need brains to be a boss. Any arsehole will do.

A bloke bought a new Mercedes and was out on the freeway for a nice evening drive. The top was down, the breeze was blowing through what was left of his hair and he decided to check it out. As the needle jumped up to 130kph, he suddenly saw flashing red and blue lights behind him.

'There's no way they can catch a Mercedes,' he thought to himself and opened her up further. The needle hit 140kph, 150kph . . . then the reality of the situation hit him. 'What am I doing,' he thought and pulled over.

The cop came up to him, took his licence without a word and examined it and the car. 'It's been a long day, this is the end of my shift and it's Friday the 13th. I don't feel like more paperwork, so if you can give me an excuse for your driving that I haven't heard before, you can go.'

The bloke thought for a moment and said, 'Last

week my wife ran off with a cop. I was afraid you were trying to give her back!'

'Have a nice weekend.'


**H**ow do you get holy water?
*Boil the hell out of it.*

### LAWS FOR WOMEN TO LIVE BY . . .

DON'T IMAGINE YOU CAN CHANGE A MAN – UNLESS HE WEARS NAPPIES.

WHAT DO YOU DO IF YOUR BOYFRIEND WALKS OUT? YOU SHUT THE DOOR.

IF THEY PUT A MAN ON THE MOON, THEY SHOULD BE ABLE TO PUT THEM ALL UP THERE.

NEVER LET YOUR MAN'S MIND WANDER – IT'S TOO LITTLE TO BE OUT ALONE.

MEN ARE ALL THE SAME – THEY JUST HAVE DIFFERENT FACES SO THAT YOU CAN TELL THEM APART.

DEFINITION OF A BACHELOR: A MAN WHO HAS MISSED THE OPPORTUNITY TO MAKE SOME WOMAN MISERABLE.

WOMEN DON'T MAKE FOOLS OF MEN – MOST OF THEM ARE THE DO-IT-YOURSELF TYPES.

BEST WAY TO GET A MAN TO DO SOMETHING – SUGGEST THEY ARE TOO OLD FOR IT.

**F**ive surgeons are discussing who makes the best patient to operate on. The first surgeon says, 'I like to see accountants on my operating table, because when you open them up, everything inside is numbered.'

The second responds, 'Yeah, but you should try electricians! Everything inside them is colour-coded.'

The third says, 'No, I really think librarians are the best. Everything inside them is in alphabetical order.'

The fourth surgeon chimes in, 'You know, I like construction workers . . . those guys always understand when you have a few parts left over at the end, and when the job takes longer than you said it would.'

But the fifth surgeon shuts them all up when he says, 'You're all wrong. Politicians are the easiest to operate on. There's no guts, no heart, no spine and the head and arse are interchangeable.'

What has four legs, is big, green, fuzzy, and if it fell out of a tree would kill you?

A pool table.

'I tell you, women drivers are a hazard to traffic. Driving to work this morning on the freeway, I looked over to my left and there was a woman in a Mustang doing 110kph with her face up next to her rear-vision mirror putting on her eyeliner.

'I looked away for a couple of seconds and when I looked back she was halfway over in my lane.

'It scared me so much I dropped my electric shaver in my coffee, and it spilled all over my mobile phone.'

A bloke goes into a restaurant for a Christmas breakfast while in his home town for the holidays. After looking over the menu he says, 'I'll just have the Eggs Benedict.'

His order comes a while later and it's served on a big, shiny hubcap. So he asks the waiter, 'What's with the hubcap?'

The waiter sings, 'Oh, there's no plate like chrome for the hollandaise!'

Did you hear about the Buddhist who refused his dentist's Novocaine during root canal work?
*He wanted to transcend dental medication.*

## The Penguin Bumper Book of Australian Jokes

A woman has twins, and gives them up for adoption. One of them goes to a family in Egypt and is named 'Amal'. The other goes to a family in Spain and they name him 'Juan'. Years later, Juan sends a picture of himself to his mother. Upon receiving the picture she tells her husband that she wishes she also had a picture of Amal. Her husband responds, 'But they are twins – if you've seen Juan, you've seen Amal.'

### STRESS MANAGEMENT

Picture yourself near a stream.
Birds are chirping in the crisp, cool mountain air.
Nothing can bother you here. No-one knows this secret place.
You are in total seclusion from that place called 'the world'.
The soothing sound of a gentle waterfall fills the air with a cascade of serenity.
The water is so clear that you can easily make out . . .

... the face of the person whose head you're holding under water.

There, now ... feeling better?

### DOG PROPERTY LAWS

IF I LIKE IT, IT'S MINE.

IF IT'S IN MY MOUTH, IT'S MINE.

IF I CAN TAKE IT FROM YOU, IT'S MINE.

IF I HAD IT A LITTLE WHILE AGO, IT'S MINE.

IF IT'S MINE, IT MUST NEVER APPEAR TO BE YOURS IN ANY WAY.

IF I'M CHEWING SOMETHING UP, ALL THE PIECES ARE MINE.

IF IT JUST LOOKS LIKE MINE, IT'S MINE.

## The Penguin Bumper Book of Australian Jokes

IF I SAW IT FIRST, IT'S MINE.

IF YOU ARE PLAYING WITH SOMETHING AND YOU PUT IT DOWN, IT AUTOMATICALLY BECOMES MINE.

IF IT'S BROKEN, IT'S YOURS.

### SIMILARITIES BETWEEN DOGS AND MEN

BOTH TAKE UP TOO MUCH SPACE ON THE BED.

BOTH HAVE IRRATIONAL FEARS ABOUT VACUUM CLEANING.

BOTH MARK THEIR TERRITORY.

NEITHER TELLS YOU WHAT'S BOTHERING THEM.

THE SMALLER ONES TEND TO BE MORE NERVOUS.

BOTH HAVE AN INORDINATE FASCINATION WITH WOMEN'S CROTCHES.

**The Penguin Bumper Book of Australian Jokes**

Neither does any dishes.

Both fart shamelessly.

Neither notices when you get your hair cut.

Both like dominance games.

Both are suspicious of the postman.

Neither understands what you see in cats.

## Top ten reasons why a dog is better than a woman

A dog's parents will never visit you.

A dog loves you when you leave your clothes on the floor.

## The Penguin Bumper Book of Australian Jokes

A DOG LIMITS ITS TIME IN THE BATHROOM TO A QUICK DRINK.

A DOG NEVER EXPECTS YOU TO TELEPHONE.

A DOG WILL NEVER GET MAD AT YOU IF YOU FORGET ITS BIRTHDAY.

A DOG DOES NOT CARE ABOUT THE PREVIOUS DOGS IN YOUR LIFE.

A DOG NEVER EXPECTS FLOWERS ON VALENTINE'S DAY.

THE LATER YOU ARE, THE HAPPIER THE DOG IS TO SEE YOU.

A DOG DOES NOT SHOP.

### LIFE LESSONS LEARNED FROM A DOG

IF YOU STARE AT SOMEONE LONG ENOUGH, EVENTUALLY YOU'LL GET WHAT YOU WANT.

Don't go out without ID.

Be direct with people; let them know exactly how you feel by piddling on their shoes.

Be aware of when to hold your tongue, and when to use it.

Leave room in your schedule for a good nap.

Always give people a friendly greeting. A cold nose in the crotch is effective.

When you do something wrong, always take responsibility (as soon as you're dragged out from under the bed).

If it's not wet and sloppy, it's not a real kiss.

**A**n overweight blonde consulted her doctor for advice. The doctor said she should run ten miles a day for 30 days. This, he promised, would help her lose the 20 pounds she'd been trying to get rid of.

The blonde followed the doctor's advice and, after 30 days, she was pleased to find that she had indeed lost the 20 pounds.

She then phoned the doctor and thanked him for the wonderful advice which produced such effective results.

At the end of the conversation, however, she asked one last question:

'How do I get home, since I'm now 300 miles away?'

**M**r Lee was terribly overweight, so his doctor put him on a diet. The doctor said, 'I want you to eat regularly for two days, then skip a day. Repeat this procedure for two weeks and the next time I see you, you'll have lost at least 5 pounds.'

When Mr Lee returned for the next visit, he shocked the doctor by losing nearly 60 pounds.

'Why, that's amazing!' the doctor said. 'Did you follow my instructions?'

Mr Lee nodded, 'I'll tell you, though. I thought I was going to drop dead that third day.'

'You mean from hunger?'

'No, from skipping.'

One night a father overheard his son saying his prayers. 'God bless Mummy and Daddy and Grandma. Goodbye Grandpa.'

Well, the father thought it was strange, but he soon forgot about it. The next day, the grandfather died.

About a month later the father heard his son saying his prayers again. 'God bless Mummy. God bless Daddy. Goodbye Grandma.'

The next day the grandmother died. And the father was getting more than a little worried about the whole situation.

Two weeks later, the father once again overheard his son's prayers. 'God bless Mummy. Goodbye Daddy.'

This alone nearly gave the father a heart attack. He didn't say anything, but got up early to go to work, so that he would miss the traffic. He stayed in all through lunch and dinner. Finally, after midnight, he went home. He was still alive!

When he got home, he apologised to his wife. 'I am sorry, dear. I had a very bad day at work today.'

'YOU THINK YOU'VE HAD A BAD DAY!?' the wife yelled. 'The postman dropped dead at the front door this morning!'

**A** 60-year-old man went to a doctor for a check-up. The doctor told him, 'You're in terrific shape. There's nothing wrong with you. Why, you might live forever; you have the body of a 35-year-old. By the way, how old was your father when he died?'

The 60-year-old responded, 'Did I say he was dead?'

The doctor was surprised and asked, 'How old is he and is he still active?'

The man replied, 'Well, he's 82 years old and he still goes skiing three times a season and surfing three times a week during the summer.'

The doctor couldn't believe it. So he said, 'Well, how old was your grandfather when he died?'

The 60-year-old replied again, 'Did I say he was dead?'

The doctor was astonished. He said, 'You mean to tell me you are 60 years old and both your father and your grandfather are alive? Is your grandfather very active?'

The man said, 'He goes skiing at least once a season and surfing once a week during the summer. Not only that,' said the man, 'my grandfather is 106 years old and next week he's getting married again.'

The doctor said, 'At 106 years why on earth would your grandfather want to get married?'

His patient looked at the doctor and said, 'Did I say he wanted to?'

Jake was on his deathbed with his wife, Betsy, maintaining a steady vigil by his side. As she held his fragile hand, her warm tears ran silently down her face, splashed onto his face, and roused him from his slumber.

He looked up and his pale lips began to move slightly. 'My darling Betsy,' he whispered.

'Hush, my love,' she said. 'Go back to sleep. Shhh. Don't talk.'

But he was insistent. 'Betsy,' he said in his tired voice, 'I have to talk. I have something I must confess to you.'

'There's nothing to confess,' replied the weeping Betsy. 'It's alright. Everything's all right. Go to sleep now.'

'No, no. I must die in peace, Betsy. I slept with your sister, your best friend and your mother.'

Betsy mustered a pained smile and stroked his hand. 'Hush now, Jake, don't torment yourself. I know all about it,' she said. 'Why do you think I poisoned you?'

---

A mob of kangaroos can only move as fast as the slowest kangaroo – so if that mob is being hunted, it's the slowest and weakest kanga at the back that is killed first. According to the principles of natural selection, as outlined by Charles Darwin, this is good for the mob as a whole, because the general speed and health of the whole group keeps improving by the regular killing-off of the weaker members.

In much the same way the human brain can only operate as fast as the slowest brain cells. Excessive intake of booze, as we all know, kills brain cells, but naturally it attacks the slowest and weakest brain cells first. In this way, regular consumption of beer eliminates the weaker brain cells, making the brain a faster and more efficient machine.

Which is why you always feel smarter after a few beers.

**A** bloke enters his favourite five-star restaurant and while sitting at his regular table notices an astonishingly beautiful woman sitting at a nearby table . . . all alone.

He calls the waiter over and asks for their most expensive bottle of Merlot to be sent over. He knows that if she accepts it, they'll be in the cot together by 10 p.m.

The waiter takes the bottle to the young lady and

indicates, with a gesture, her benefactor. She examines the label and then quickly scrawls a note which she has the waiter deliver.

It read, 'For me to accept this bottle, you'd need to have a BMW 7 series in your garage, $2 million in the bank and seven inches in your trousers.'

The bloke reads the note and sends one of his own back to her. It reads, 'Just so you know, I happen to have a Ferrari Testarosa, a BMW 850IL and a Mercedes S600 in the garage. Plus I have $20 million in the readies. But, not even for a woman as beautiful as you, would I cut off three inches. Please return the bottle.'

**T**wo engineers went moose hunting in the backwoods of British Columbia. Although they'd never been moose hunting before, they managed to bag a beauty. The only trouble was they were about a mile from their truck and were having a very tough time dragging the huge animal by the hind legs – when a wildlife biologist happened upon them.

First of all, he established that he disapproved of hunting and believed that moose should be protected. But he couldn't help displaying his profound knowledge. 'The hair follicles on a moose have a grain to them,' he said, 'that causes the hair to lie towards the back. The way you are dragging the moose increases your coefficient to friction by a huge margin. But if you grab by the antlers and pull, you'll find the work required to be quite minimal.'

Thanking him, the engineers started dragging the moose by the antlers. After an hour, one engineer said to the other, 'I can't believe how easy it is to move the moose this way. We're lucky to have run across that biologist.'

'Yeah,' said the other engineer, 'but we're getting further and further away from our truck.'

Two wildlife biologists are following the tracks of a radio-collared grizzly bear when, all of a sudden, the immense animal crashes out of the brush and heads right for them. Scrambling up the nearest tree, they find the bear is climbing up the trunk after them. The first biologist takes off his heavy hiking boots and pulls a pair of sleek running shoes from his backpack. His colleague gives him a puzzled look and says, 'What the hell are you doing?'

He says, 'I figure when the bear gets close to us we'll jump down and make a run for it.'

'Are you crazy? We both know you can't outrun a fully grown grizzly bear.'

'I don't have to outrun the bear. I only have to outrun you.'

Two farm boys are sitting side by side on a post-and-rail fence when a young heifer strolls by.

'If only,' says the first boy, 'that heifer was a girl.'

'If only,' says the other, 'it was dark.'

Three couples approached the vicar of the local Anglican church, who told them that if they wished to join his congregation, they'd have to go without sex for a fortnight – and then come back and tell him how it went.

The first couple was elderly. The second couple were in their 40s. The final couple was newly wed.

After a fortnight, the couples returned to the minister. The retired couple said they'd had no difficulties at all. The couple in their 40s said it had been tough for the first week but, after that, they'd managed. But the newly weds said it was fine until she'd dropped the can of paint.

'Can of paint!' said the minister.

'Yeah,' said the newly wed bloke. 'My wife dropped the can and when she bent over to pick it up I had to have her right there and then. I'm sorry, reverend, but lust took over.'

The Minister shook his head and said that, sadly, they would not be welcome in his church.

Whereupon the young woman burst into tears. 'We're not welcome at Mitre 10 either.'

**A** young couple check into a cheap hotel. The husband goes downstairs for a drink at the bar but she's so tired she plonks herself on the bed for a rest.

No sooner has she laid down than a train thunders by the window, shaking the room so hard she's tossed onto the floor.

She climbs onto the bed and, once again, a passing train shakes the room so violently she's back on the floor.

Furious, she calls the front desk and asks for the manager, who says he'll come straight up. The manager admits that the train does pass close to the hotel but can't believe that the effect on hotel guests could be so violent.

'Look, lie here on the bed,' says the young woman, 'and see for yourself.'

So he lies down next to her.

At that moment the husband walks in, sees a stranger lying with his wife and yells, 'What the hell are you doing here?'

'Would you believe I'm waiting for a train?'

## The Penguin Bumper Book of Australian Jokes

**M**um was at the end of her tether. Her five-year-old child was hyperactive, had attention deficit disorder, and was a constant bed-wetter. Child psychiatrists couldn't do a thing with him.

So she went to another psychiatrist, seeking help for herself.

'You're far too upset and worried about your child. So I'm going to give you a prescription for Prozac.'

'Prozac? Isn't that pretty strong stuff?'

'Yes, but you need a circuit breaker. And in my experience, if you're calmer, it might, just might, calm your son down a little.'

On her next visit the psychiatrist asked, 'Has the Prozac helped?'

'Yes,' the mother answered. 'It does wonders for me.'

'And is your son any better?' he asked.

'Who gives a fuck?' she replied.

**A** bloke walks into a bar and asks for a beer.

'No trubs. That'll be a cent.'

'One cent?'

'Yep, one cent.'

Delighted, the customer looks up at the menu that's been chalked on the blackboard. 'Could I have a steak with chips, peas and a fried egg?'

'Yep,' says the barman. 'That'll be four cents.'

'Four cents? Look, I'd like to thank the owner.'

The barman says, 'He's upstairs with my wife.'

'What's he doing with your wife?'

'The same as I'm doing to his business.'

**B**efore I went for a walk last night, my kids asked me how long I'd be gone. I said, 'The whole time.'

**S**o what's the speed of dark?

**H**ow come you don't ever hear about gruntled employees?

### The Penguin Bumper Book of Australian Jokes

A 90-year-old was having his check-up and the GP asked him how he was feeling. 'Never better, never better. I've got a 22-year-old wife who's pregnant and having my child.'

The GP thought about this for a while. 'Let me tell you a story. I knew a bloke who loved hunting. He never missed a season. But one day he left home in a hurry and instead of his gun, he accidentally grabbed his umbrella. And there he was in the wetlands when suddenly a duck appeared in front of him. And he lifted up the umbrella, pointed it at the duck and squeezed the handle. And do you know what happened?'

The old bloke slowly shook his head. 'No, no idea.'

'Well, the duck dropped dead in front of him.'

'But that's impossible,' said the patient. 'Someone else must have shot that duck.'

'Well, that's what I'm getting at,' said the GP.

Two old dears were sunning themselves outside the nursing home when it started to rain.

One pulled out a French letter, cut off the end and put it over her cigarette.

'What's that?' said the other.

'A condom.'

'What's it for?'

'Well, I can keep smoking in the rain.'

'Where did you get it?'

'You can get them at any chemist.'

Next day, the other old dear hobbled into the local chemist and asked for a packet of condoms.

The chemist looked at her. A woman in her 80s wanting condoms? Then he asked, very politely, what brand she preferred.

'That doesn't matter,' she said, 'as long as it fits on a camel.'

Taking a seat in his chambers, the judge faced the opposing lawyers.

'Gentlemen, both of you have tried to pervert the course of justice by giving me a bribe.'

Both lawyers looked uncomfortable. 'You, sir, gave me $15 000. And you, sir, gave me $10 000.'

Whereupon his honour reached into his gown and

pulled out a cheque book. And wrote out a cheque. Which he handed to the first lawyer. 'Now, I'm returning $5000. And we're going to decide this case solely on its merits.'

A widower and a widow meet in a twilight home. They like each other, laugh at the same jokes and, after a few months, the widower asks the widow for her hand in marriage.

Whilst attracted to the idea she decides to approach the proposal in a responsible, logical manner.

'Before I answer you I have a couple of questions. How's your health?'

'Fine, fine. I'm not getting any younger but everything was OK at the last check-up.'

'Good, now while I think we're too old for a pre-nup, I've got to protect myself. How are you off financially?'

'So-so. I'm not rolling in it. But I'm comfortable. We won't have to eat into your capital.'

'And how's your sex life?'

'Infrequently,' he says.

The widow thinks about this for a moment. 'Is that one word, or two?'

## SCIENCE AS SEEN BY STUDENTS

This is a list of comments from test papers, essays, etc. submitted to science and health teachers.

$H_2O$ IS HOT WATER, AND $CO_2$ IS COLD WATER.

TO COLLECT FUMES OF SULPHUR, HOLD A DEACON OVER A FLAME IN A TEST TUBE.

WHEN YOU SMELL AN ODOURLESS GAS, IT IS PROBABLY CARBON MONOXIDE.

WATER IS COMPOSED OF TWO GINS, OXYGIN AND HYDROGIN. OXYGIN IS PURE GIN. HYDROGIN IS WATER AND GIN.

A SUPER SATURATED SOLUTION IS ONE THAT HOLDS
MORE THAN IT CAN HOLD.

MAGNET: SOMETHING YOU FIND CRAWLING ALL OVER
A DEAD CAT.

MOMENTUM: WHAT YOU GIVE A PERSON WHEN THEY
ARE GOING AWAY.
VACUUM: A LARGE, EMPTY SPACE WHERE THE
POPE LIVES.

ARTIFICIAL INSEMINATION IS WHEN THE FARMER DOES
IT TO THE COW INSTEAD OF THE BULL.

THE PISTOL OF THE FLOWER IS ITS ONLY PROTECTION
AGAINST INSECTS.

A FOSSIL IS AN EXTINCT ANIMAL. THE OLDER IT IS,
THE MORE EXTINCT IT IS.

TO REMOVE DUST FROM THE EYE, PULL THE EYE DOWN
OVER THE NOSE.

FOR A NOSEBLEED, PUT THE NOSE MUCH LOWER THAN
THE HEART UNTIL THE HEART STOPS.

## The Penguin Bumper Book of Australian Jokes

For head colds, use an agonizer to spray the nose until it drops into your throat.

Germinate: To become a naturalised German.

The times are a fight between the earth and moon. All water tends towards the moon, because there is no water on the moon, and nature abhors a vacuum. I forget where the sun joins in this fight.

Blood flows down one leg and up the other.

**A**n Australian businessman was scanning the books for sale at the new Hong Kong airport when he noticed a thick paperback entitled 'How to Woo'. Given that he was scheduled to spend quite a lot of time in that part of the world he thought it might, just might, prove useful. Knowledge of the appropriate social etiquette might well improve his sex life.

Settling back in his seat after takeoff, in a Boeing heading for Beijing, he was devastated to discover that he'd just purchased volume two of the Hong Kong telephone directory.

**G**azza keeps himself supplied with fish by chucking illegal traps into the local river. One day, around sunset, Gazza is down at the river pulling in two of his traps, both chockers with fish, when he becomes aware of a bloke standing behind him on the bank.

'Do you know who I am?' says the bloke.

'No idea,' says Gazza, 'who are you?'

'I'm the Fisheries Inspector,' says the bloke.

'Thank Christ for that!' says Gazza. 'I thought you might have been the bloke who owns these fish traps.'

**T**he old man and woman remained married for years even though they hated each other. When they had a confrontation, screams and yelling could be heard deep into the night. A constant threat was heard by the neighbours. 'When I die I will dig my way up and out of the grave to come back and haunt you for the rest of your life!'

Neighbours believed he practised black magic and was responsible for missing cats and dogs. He was feared and enjoyed the respect it garnered.

He died abruptly under strange circumstances and the funeral had a closed casket. After the burial, the wife went straight to the local bar and began to party as if there was no tomorrow. The gaiety was such that the neighbours approached in a group to ask: 'Are you not afraid? Concerned? Worried? This man who practised black magic stated when he died he would dig his way up and out of the grave to come back and haunt you.'

The wife put down her drink and said, 'Let the old bastard dig. I had him buried upside down.'

A little old lady went into the bank one day, carrying a bag of money. She insisted that she must speak

# The Penguin Bumper Book of Australian Jokes

with the president of the bank to open a savings account because, 'It's a lot of money!'

After much humming and haaing, the bank staff finally ushered her into the president's office.

The bank president then asked her how much she would like to deposit. She replied, 'I've got $165 000!' and dumped the cash out of her bag onto his desk.

The president was, of course, curious as to how she came by all this cash. So he asked her, 'Ma'am, I'm surprised you're carrying so much cash around. Where did you get this money?'

The old lady replied, 'I make bets.'

The president then asked, 'Bets? What kind of bets?'

The old woman said, 'Well, for example, I'll bet you $25 000 that your balls are square.'

'Ha!' laughed the president. 'That's a stupid bet. You can never win that kind of bet!'

The old lady challenged, 'So, would you like to take my bet?'

'Sure,' said the president, 'I'll bet $25 000 that my balls are not square!'

The little old lady then said, 'OK, but since there is a lot of money involved, may I bring my lawyer with me tomorrow at 10 a.m. as a witness?'

'Sure!' replied the confident president.

That night, the president got very nervous about the bet and spent a long time in front of a mirror checking his balls, turning from side to side, again and again. He thoroughly checked them out until he was sure that there was absolutely no way his balls were square and that he would win the bet.

Next morning, at precisely 10 a.m. the little old lady appeared with her lawyer at the president's office. She introduced the lawyer to the president and repeated the bet: '$25 000 says the president's balls are square!'

The president agreed with the bet again and the old lady asked him to drop his pants so they could all see.

The president complied.

The little old lady peered closely at his balls and then asked if she could feel them.

'Well, OK,' said the president, '$25 000 is a lot of money, so I guess you should be absolutely sure.'

Just then, he noticed that the lawyer was quietly banging his head against the wall.

The president asked the old lady, 'What the hell's the matter with your lawyer?'

She replied: 'Nothing, except I bet him $100 000 that at 10 a.m. today I'd have the bank president's balls in my hand.'

Two aerials meet on a roof, fall in love and get married.

The ceremony was rubbish but the reception was brilliant.

Two specialists met in the hallway of St Vincent's Private Hospital, in Sydney.

'I'm worried about that new nurse. She does everything backwards.'

'Backwards?'

'Yes, just yesterday I told her to give a patient two milligrams of Percocet every ten hours. And she gave him ten milligrams every two hours. He damn near died on us!'

'That's nothing,' said the other. 'Last week I told her to give a patient an enema every 24 hours. And she started to give him 24 enemas in one hour. If I hadn't intervened, the poor bloke would have exploded.'

Whereupon they heard a blood-curdling scream from down the hall. 'Oh my God! I've just realised I told her to prick Mr Smith's boil.'

### 'LET'S PICK ON MEN INSTEAD OF BLONDES' TIME . . .

**W**hy do only ten per cent of men make it to Heaven?
*Because if they all went, it would be Hell.*


**H**ow are husbands like lawn mowers?
*They're hard to get started, they emit noxious odours and half the time they don't work.*


**H**ow do men define a '50/50' relationship?
*We cook – they eat; we clean – they dirty; we iron – they wrinkle.*


**H**ow do men exercise on the beach?
*By sucking in their stomachs every time they see a bikini.*

**The Penguin Bumper Book of Australian Jokes**

**H**ow do you get a man to stop biting his nails?
*Make him wear shoes.*

**H**ow is Colonel Sanders like the typical male?
*All he's concerned with are legs, breasts and thighs.*

**W**hat do most men consider a gourmet restaurant?
*Any place without a drive-through window.*

**W**hat do you do with a bachelor who thinks he's God's gift to women?
*Exchange him.*

**W**hat's a man's idea of honesty in a relationship?
*Telling you his real name.*

**What's the best way to force a man to do sit-ups?**
*Put the remote control between his toes.*


**What's the difference between Big Foot and an intelligent man?**
*Big Foot's been spotted several times.*


**What's the smartest thing a man can say?**
*'My wife says . . .'*


**Why are all dumb blonde jokes one-liners?**
*So men can understand them.*


**Why did God create man before woman?**
*Because you're always supposed to have a rough draft before creating your masterpiece.*

**Why** do men need instant reply on TV sports?
*Because after 30 seconds they forget what happened.*

**Why** is it good that there are female astronauts?
*When the crew gets lost in space, at least the woman will ask for directions.*

**Why** is psychoanalysis a lot quicker for men than for women?
*When it's time to go back to his childhood, he's already there.*

**Man** goes to the doctor with a strawberry growing out of his head.
*Doctor says, 'I'll give you some cream to put on it.'*

**A** bloke walks into the psychiatrist's office wearing only clingwrap for shorts.
*The shrink says, 'Well, I can see you're nuts.'*

**W**hat's brown and sounds like a bell?
*DUNG.*

**A** very religious man lived right next door to an atheist. While the religious one prayed day in and day out, and was constantly on his knees in communion with his Lord, the atheist never even looked twice at a church.

However, the atheist's life was good, he had a well-paying job and a beautiful wife, and his children were healthy and good-natured. Whereas the pious man's job was strenuous and his wages were low, his wife was cheating on him and his kids wouldn't give him the time of day.

So, one day, deep in prayer as usual, he raised his eyes towards heaven and asked: 'Oh God, I honour you every day, I ask your advice for every problem and confess to you my every sin. Yet my neighbour, who doesn't even believe in you and certainly never prays, seems blessed with every happiness while I go poor and suffer many an indignity. Why is this?'

And a great voice was heard from above . . .

'BECAUSE HE DOESN'T BOTHER ME ALL THE TIME!'

**A** man is in bed with his wife when there is a rat-a-tat-tat on the door. He rolls over and looks at his clock and it's half past three in the morning.

'I'm not getting out of bed at this time,' he thinks, and rolls over. Then, a louder knock follows. 'Are you going to answer that?' asks his wife.

So he drags himself out of bed, and goes downstairs. He opens the door and there's a man standing there. It doesn't take the homeowner long to realise the bloke is drunk.

'Hi there,' slurs the stranger, 'can you give me a push?'

'No, get lost, it's half past three. I was in bed,' says the man, and slams the door.

He goes back to bed and tells his wife what happened. She says, 'Dave, that wasn't very nice of you. Remember that night we broke down in the pouring rain on the way to pick the kids up from the babysitter and you had to knock on that man's house to get us started again? What would have happened if he'd told us to get lost?'

'But the guy's drunk!' says the husband.

'It doesn't matter,' says the wife. 'He needs our help and it would be the Christian thing to help him.'

So the husband gets out of bed again, gets dressed and goes downstairs. He opens the door and, not being able to see the stranger anywhere, shouts: 'Hey? Do you still want a push?'

And he hears a voice cry out, 'Yeah, please.'

So, still being unable to see the stranger he shouts: 'Where are you?'

And the stranger replies, 'I'm over here, on your swing!'

**W**hat do you call a fish with no eyes?
*A fsh.*

### The Penguin Bumper Book of Australian Jokes

**W**e are reliably informed that the following questions were submitted to the Olympic Committee via their website, prior to the 2000 Games.

'I've seen lots of documentaries about Australia on television and have never seen it rain. So how do your plants grow?' (UK)

'I plan to take some daytrips during the Olympics. Which direction should I drive – Perth to Darwin or Darwin to Perth – to avoid driving with the sun in my eyes?' (Germany)

'I want to walk from Perth to Sydney for the Olympics – can I follow the railroad tracks?' (Sweden)

'Is it safe to run around in the bushes in Australia?' (Sweden)

'Are there any ATMs in Australia? Can you send me a list of them in Brisbane, Cairns, Townsville and Hervey Bay?' (UK)

'Where can I learn underwater welding in Australia?' (Portugal)

'Do the camels in Australia have one hump or two?' (UK)

'Can I bring cutlery into Australia?' (UK)

'I want to go swimming at Bondi Beach. Will I turn blue?' (Germany)

'Do you have perfume in Australia?' (France)

'Do you celebrate Christmas in Australia?' (France)

'Can you give me some information about hippo racing in Australia?' (USA)

'Are there supermarkets in Sydney and is milk available all year round?' (Germany)

'Please send a list of all doctors in Australia who can dispense rattlesnake serum.' (USA)

'Which direction is north in Australia?' (USA)

'I have a question about a famous animal in Australia, but I forget its name. It's a kind of bear and lives in trees.' (USA)

---

A neutron walks into a bar. 'I'd like a beer,' he says.

The bartender promptly serves up a beer.

'How much will that be?' asked the neutron.

'For you?' replies the bartender. 'No charge.'

**A** Vaucluse socialite is planning a party – and on the invitation she writes, 'Please come dressed as a human emotion.'

The host opens the door to reveal the first guest – who's covered in green paint with the letters 'N' and 'V' painted on his chest. 'That's a terrific outfit. But what emotion are you?'

And the bloke says, 'I'm green with envy.'

The next guest is a woman covered in a pink body stocking with a feather boa wrapped around her naughty bits. 'That a great costume. But what emotion are you?'

And she says, 'I'm tickled pink.'

The third and fourth guests are a couple of visitors from New York – and they're stark naked. One has his penis stuck in a bowl of custard and the other has his stuck in a pear. The host is quite shocked and bundles them indoors before they get arrested. 'And what emotions are you supposed to be?'

The first New Yorker says, 'Well, I'm fuckin' dis-custard, and my friend has come in dis-pear.'

**THINGY** n.
Female: Any part under a car's hood.
Male: The strap fastener on a woman's bra.


**VULNERABLE** adj.
Female: Fully opening up one's self emotionally to another.
Male: Playing football without a helmet.


**COMMUNICATION** n.
Female: The open sharing of thoughts and feelings with one's partner.
Male: Scratching out a note before suddenly taking off for a weekend with the boys.


**COMMITMENT** n.
Female: A desire to get married and raise a family.
Male: Not trying to pick up other women while out with one's girlfriend.

ENTERTAINMENT n.
Female:   A good movie, concert, play or book.
Male:     Anything that can be done while drinking.


FLATULENCE n.
Female:   An embarrassing by-product of digestion.
Male:     An endless source of entertainment, self-expression and male bonding.


MAKING LOVE n.
Female:   The greatest expression of intimacy a couple can achieve.
Male:     Call it whatever you want just as long as we end up in bed.


REMOTE CONTROL n.
Female:   A device for changing from one TV channel to another.
Male:     A device for scanning through all 75 channels every three minutes.

Five doctors went duck hunting one day. Included in the group were a GP, a paediatrician, a psychiatrist, a surgeon and a pathologist. After a time, a bird came winging overhead. The first to react was the GP who raised his shotgun, but then hesitated.

'I'm not quite sure it's a duck,' he said. 'I think that I will have to get a second opinion.' And, of course, by that time the bird was long gone.

Another bird appeared in the sky. This time, the paediatrician took aim. He too, however, was unsure if it was really a duck in his sights and besides, it might have babies. 'I'll have to do some more investigations,' he muttered, as the creature made good its escape.

Next to spy a bird flying was the sharp-eyed psychiatrist. Shotgun shouldered, he was more certain of his intended prey's identity.

'Now I know it's a duck, but does it know it's a duck?' The fortunate bird disappeared while the fellow wrestled with this dilemma.

Finally, a fourth fowl sped past and this time the surgeon's weapon pointed skywards. BOOM!! The surgeon lowered his smoking gun and turned nonchalantly to the pathologist beside him.

'Go see if that was a duck, will you?'

# The Penguin Bumper Book of Australian Jokes

**A** man takes the day off work and decides to go out golfing. He is on the second hole when he notices a frog sitting next to the green. He think nothing of it and is about to shoot when he hears, 'Ribbit nine iron'. The man looks around and doesn't see anyone. Again he hears, 'Ribbit nine iron.'

He looks at the frog and decides to prove the frog wrong and grabs his nine iron. Boom! He hits it ten inches from the cup. He's shocked. 'This is amazing. You must be a lucky frog, eh?'

The frog replies, 'Ribbit lucky frog.'

The man decides to take the frog with him to the next hole. 'What do you think, frog?' the man asks.

'Ribbit three wood.'

The bloke takes out a three wood and Boom! Hole-in-one. The man is befuddled and doesn't know what to say. By the end of the day, he's played the best game of golf in his life and asks the frog, 'OK, where to next?'

The frog replies, 'Ribbit Las Vegas.'

They go to Las Vegas and the bloke says, 'OK frog, now what?'

The frog says, 'Ribbit roulette.'

Upon approaching the roulette table, the man asks, 'What do you think I should bet?'

The frog replies, 'Ribbit $3000, black six.' This is a very long shot, but after the golf game he thinks what the heck. Boom! Tonnes of cash come sliding back across the table.

The man takes his winnings and reserves the best room in the hotel. He sits the frog down and says, 'Frog, I don't know how to repay you. You've won me all this money and I've played the best golf game of my life. I am forever grateful.'

The frog replies, 'Ribbit kiss me.'

He thinks, why not. After all the frog did for him he deserves it. With a kiss, the frog turns into a gorgeous 15-year-old girl.

'And that, Your Honour, is how the girl ended up in my room. So help me God, or my name isn't William Jefferson Clinton.'

**A** man walked into the doctors.
The doctor said, 'I haven't seen you in a long time.'
The man replied, 'I know. I've been ill.'

A tourist in Vienna is going through a graveyard and all of a sudden he hears some music. No-one is around, so he starts searching for the source. He locates the origin and finds it is coming from a grave with a headstone that reads: Ludwig van Beethoven, 1770–1827.

He then realises that the music is the Ninth Symphony and it is being played backwards! Puzzled, he leaves the graveyard and persuades a friend to return with him. By the time they arrive back at the grave, the music has changed. This time it's the Seventh Symphony but, like the previous piece, it's being played backwards. Curious, the men agree to consult a music scholar.

When they return with the expert, the Fifth Symphony is playing, again backwards. The expert notices that the symphonies are being played in the reverse order in which they were composed, the ninth, then the seventh, then the fifth.

By the next day the word has spread and a throng has gathered around the grave. They are all listening to the Second Symphony being played backwards.

Just then the graveyard's caretaker ambles up to the group. Someone in the group asks him if he has an explanation for the music.

'Don't you get it?' the caretaker says incredulously. 'He's decomposing!'

### WORLD'S BEST FRUITCAKE

Ingredients:

1 cup butter
1 cup sugar
4 large eggs
1 cup dried fruit
1 teaspoon baking power
1 teaspoon baking soda
1 tablespoon lemon juice
1 cup brown sugar
1 cup nuts
1 or 2 quarts of aged whisky

# The Penguin Bumper Book of Australian Jokes

Before you start, sample the whisky to check for quality. Good, isn't it?

Now, go ahead.

Select a large mixing bowl, measuring cup etc. Check the whisky again as it must be just right. To be sure the whisky is of the highest quality, pour 1 level cup into a glass and drink it as fast as you can. Repeat.

With an eclectic mixer, beat 1 cup of butter in a large fluffy bowel. Add 1 teaspoon of sugar and beat the hell out of it again.

Meanwhile, at this parsnicular point in time, wake sure that the whixey hasn't gone bad while you weren't lookin'. Open second quart if nestessay.

Add 2 large leggs, 2 cups fried druit an beat til high. If druit getsshtuck in peaters, just pry the monsters loosh with a drewscriber.

Exasmple the whiksty again, shecking confistancy, then shift 2 cups of salt or destergent or whatever – like, anyone gives a shit.

Chample the whitchy shum more.

Shift in shum lemon zhoosh. Fold in chopped sputter and shrained nuts. Add 100 babblespoons of brown booger or whushever's closhest and mix well. GReash ubben and turn the cakey pan to 350 decrees. Now pour the whole pissin' mesh into the washin' machine and set on sinsh shycle.

Check dat whixny wunch more and pash out.

### CALORIES THAT DON'T COUNT

**1.** FOOD ON FOOT. All food eaten while standing has no calories. Exactly why, it is not clear. But the current theory relates to gravity. The calories apparently bypass the stomach flowing directly down the legs and through the soles of the feet into the floor, like electricity. Walking appears to accelerate this process, so that an ice-cream or hot dog eaten at the Easter Show actually has a calorie deficit.

**2.** TV FOOD. Anything eaten in front of the TV has no calories. This may have something to do with radiation leakage, which negates not only the calories in the food but all recollections of having eaten it.

**3.** UNEVEN EDGES. Pies and cakes should be cut neatly in even wedges or slices. If not, the responsibility falls on the person putting them away to 'straighten up the edges' by slicing away the offending irregularities, which have no calories when eaten.

**4.** BALANCED FOOD. If you have a glass of punch in your right hand, anything eaten with the other hand has no calories. Several principles are at work here. First of all, you're probably standing up at a wedding reception (see FOOD ON FOOT). Then there's the electronic field: a wet glass in one hand forms a negative charge to reverse the polarity of the calories attracted to the other hand. It's not quite known how it works. But it's reversible if you're left-handed.

**5.** FOOD FOR MEDICINAL PURPOSES. Food used for medicinal purposes NEVER counts. This includes hot chocolate, malted milk, toast and Sara Lee cheesecake.

**6.** WHIPPED CREAM, SOUR CREAM, BUTTER. These all act as a poultice that actually 'draws out' the calories when placed on any food, leaving them calorie-free. Afterwards you can eat the poultice too, as all calories are neutralised by it.

**7.** FOOD ON TOOTHPICKS. Sausages, mini-franks, cheese and crackers are all fattening UNLESS impaled on frilled toothpicks. The insertion of a sharp object allows the calories to leak out the bottom.

**8.** CHILDREN'S FOOD. Anything produced, purchased or intended for minors is calorie-free when eaten by adults. This category covers a wide range, beginning with a spoonful of baby-food custard, consumed for demonstration purposes, up to and including cookies baked to send to college.

**9.** CHARITABLE FOODS. Girl Guides' biscuits, cakes and ice-creams all have a religious dispensation from calories.

**10.** CUSTOM-MADE FOOD. Anything somebody makes 'just for you' must be eaten regardless of the calories, because to do otherwise would be uncaring and insensitive. Your kind intentions will not go unrewarded.

How do crazy people go through the forest?
*They take the psycho path.*

What did the fish say when he hit a concrete wall?
*'Dam!'*

**The Penguin Bumper Book of Australian Jokes**

**W**hat do prisoners use to call each other?
*Cell phones.*

**W**hat do the letters D.N.A. stand for?
*National Dyslexics Association.*

**W**hat do you call cheese that isn't yours?
*Nacho cheese.*

**W**hat do you get from a pampered cow?
*Spoiled milk.*

**W**hat lies at the bottom of the ocean and twitches?
*A nervous wreck.*

**The Penguin Bumper Book of Australian Jokes**

What's the difference between roast beef and pea soup?
*Anyone can roast beef.*


Where do you find a dog with no legs?
*Right where you left him.*


Why are there so many Smiths in the phone book?
*They all have phones.*


Why do bagpipers walk when they play?
*They're trying to get away from the noise.*


Why do gorillas have big nostrils?
*Because they have big fingers.*

**What's** the difference between an oral thermometer and a rectal thermometer?
*The taste.*


**What** is a zebra?
*26 sizes larger than an 'A' bra.*


**Did** you hear about the flasher who was thinking about retiring?
*He decided to stick it out for one more year.*


**What** do you get when you cross a pitbull with a collie?
*A dog that runs for help . . . after it bites your leg off.*

The scene is Golgotha. The sun is hiding its face in shame. The heavens rumble and, again and again, the unnatural darkness is punctuated by the harshest lightning – burning into the retinas of the small gathering on the hillside an unforgettable and harrowing image: three crosses, silhouetted against the sporadically illuminated backdrop of menacing clouds.

The Lord, crucified between two thieves, is crying out. 'God, why has thou forsaken me?'

But now there's a change in his voice. He is calling feebly for Peter.

'Peter! Peter!'

Peter approaches the roughly hewn cross, guarded by formidable centurions. Looking up at the Messiah, he calls out, 'Yes Lord, yes!'

'Peter! Peter!' repeats Jesus.

'Lord, speak to me! What is it?'

'Peter, guess what? I can see your house from up here!'

1972: Long hair.
2002: Longing for hair.

1972: The perfect high.
2002: The perfect high-yield mutual fund.

1972: Keg.
2002: EKG.

1972: Acid rock.
2002: Acid reflux.

1972: Growing pot.
2002: Growing pot belly.

1972: Sydney Harbour bridge.
2002: Dental bridge.

1972: Trying to look like Marlon Brando or Elizabeth Taylor.
2002: Trying NOT to look like Marlon Brando or Elizabeth Taylor.

1972: Seeds and stems.
2002: Roughage.

1972: Popping pills, smoking joints.
2002: Popping joints.

1972: Being caught with *Hustler* magazine.
2002: Being caught with *Hustler* magazine.

1972: Killer weed.
2002: Weed killer.

1972: Getting out to a new, hip joint.
2002: Getting a new hip joint.

1972: Rolling Stones.
2002: Kidney stones.

1972: Being called into the principal's office.
2002: Calling the principal's office.

1972: Screw the system!
2002: Upgrade the system.

1972: Peace sign.
2002: Mercedes logo.

1972: Parents begging you to get your hair cut.
2002: Children begging you to get their heads shaved.

1972: Take acid.
2002: Antacid.

1972: Passing the driver's test.
2002: Passing the vision test.

## SIX PRESIDENTS ON A SINKING SHIP . . .

Ford says: 'What do we do?'
Bush says: 'Man the lifeboats.'
Reagan says: 'What lifeboats?'
Carter says: 'Women first.'
Nixon says: 'Screw the women.'
Clinton says: 'Do you think we have time?'

# The Penguin Bumper Book of Australian Jokes

A farmer is sitting in the neighbourhood bar getting pissed. A man comes in and asks the farmer, 'Hey, why are you sitting here on this beautiful day getting drunk?'

Farmer: 'Some things you just can't explain.'
Man: 'So what happened that's so horrible?'
Farmer: 'Well, today I was sitting by my cow milking her. Just as I got the bucket about full, she took her left leg and kicked over the bucket.'
Man: 'OK, but that's not so bad.'
Farmer: 'Some things you just can't explain.'

Man: 'So what happened then?'
Farmer: 'I took her left leg and tied it to the post on the left.'
Man: 'And then?'
Farmer: 'Well, I sat back down and continued to milk her. Just as I got the bucket about full, she took her right leg and kicked over the bucket.'
Man: 'Again?'
Farmer: 'Some things you just can't explain.'

## The Penguin Bumper Book of Australian Jokes

Man: 'So, what did you do then?'
Farmer: 'I took her right leg this time and tied it to the post on the right.'
Man: 'And then?'
Farmer: 'Well, I sat back down and began milking her again. Just as I got the bucket about full, the stupid cow knocked over the bucket with her tail.'
Man: 'Hmmm...'
Farmer: 'Some things you just can't explain.'

Man: 'So, what did you do?'
Farmer: 'Well, I didn't have any more rope, so I took off my belt and tied her tail to the rafter. In that moment, my pants fell down and my wife walked in ... Some things you just can't explain.'

Chinese couple gets married – and she's a virgin.

On the wedding night, she cowers naked under the bedsheets as her husband undresses. He climbs in next to her and tries to be reassuring: 'My darring, I know dis you firs time and you bery frighten. I plomise you, I give you anyting you want, I do anyting you want. What you want?'

'I wan numma 69,' she replies.

He looks at her very puzzled and says, 'You want . . . Beef with Snowpeas?'

**S**everal blokes are sitting around in the locker room after working out. Suddenly a mobile phone on one of the benches rings. One of the men picks it up, and the following conversation ensues:

'Hello?'

'Honey, it's me. Are you at the gym?'

'Ummm, yes.'

'Great! I am at the mall two blocks from where you are and I just saw this beautiful mink coat. It's absolutely gorgeous! Can I buy it, please?'

'What's the price?'

'Only $15 000.'

'Well, OK, go ahead and get it, if you like it that much . . .'

'Ahhh . . . and I also stopped by the Mercedes

dealership and saw the brand-new 200Z models. I saw one I really liked and spoke with the salesman and he gave me a really good price . . . and since we really need to exchange the BMW that we bought last year . . .'

'What price did he quote you?'

'Only $60 000 . . .'

'Well, OK. But for that price I want it with all the options.'

'Great! But before we hang up, just one more thing . . .'

'What's that?'

'Now, this might look like a little bit much, but I was reconciling your bank account and . . . ummm . . . well, I stopped by the real estate agent this morning and saw that house we had looked at last year. It's on sale! Remember? The one on the harbour?'

'So, how much are they asking?'

'Only three million . . . and I see that we have that much in the bank to cover . . .'

'Well, then go ahead and buy it, but just bid $2 800 000. OK?'

'OK, sweetie . . . Thanks! I'll see you later! I love you!!!'

'Bye, I do too . . .'

Slowly shaking his head, the bloke closes the phone's flap. Then he holds it up and asks: 'Hey, does anyone know who this belongs to?'

One of the USA's largest soup manufacturers announced today that they will be stocking America's shelves this week with their newest soup creation, 'Clinton Soup', which will honour one of the nation's most distinguished men. It consists primarily of a small weenie in hot water.

When Clinton was asked what he thought about foreign affairs, he replied, 'I don't know, I never had one.'

If you came across Bill Clinton struggling in a raging river and you had a choice between rescuing him or getting a Pulitzer Prize-winning photograph, what shutter speed would you use?

Clinton's mother prayed fervently that Bill would

grow up and be president. So far, half of her prayer has been answered.

American Indians nicknamed Bill Clinton 'Walking Eagle' because he is so full of crap he can't fly.

Clinton did the work of three men: Moe, Larry and Curly.

Revised judicial oath: 'I solemnly swear to tell the truth as I know it, the whole truth as I believe it to be, and nothing but what I think you need to know.'

### WHY DID THE CHICKEN CROSS THE ROAD?

JOHN HOWARD:
The chicken never ever crossed the road. And it was not forcibly removed from its mother! Anyway, that's a matter for the states and is of no interest to us. The United Nations should butt out.

KIM BEAZLEY:
There WAS a chicken and it DID cross the road. This is a deliberate act by the government to hide the fact that chickens continue to cross Australian roads.

## The Penguin Bumper Book of Australian Jokes

NATASHA STOTT DESPOJA:
What if it was not a chicken but a bantam? Minority sectors of our community shouldn't be discriminated against based purely on the size of their legs and breasts.

SUSIE O'NEILL:
It was a rather sus chicken, don't you think? Pretty big for its age.

EVELYN SCOTT:
To demonstrate a commitment to reconciliation with indigenous chickens.

PETER COSTELLO:
According to documentation submitted to the Live Foods Processing Authority, the chicken in question was uncooked at the time of its journey and therefore will not incur a GST charge. However, if that chicken actually crossed the road for profit, regardless of its raw/cooked status, the road crossing would be considered by the ATO to be a service for which GST will be imposed.

PAULINE HANSON:
Please explain.

# The Penguin Bumper Book of Australian Jokes

REV. FRED NILE:
Because the chicken was gay! Isn't it obvious? Can't you people see the plain truth in front of your face? The chicken was going to the 'other side'. That's what 'they' call it: the 'other side'. Yes, my friends!

JOHN MARSDEN:
The chicken was an adult. It's a free country. Those little devils peck so deliciously hard!

ROBERT DE NIRO:
Are you telling me the chicken crossed that road? Is that what you're telling me?

ERNEST HEMINGWAY:
To die. In the rain.

MARTIN LUTHER KING JR:
I envision a world where all chickens, be they black or white or brown or red or speckled, will be free to cross roads without having their motives called into question.

GRANDPA:
In my day, we didn't ask why the chicken crossed the road. Someone told us that the chicken crossed the road, and that was good enough for us.

ARISTOTLE:
It is the nature of chickens to cross the road.

KARL MARX:
It was a historical inevitability.

SADDAM HUSSEIN:
It was an unprovoked act of rebellion and violence by a counter-revolutionary terrorist chicken and we were forced to defend ourselves from the menace by dropping 500 tons of nerve gas on it.

RONALD REAGAN:
What chicken, Mommy?

CAPTAIN JAMES T. KIRK:
To boldly go where no chicken has gone before.

FOX MULDER:
You saw it cross the road with your own eyes. How many more chickens have to cross before you believe it's true?

BILL GATES:
We have just released eChicken 2000, which will not only cross roads, but will lay eggs (only in the

proprietary brown_ms.egg format), file your important documents and balance your chequebook. Internet Explorer is an inextricable part of eChicken.

THE CIA:
Who told you about the chicken? Did you see the chicken? There was no chicken. Please step in the car, sir.

EINSTEIN:
Did the chicken really cross the road or did the road move beneath the chicken?

BILL CLINTON:
I did not cross the road with THAT chicken. What do you mean by chicken? Could you define the word 'chicken'?

JULIUS SUMNER-MILLER:
Why is it so? Just as this chicken crosses the road, so there's a glass and a half of full cream dairy milk . . .

ACADEMIC ECONOMIC RATIONALIST:
Deregulation of the chicken's side of the road was threatening its dominant market position. The chicken was faced with significant challenges to create and

develop the competencies required for the newly competitive market. The AER, in a partnering relationship with the client, helped the chicken by using the Poultry Integration Model (PIM). AER helped the chicken use its skills, methodologies, knowledge, capital and experiences to align the chicken's people, processes and technology in support of its overall strategy within a Program Management framework. AER convened a diverse cross-spectrum of road analysts and best chickens along with AER consultants with deep skills in the transportation industry to engage in a two-day itinerary of meetings in order to leverage their personal knowledge capital, both tacit and explicit, and to enable them to synergise with each other in order to achieve the implicit goals of delivering and successfully architecting and implementing an enterprise-wide value framework across the continuum of poultry cross-median processes. The meeting was held in a park-like setting, enabling and creating an impactful environment which was strategically based, industry-focused, and built upon a consistent, clear and unified market message and aligned with the chicken's mission, vision and core values. This was conducive towards the creation of a total business integration solution. The AER helped the chicken change to become more successful.

If you come home to a house full of love, warmth and understanding . . . you're in the wrong house.

I'd rather have a bottle in front of me than a frontal lobotomy.

A lawyer specialising in divorce kicks the bucket and finds himself standing, knee-deep in clouds, at the Pearly Gates. St Peter opens one gate, just a little, and asks, 'What have you done to merit admission into Heaven?' The lawyer ponders the question and then says, 'Well, a week ago I gave 20 cents to a homeless person.'

St Peter asks Gabriel to check the accounts and Gabriel runs a finger up and down the columns, finally nodding in affirmation.

St Peter says, 'Fine, fine. But it's not really quite enough to get you into Heaven.'

'Wait! Wait!' the lawyer says, remembering. 'There's more. Three years back I gave another homeless person 20 cents.'

St Peter looks at Gabriel, seeking confirmation. Gabriel returns to the accounts book and, after a moment or two of turning the pages, affirms the donation.

St Peter then whispers to Gabriel, 'What should we do with this bloke?'

Gabriel looks at the lawyer, barely able to conceal his contempt. 'Let's give him back his 40 cents and tell him to go to hell.'

The RAAF have an ultra-secret base, run in collaboration with the Pentagon, near Pine Gap. It appears on no maps. Commercial flights are forbidden to come within 500kms.

Late one arvo, the RAAF people at the base are astonished to see a Cessna approaching the runway. When it lands, they impound the aircraft and haul the pilot into an interrogation room.

His story? Well, he was holidaying in Alice Springs and had been taking a few flights to see the highlights, like Uluru. On this occasion, he'd miscalculated the distances and was almost out of fuel.

The air force people aren't convinced. They implement a full ASIO background check and hold him overnight.

Next morning, they're finally persuaded that he really was lost and wasn't a spy. They give him some Avgas, bully him with a 'you have never been here ... you saw nothing ... you know nothing ...' briefing, telling him that he could go to jail if he tells anybody anything, and send him on his way.

Imagine their astonishment when, the very next day, he turns up again. Once again, the Cessna violates the top-secret airspace and lands. And taxis to their terminal.

Once again, MPs surround the plane ... which, this time, has two people inside it.

The pilot jumps out and says, 'Do anything you want to me, but my wife is in the plane, and you have to tell her where I was last night.'

'I have to say,' said the GP, 'that you're in very, very good shape for a bloke your age. Incidentally, what is your age?'

'I'm 82,' the patient said.

'Eighty-two? Really? How do you stay so healthy? You have the blood pressure, the heart rate and the appearance of a bloke 20 years younger.'

'It's like this, doctor. My wife and I agreed, when we got married, that whenever she got angry with me she'd go into the kitchen and count to ten. And I'd go outside to calm down.'

'And the result?'

'Doctor, I've enjoyed the benefits of an outdoor life.'


I just got skylights put in my place. The people who live above me are furious.


Why do they sterilise needles for lethal injections?

## The Penguin Bumper Book of Australian Jokes

If it's tourist season, why can't we shoot them?

A little bloke ventures into a bikers' bar at Cessnock, scene of many a turf war between rival gangs.

Clearing his throat he asks the hulking figures sitting at the bar, 'Which one of you gentleman owns the Rottweiler that's tied up outside?'

The biggest of the blokes, wearing biker leathers, with every visible inch of his epidermis covered in tattoos, says, 'That's my dog. Why?'

'Well, sir,' said the little bloke, very nervously, 'I'm afraid my dog has just killed your dog.'

The giant bikie roars in anger and disbelief. 'What kind of dog could kill a Rottweiler?'

'It's a Jack Russell. A four-week-old puppy.'

'How could your fuckin' puppy kill my Rottweiler?'

'Sir, it appears that he choked on it.'

**A** blonde was driving through the bush, back o' Bourke, when she saw another blonde in the middle of a wheatfield. To her astonishment, she seemed to be rowing a boat. Pulling to the side of the road, the blonde stared in disbelief at the blonde in the middle distance.

Finally she called out to the blonde in the boat, 'Why are you rowing a boat?'

The blonde stopped rowing and called back, 'Because it's an ocean of wheat.'

The blonde by the car was unimpressed. 'It's dumb blondes like you that give the rest of us a bad name,' she yelled.

The blonde in the boat simply shrugged her shoulders and returned to her rowing.

Beside herself with rage, the blonde at the side of the road shook her fist at the blonde in the boat, 'I'd like to come out there and toss you out of that silly dinghy, but I can't swim.'

**D**riving in the middle of nowhere, a bloke notices that he's getting low on diesel so pulls into an isolated service station. Just a couple of pumps in front of a shed.

He fills the tank and as he goes in to pay notices an old dog asleep in the doorway. And beside it, a crudely lettered sign saying, 'DANGER. BEWARE OF THE DOG!'

So he stops and calls to the bloke at the till. 'Is this the dog I'm supposed to beware of?'

'Yes, that's him.'

'Well, he doesn't look all that dangerous. In fact, he looks absolutely and utterly harmless. Why the sign?'

'Because,' the owner said, 'silly buggers like you keep tripping over him.'

**A** couple in their late 60s went to a doctor specialising in sex therapy.

'And what can I do for you?' the doctor asked the old couple.

'We want you to watch us having a fuck.'

The doctor was puzzled but, having learnt to be non-judgemental, agreed. But he insisted that, first of all, he give them a thorough medical examination.

They seemed in good nick so he told them to get on with it.

They cleared the In and Out trays from his desk and had sexual intercourse while he watched them as requested. 'Well, there's nothing wrong with the way you have intercourse,' he said, charging them his standard $50.

They came back week after week. They'd make an appointment, have sexual intercourse while he watched, get dressed, write out the cheque and leave.

After months of this routine the doctor decided enough was enough. 'Look, there seems to be no point to this. Everything's fine. You're having no dysfunctionality. What exactly are you trying to find out?'

The old bloke said, 'We're not trying to find out anything. I'm married, so we can't go to my house. She's married, so we can't go to hers. The Flag Inn charges $120. The Hilton charges $250. We do it here for $50 and get half back on health insurance.'

A woman was walking her Pekinese when she noticed a funeral procession slowly approaching. The black hearse was followed by a second black hearse ... and walking behind it was a solitary mourner, a woman with a Rottweiler on a leash.

And, at a respectful distance, were no less than 200 women walking in single file, each dangling dog leashes but ... without dogs.

Unable to contain her curiosity, the woman on the footpath approached the woman with the Rottweiler and said, 'I'm sorry for your loss, and it's probably a bad time to disturb you, but I've never seen a funeral like this. Who's is it?'

'The first hearse,' the woman with the Rottweiler replied, 'is my husband.'

'How sad. And how did he die?'

The widow replied, 'My Rottweiler killed him.'

'Forgive me for asking, but who's in the second hearse?'

The widow said, 'My mother-in-law. She was trying to help my husband when the Rottweiler went for her throat.'

A moment of silence passed.

'Can I borrow your dog?'

'Join the queue.'

A couple of blokes were playing golf at Royal Melbourne. One pulled out a cigar but couldn't find a lighter. 'Do you have a light?' he asked his mate.

'Yep,' said the friend, who reached into his golf bag and pulled out an immense Bic lighter. At least four times as big as any other Bic lighter you've ever seen.

'Where did you get that monstrous Bic?'
'From my genie.'
'From your genie?'
'Yep. I've got a genie. Right here in my golf bag.'
'Bullshit.'
'No, it's dinkum. Have a look for yourself.'

And he opened his golf bag and out popped the genie.

'For chrissake,' said his friend, absolutely astonished. But collecting his senses he said, 'Any chance of having a wish granted? Just one?'

'By all means,' said the genie.
'Well, I'd like a million bucks.'

The genie climbed back into the golf bag and, for a few moments, absolutely nothing happened.

Then, suddenly, the sky darkened, as if the sun had been hidden by thunder clouds. But when they looked up they saw, instead, a million ducks flying overhead.

'But I asked for a million bucks, not ducks!'
'Did I tell you the genie is half-deaf? Sorry.'
'Half-deaf?'
'Yep, do you really think I asked him for a 12-inch Bic?'

**V**erily I say unto you. The Lord appeared to Adam and sayeth, 'I've got some good news and bad news.'

Adam shielded his face from the sight of the Lord with an upraised arm and said, 'Well, give me the good news first.'

And the Lord speaketh, 'I've got two new organs for you. One is called a brain. This will allow you to solve problems, pose questions, create hypotheses – and have intelligent conversations with Eve.'

'And the bad news?' asked Adam.

And the Lord sayeth, 'The other organ I have for you is called a penis. It will give you great pleasure and allow you to reproduce your now intelligent life form and populate this planet.'

Adam, very excited, said, 'These are great gifts! But I don't see where the bad news comes in.'

The Lord looked down upon Adam and said, with infinite sorrow, 'You will never be able to use these two gifts at the same time.'

---

A blonde was having trouble with the powerboat her merchant banking friend had given her. No matter how hard she tried, she couldn't get it to gain any speed. It was sluggish in manoeuvring and heavy in the water.

After trying for hours to get the boat running properly she appealed to a bloke at a nearby marina for help. He checked the engine – it was fine. And the propeller was the correct size and pitch.

So he jumped into the water to check beneath the boat – and came up choking with laughter.

Under the boat, still strapped securely in place, was the trailer.

# The Penguin Bumper Book of Australian Jokes

**T**he four-year-old was sitting in grandpa's lap as he read her a fairy story.

As he read, she reached up and touched his old, wrinkled cheek. Then she stroked her own chubby, smooth cheek. Then she touched his again.

'Grandpa,' she said. 'Can I ask you a question?'

'Of course, my dear.'

'Did God make you?'

'Yes, He made me a long, long time ago.'

'And did God make me too?'

'Yes, my child. God made you, just a little while ago.'

Comparing their respectives faces, she said, 'God's getting better at it now, isn't He?'

**H**aiku are very short, very formally structured Japanese poems, each of three lines and each containing the same number of syllables.

Here are the haiku used to replace the Microsoft error messages.

Three things are certain
Death, taxes and lost data
Guess which has occurred?

Yesterday it worked
today it is not working.
Windows is like that.

A crash reduces
your expensive computer
to a simple stone.

The website you seek
cannot be located but
countless more exist.

First snow then silence.
This $1000 screen dies
so beautifully.

Chaos reigns within.
Reflect, repent, and reboot.
Order shall return.

# The Penguin Bumper Book of Australian Jokes

You step in the stream
but the water has moved on.
This page is not here.

The Tao that is seen
is not the true Tao until
you bring fresh toner.

Out of memory.
We wish to hold the whole sky.
But we never will.

With searching comes loss
and the presence of absence.
'My novel' not found.

Stay the patient course.
Of little worth is your ire.
The network is down.

Windows NT crashed.
I am the Blue Screen of Death.
No-one hears your screams.

**The Penguin Bumper Book of Australian Jokes**

Having been erased
the document you're seeking
must now be retyped.

A file that big?
It might be very useful.
But now it is gone.

Serious error.
All short-cuts have disappeared.
Screen. Mind. Both are blank.

### THINGS YOU LEARN FROM TV AND FILLUMS

ONE OF A PAIR OF TWINS IS ALWAYS BORN EVIL.

SHOULD YOU DECIDE TO DEFUSE A BOMB, DON'T WORRY WHICH WIRE TO CUT. YOU'LL ALWAYS CHOOSE THE RIGHT ONE.

### The Penguin Bumper Book of Australian Jokes

Most laptop computers are powerful enough to override the communications system of any invading alien.

It does not matter if you are heavily outnumbered in a fight involving martial arts. Your enemies will wait patiently to attack you one by one, by dancing around in a threatening manner until you have knocked out their mates.

When you turn out the light by the bed, everything in the bedroom will still be clearly visible. Just slightly bluish.

If you're blonde and pretty, it's possible to become a world expert on nuclear fission at the age of 23.

Honest and hardworking policemen are always gunned down three days before their retirement.

During all investigations, it will be necessary for the cops to visit a strip club.

**The Penguin Bumper Book of Australian Jokes**

ALL BEDS HAVE SPECIAL L-SHAPED COVER SHEETS THAT REACH UP TO THE ARMPITS OF A WOMAN BUT ONLY TO WAIST LEVEL ON THE BLOKE BESIDE HER.

ALL SHOPPING BAGS CONTAIN AT LEAST ONE STICK OF FRENCH BREAD.

ANY FOOL CAN LAND A PLANE PROVIDING THERE IS SOMEONE IN THE CONTROL TOWER TO TALK YOU DOWN.

IN WAR YOU WON'T DIE UNLESS YOU MAKE THE MISTAKE OF SHOWING SOMEONE A PICTURE OF YOUR SWEETHEART.

SHOULD YOU WISH TO PASS YOURSELF OFF AS A GERMAN OR RUSSIAN OFFICER, IT WILL NOT BE NECESSARY TO SPEAK THE LANGUAGE. A GERMAN OR RUSSIAN ACCENT WILL DO.

THE EIFFEL TOWER CAN BE SEEN FROM ANY WINDOW IN PARIS.

A MAN WILL SHOW NO PAIN WHILE TAKING THE WORST BASHING BUT WILL WINCE WHEN A WOMAN TRIES TO CLEAN HIS WOUNDS.

## The Penguin Bumper Book of Australian Jokes

Whenever a large pane of glass is visible, someone will be thrown through it.

When staying in a haunted house, women should investigate any strange noises alone in their sexiest undies.

Word processors never display a cursor on the screen but will always say: 'Enter Password Now'.

Even when driving down a perfectly straight road, it is necessary to turn the steering wheel vigorously from left to right every few moments.

All bombs are fitted with electronic timing devices with large red read-outs so you know exactly when they're going to go off.

Detectives can only solve a case once they've been suspended from duty.

If you decide to start dancing in the street, everyone you meet will know all the steps.

# The Penguin Bumper Book of Australian Jokes

Police departments give their officers personality tests to make sure they are deliberately assigned to a partner who's their total opposite.

When alone, all foreign spies or military officers prefer to speak to each other in English.

## The following is a question given in a Sydney University chemistry exam

'Is Hell exothermic (gives off heat) or endothermic (absorbs heat)? Support your answer with a proof.'

Most of the students wrote proofs of their beliefs using Boyle's Law (gas cools off when it expands and heats up when it is compressed) or some variant. One student, however, wrote the following:

First, we need to know how the mass of Hell is changing in time. So, we need to know the rate that souls are moving into Hell and the rate they are leaving. I think that we can safely assume that once a soul gets to Hell, it will not leave. Therefore, no souls are leaving. As for how many souls are entering Hell, let's look at the different religions that exist in the world today. Some of these religions state that if you are not a member of their religion, you will go to Hell. Since there are more than one of these religions and since people do not belong to more than one religion, we can project that all people and all souls go to Hell. With birthrates and death rates as they are, we can expect the number of souls in Hell to increase exponentially. Now, we look at the rate of change of the volume in Hell because Boyle's Law states that in order for the temperature and pressure in Hell to stay the same, the volume in Hell has to expand as souls are added. This gives two possibilities:

**1.** If Hell is expanding at a slower rate than the rate at which souls enter Hell, then the temperature and pressure in Hell will increase until all Hell breaks loose.

**2.** Of course, if Hell is expanding at a rate faster than the increase of souls in Hell, then the temperature and pressure will drop until Hell freezes over.

So which is it?

If we accept the postulate given to me by a girl during my first year at Sydney Uni, 'That it will be a cold night in Hell before I sleep with you,' and take into account the fact that I still have not succeeded in having sexual relations with her, then (2) cannot be true, and thus I am sure that Hell is exothermic.

---

A blonde was pulled over for speeding. As the motorcyle officer walked to her car window, flipping open his ticket book, she said, 'I bet you are going to sell me a ticket to the Highway Patrolmen's Ball.'

He replied, 'Highway patrolmen don't have balls.'

## The horse race

LINE-UP:
1. Passionate Lady
2. Bare Belly
3. Silk Panties
4. Conscience
5. Jockey Shorts
6. Clean Sheets
7. Thighs
8. Big Dick
9. Heavy Bosom
10. Merry Cherry

THEY'RE OFF!!!
Conscience is left behind at the gate.
Jockey Shorts and Silk Panties are off in a hurry.
Heavy Bosom is being pressured.
Passionate Lady is caught by Thighs
and Big Dick is in a dangerous spot!

AT THE HALF...
It's Bare Belly on top, Thighs open and Big Dick is pressed in.
Heavy Bosom is being pushed hard against Clean Sheets.

Passionate Lady and Thighs are working hard on Bare Belly.
Bare Belly is under terrific pressure from Big Dick.

AT THE STRAIGHT...
Merry Cherry cracks under the strain.
Big Dick is making a final drive.
Bare Belly is in and Passionate Lady is coming.

AT THE FINISH...
It's Big Dick giving everything he's got
and Passionate Lady takes everything Big Dick has to offer.
It looks like a dead heat but Big Dick comes through with one final thrust and wins by a head...
Bare Belly shows...
Thighs weakens...
Heavy Bosom pulls up...
and Clean Sheets never had a chance.

## New Maths

Ratio of an igloo's circumference to its diameter: Eskimo Pi

2000 pounds of Chinese soup: Won ton

Time between slipping on a peel and hitting the pavement: 1 bananosecond

Weight an evangelist carries with God: 1 billigram

Half of a large intestine: 1 semicolon

100 aches: 1 kilohurtz

Basic unit of laryngitis: 1 hoarsepower

1 million microphones: 1 megaphone

2000 mockingbirds: 2 kilomockingbirds

52 cards: 1 decacards

### The Penguin Bumper Book of Australian Jokes

**H**e had never been a popular man and eulogies would be few and far between. The rabbi's contribution to the service was limited because the deceased had rarely, if ever, attended his synagogue. Struggling to make the best of things, the rabbi asked the not particularly mournful mourners attending if any of them wanted to say something about the dearly departed. There was a long silence. An embarrassing silence. Finally there was a voice from the rear.

'Well, he wasn't as bad as his brother.'

**T**here is one issue on which every husband and wife are in agreement.

Neither like sucking cocks.

**A** bloke was visiting his grandparents. As he walked up the garden path he noticed grandpa sitting on the verandah, in his rocking chair, bare from the waist down.

'Grandpa! What are you doing?' he asked, concerned that passers-by might see the old fellow. And the old fellow's old fellow.

Looking off into the distance, grandpa remained silent.

'Grandpa, what are you doing sitting out here like this?' the grandson asked again.

The old man looked at him and said, 'Well, last week I sat out here with no shirt on, and I got a stiff neck. So today's your grandma's idea.'

Two old blokes were playing cards one Saturday evening, as they had for decades. Bill, the oldest, was having a problem identifying the suits – and usually sought help from his missus.

At the end of the card game, Fred said to Bill, 'You did very, very well tonight. You didn't need any help. Not from your wife, not from anyone. How come?'

And Bill said, 'Ever since Maud sent me to that memory school, I haven't had any problems at all.'

'Memory school?'

'Yes,' said Bill, 'memory school. They teach you to remember things by association. Like, "Oh, what's that flower that's red with thorns?".'

'You mean, a rose?'

'Yeah, a rose.'

Bill turned and yelled, 'Hey, Rose! What's the name of that memory school you've been sending me to?'

It was a bus tour for senior citizens. When they arrived at the Three Sisters, in the Blue Mountains, the driver parked the bus and the passengers made their doddering, unsteady descent to the footpath. As they filed past, one elderly lady stopped and whispered in the driver's ear. 'I've been sexually harassed.'

A few seconds later, another old dear stopped and whispered in his ear. 'Driver, I've been sexually harassed.'

This kept happening. Soon seven pensioners had complained – whilst others pointed to an old bloke who was crawling around the floor of the bus, looking beneath the seats.

The driver approached him, tapped him on his back and said, 'Excuse me sir, I'd like to have a word with you.'

The old bloke looked up and said, 'Of course you can. But not right at the moment. You see, I've lost my toupee and am trying to find it. I thought I'd found it seven times – but they were parted in the middle, and mine's parted on the side.'

### EXCERPTS FROM LETTERS SENT TO LANDLORDS . . .

- I want some repairs done to my stove as it has backfired and burnt my knob off.
- This is to let you know that there's a smell coming from the man next door.
- The toilet is blocked and we cannot bathe the children until it's fixed.
- I'm writing on behalf of my sink, which is running away from the wall.
- The toilet seat is cracked. Where do I stand?
- The bloke next door has a large erection in his backyard. This is unsightly and dangerous.
- I want your permission to remove my drawers in the kitchen.
- As I told you in my last letter, the garden path is in

urgent need of repair. Yesterday my wife tripped on it and is now pregnant.
- Please send a plumber to look at my water. It is a funny colour and not fit to drink.
- I want to complain about the neighbour. Every morning at 5.30 his cock wakes me up and it's getting too much.

**A** cocktail party. A blonde approaches a colonel in full dress uniform. Flirtatiously she asks him, 'When was the last time you had sex?'

'Nineteen forty-three,' he replied.

'You poor thing. You really need to enjoy yourself more.'

'I don't understand you,' he said, glancing at his watch. 'It's only 2014 now.'

**A** brunette and a blonde are running a small hobby farm. They decide that their cows need a bull. The brunette takes $600 from their joint account and goes to a local sale. And her bid of $599 is successful.

Having bought the bull, she goes to the local post office and says, 'I'd like to send a telegram to my partner that says, HAVE FOUND THE BULL FOR OUR PROPERTY. BRING THE TRAILER.'

The bloke behind the counter says, 'Telegrams are 75 cents a word.'

She thinks about it for a moment. 'Then I'll send one word.'

'And what word would that be?'

'COMFORTABLE.'

'But will your friend understand this message?'

The brunette says, 'My friend is a blonde and reads very, very slowly. When she gets this she will see "Com-for-da-ble".'

---

**T**he Godfather, accompanied by his attorney, a man who spent a lifetime working for the mafia, storms into an office to confront his accountant. 'Where's the three million bucks you embezzled from me?' snarls the Godfather.

The accountant doesn't say a word. So the Godfather asks again, 'OK, you cocksucker, where's the three million bucks?'

The attorney interrupts. 'Godfather, the man is a deaf mute and cannot understand you. But I can interpret.'

And the Godfather says, 'Interpret away. Ask him where the fucking money is!'

Using sign language, the accountant obliges. And the accountant signs back, 'I don't know what you're talking about.'

The attorney translates for the Godfather. 'He doesn't know what you're talking about.'

Now the Godfather pulls out a huge revolver, puts the barrel to the temple of the accountant, cocks the trigger, and says, 'Ask him again where the fucking three million is!'

The attorney signs the accountant, 'The Godfather wants to know where the money is.'

The accountant, hands shaking, signs back. 'OK, OK! I give up. The money's hidden in a box on top of the wardrobe.'

The Godfather asks, 'Well, what did the little bastard say?'

The attorney interprets for the Godfather. 'He says that you don't have the guts to pull the trigger.'

# The Penguin Bumper Book of Australian Jokes

What do you call a girl with no arms or legs at the beach?
*Sandy.*

### How to clean a cat . . .

**1.** Thoroughly clean your toilet.

**2.** Add the right amount of shampoo to the toilet water and lift both the seat and the lid.

**3.** Get the cat and stroke it while you carry it to the bathroom.

**4.** In one smooth movement, drop the cat into the loo. And close both lids. It's probably a good idea to stand on the lid so he can't escape. Do not let any part of your body get too close to the cat – as his paws and claws will be reaching for anything they can get.

**5.** Flush the toilet four times. This provides a 'power wash and rinse' which is very effective.

**6.** Have someone open the back door and ensure there are no people between the toilet and the garden.

**7.** Lift the lid and the seat very quickly and jump into the shower recess.

**8.** The freshly cleaned cat will explode from the loo and run outside dripping water everywhere.

**A** young maths teacher, new to the school and the class, was writing an assignment on the blackboard. It involved chalking up a lot of equations and as she reached higher and higher up the board there was a giggle from one of the boys in the class.

She turned and said, 'What's so funny?'

'I just saw one of your garters.'

'Get out of this classroom,' she yelled, 'you're lucky I don't send you straight to the headmaster for the strap. I don't want to see you for three days!'

She returned to the blackboard, reaching to the very top to complete an equation. Whereupon there was an even louder giggle from another little boy.

'WHAT'S SO FUNNY?'

'I just saw both of your garters.'

'Get out of my classroom! I don't want to see you for three weeks!'

In her embarrassment, she dropped the duster and bent to pick it up. This time there was an eruption of laughter from another young student. But by the time she identified him, he was already walking out of the class.

'And where do you think you're going?'

'From what I just saw, my schooldays are over.'

**A**fter eating, do amphibians need to wait an hour before getting OUT of the water?

**W**hy don't they just make mouse-flavoured cat food?

**I**f you're sending someone some styrofoam, what do you pack it in?

**A**n old farmer is walking his boundaries when he comes close to his neighbour's barn and sees a big sign. 'HORSE FOR SALE. $10.'

And there's his neighbour, an old Italian, brushing down a marvellous looking stallion.

'Hello, Luigi. Your horse is for sale?'

'Yep, yep, dissa isa da horse for-a-sale.'

'But he's a fine looking animal. Why would you want to sell him?'

'Well,' says the Italian, 'he no looka so good any more.'

The farmer is convinced that he's got a big, big bargain. He gives the Italian $10, puts on a halter and leads the horse back to the homestead. But when he tries to coax the horse into the horse yards, the horse misses the gate completely and walks head first into a tree.

'That Italian bastard! He sold me a blind horse.'

And he storms across the paddocks to give the Italian a piece of his mind.

'You're a cheat! That horse is blind and you didn't even tell me!'

'I tella you,' cries the Italian farmer, 'I tella you! I say, "He no looka so good any more".'

**A** woman took her ailing husband to the doctor's surgery.

When it was over, the GP took the woman aside and whispered. 'Your husband is suffering from a very severe stress disorder. And if you don't do the following, I'm afraid he'll almost certainly have a massive stroke.'

'What am I supposed to do?'

'Well, each morning fix him a big breakfast. Always be pleasant. Make him a three-course lunch. And always have a particularly nice evening meal for him. And don't ask him to do work around the house. Don't discuss any problems with him – the stress could be fatal. Whatever you do, no nagging. And most importantly, make love several times a week. Do this for the next 12 months and I'm pretty certain he'll regain his health.'

Back in the car the husband asked his wife, 'What did the doctor whisper to you?'

'He said you're fucked,' she replied.

**A**fter years and years in the computer business, Frank is tired of the stress. So he leaves the big company, buys 50 acres of land at Woori Yallock and builds himself a nice little hut. He sees the postman once a week and gets groceries once a month. He feeds kookaburras and kangaroos. And he loves the peace and quiet.

After six months of isolation, he's watching the sunset when someone drives up in a 4WD. 'The name's Arthur. I'm one of your neighbours. And I'm having a party Saturday. Thought you'd like to come.'

'Fine,' says Frank, 'after six months I'm ready to meet some locals.'

As the neighbour leaves he says, 'I better warn you. There's going to be some drinking.'

'No problem. After a career in the computer business, I can drink with the best of them.'

'And there may be some fighting, too.'

'Look, I get along pretty well with people. I'll be there. Thanks again.'

Another warning from the neighbour. 'There's likely to be some wild sex.'

'Not a problem. I've been all alone for six months. By the way, what should I wear?'

'Whatever you like. There's only going to be the two of us.'

The young woman, her elderly husband and a young, handsome sailor are shipwrecked on an island. One morning, the sailor climbed a palm tree, looked down and yelled, 'Stop making love!'

'What are you talking about?' the husband called up the palm tree. 'We're not making love.'

'Sorry,' said the sailor, 'but from up here it looked like you were.'

So the husband decided to climb the palm tree, which he did with considerable difficulty. And looking down he said, 'You know, he's absolutely right. I'd swear the two of you were making love.'

---

Two old mates were enjoying a few beers at the pub when one said to the other, 'If I asked you a question, would you promise to answer it honestly?'

'Of course.'

'Well, why do you think all the blokes around here find my wife so attractive?'

'Oh, that? It's because of her speech impediment.'

'Her speech impediment? My wife doesn't have a speech impediment.'

'You must be the only bloke around here,' said the friend, 'who hasn't noticed that she can't say "No".'

# The Penguin Bumper Book of Australian Jokes

The poorly reviewed novelist visits the GP to see what a succession of imaging tests have produced.

'We used X-ray,' says the doctor, 'and ultrasound and you won't have forgotten the discomfort of the MRI machine. And I've got good news and bad news. The good news? Yes, we did find a creative bone in your body. The bad news? It was very untalented.'

## How to speak New Zulland . . .

The Kiwese language continues to fascinate. Here are some examples of Kiwese collected at Bondi whilst purchasing fush and chups.

BETTING: Hitting a ball with a wooden thing called a 'bet'. Betting gloves, for example, are worn by 'betsmen' in crucket.

BRIST: Part of the human anatomy between the 'nick' and the 'billy'.

### The Penguin Bumper Book of Australian Jokes

BUGGER: As in 'mine is bugger than yours'.

BUZZNESS: Activity, generally profit-making, as in 'I hev a muxed buzzness. One of my bug selling lines is mulk.'

CHUPS: Potatoes cut into small, long pieces and fried. Often eaten with fush (see below), hence 'fush 'n' chups'.

COLOUR: Terminator, murderer, person who kills.

CUSS: Kiss

DIMMER KRETZ: Those who believe in democracy.

DUCK HID: Term of abuse directed mainly at males.

EKKA DYMOCKS: University staff.

ERROR BUCK: Language spoken in countries like 'Surria', 'E-Jupp' and 'Libinon'.

ERROR ROUTE: As in 'Arnotts mulk error route buskets'.

FITTER CHENEY: A type of long, flat pasta not to be confused with 'rugger tony'.

FUSH: Edible sea creature, often eaten with chups (see above).

GUESS: Flammable vapour used in stoves.

SENDELS: Thongs, open shoes.

The madam at the Touch of Class opened the door to see one of the frailest, oldest blokes in the history of the brothel.

'Can I help you?'

'I want Natalie.'

'Sir, Natalie is one of our most expensive ladies. And one of the most energetic. Perhaps someone less expensive? Less energetic?'

'No, I must see Natalie.'

So Natalie came and inspected the old bloke who

gave her a big, toothless smile. 'Do you realise that I charge $1000 per visit?'

Without hesitation, the old codger reached into his kick and handed her ten $100 bills. They went upstairs for an hour and, afterwards, the old man left with a smile on his face.

The next night he returned to the bordello, again asking the madam for Natalie. The madam said that no-one had ever come back two nights in a row and that there were no discounts. It was still $1000. Again, the old bloke produced the money and he and Natalie went upstairs.

When he showed up the third consecutive night, no-one could believe it.

Again he handed over the $1000 and at the end of proceedings, Natalie asked him, 'Nobody has ever booked me three nights in a row. Where are you from?'

He said, 'I'm from Adelaide.'

'Is that right?' said Natalie. 'My family lives there.'

'I know,' said the old bloke, 'and I'm sad to say your father's dead and I'm his lawyer. In his Will he left you three thousand dollars.'

# The Penguin Bumper Book of Australian Jokes

Every bloke knows there are days in the month when it is dangerous to talk to a woman. Here is a guide for husbands, boyfriends or 'significant others' that can minimise the problem.

DANGEROUS
What's for dinner?
SAFE
Can I help you with dinner?
SAFEST
Where would you like to go for dinner?

DANGEROUS
What are you so angry about?
SAFE
Could we be over-reacting?
SAFEST
Here's $50

DANGEROUS
You're not wearing THAT!
SAFE
You've always looked good in brown.
SAFEST
Hey! Look at you!

**DANGEROUS**
What did you do all bloody day?
**SAFE**
I hope you didn't overdo things today?
**SAFEST**
I've always loved you in that dressing-gown.

God, sitting on His Throne, is gazing down at Earth with a sad expression. St Peter explains this to a recently arrived merchant banker. 'You'll understand his feelings. Earth is yet to turn a profit.'

It is Christmas, near the Woomera Detention Centre. Someone rings the bell. The wife opens the door and sees a man outside, looking very sad and hungry. He asks, 'Would you take in an asylum seeker at Christmas?'

She says, 'I'll have to ask my husband.'

She goes into the lounge and says, 'Darling,

there's a poor man outside wondering if we'd take an asylum seeker in for Christmas.'

He puts down the remote control and thinks about it for a moment. 'Well, I suppose so. But I'd rather it was a turkey.'

**W**hy do Americans hate playing hide and seek?
*Because nobody wants to look for them.*

**A**n SS man talks to a Jew in Auschwitz.

'You will die today. But I will give you one last chance. I have a glass eye. If you can tell me which one, I will spare you.'

The Jew looks at the SS man and says, 'It is the left one.'

'How did you guess?'

The Jew replies, 'It looks more human.'

**D**ad calls a meeting of the family. They sit around the laminex table in the kitchen – Mum and the five children. 'I've called the family together,' he says, 'to tell you that, because of the economic downturn, the rise in inflation and the collapse of our share portfolio, I'm going to have to let three of you go.'

**A** bar. Two blokes are sitting side by side, on their bar stools, sipping their beers. But one keeps moaning and groaning and shaking his head. And from time to time he says, 'Fuck the bastards!'

After twenty minutes of this, the other bloke says, 'If you keep talking politics, I'm leaving.'

**T**wo Russian mafiosi are sitting in a bar in Moscow, boasting of their ill-gotten gains. They talk about their new Mercedes and their new condos and now attention turns to their new clothes.

'How much did you pay for that tie?' asks the first.

'This tie? Pure Italian silk. Three hundred dollars.'

'Three hundred dollars! Is that all? You were ripped off my friend. This tie cost me $800.'

It's the 38th parallel in Korea and, every day, a North Korean presents himself to the guards. And on every occasion, he has a bag of rice on the handlebars of his bicycle.

Every time they take the rice and send it to be analysed to make sure that it is really rice. And the results always come back. Pure rice. Nothing else.

After this procedure's been going on for months, the guards plead with the North Korean to tell them what the hell he's been smuggling. In return, they promise not to bother him any more.

'Bicycles,' he says.

The Chinese had the horse for thousands of years but never thought of riding it. And the ancient

Egyptians had the horse for centuries before someone thought of having it pull a cart. When an inventor came up with the idea of a chariot, he presented the concept to the Pharaoh and his high priests. The Pharaoh was concerned about the safety considerations. 'A beast pulling a wheeled vehicle? It looks somewhat dangerous.'

'No, sire,' said the inventor, 'in the event of a front-end collision, the horse absorbs most of the impact.

**V**ladimir Putin is sitting in his office, at the Kremlin, when his secretary tells him there are two visitors in the anteroom. One is the patriarch of the Russian Orthodox Church, and the other is Jim Wolfensen, the Australian who heads the World Bank.

The patriarch wants to discuss the influx of American religions into Russia, which is causing enormous concern to the Orthodox hierarchy. Mr Wolfensen wants to discuss Russia's debt crisis.

'Who shall I show in first, Mr President?' asks the secretary.

'The patriarch. I'll only have to kiss his hand.'

## COMPUTER ALERT! COMPUTER ALERT! DANGEROUS VIRUSES!

The Clinton Virus. Gives you a seven-inch hard drive with no memory.

The Viagra Virus. Makes a new hard drive out of an old floppy.

The Ronald Reagan Virus. Saves your data, but forgets where it's stored.

Lewinsky Virus. Sucks all the memory out of your computer, then emails everyone about what it did.

Mike Tyson Virus. Quits after two bytes.

Dr Jack Kevorkian Virus. Deletes all old files.

'Doctor, why do men always want to marry a virgin?'
'*To avoid criticism.*'

**P**rior to his marriage, the businessman, a high-ranking executive with a global corporation, had his lawyer prepare a pre-nup to protect his assets in the event of a future divorce. And he insisted that his lawyer serve as his best man in the nuptials.

And just when the priest asked him whether he would take the woman as his wife ... the lawyer stepped forward and said, 'My client doesn't have to answer that.'

**T**wo blokes are sitting in a bar discussing their sex lives. 'Last night, I asked the missus if we could try sex doggy style.'

'I bet she was furious.'

'No, that's exactly what we did. We did it doggy style. I sat up and begged. She rolled over and played dead.'

They'd been married for 25 years and were celebrating his 60th birthday. He was happily unwrapping his presents when he came upon a funny old brass lamp, and he gave it a bit of a rub with the tissue paper.

There was a puff of smoke and a genie appeared. 'Because you've been such a loving couple all these years, I'll give each of you one wish.'

The wife said, 'Well, we've been so poor all these years. I've never been able to travel anywhere outside Australia. I wish we could travel all over the world!'

The genie waved his hand and POOF! She had a handful of first-class tickets.

Now it was his turn. Pausing for a moment, he said, 'Look, to be perfectly frank, I'd like to be married to a woman 30 years younger than me.'

And the genie waved his hand and POOF! He was 90!

It's Murrurundi and a lawyer from Sydney is representing the State Rail Authority in a law suit. It seems that a cattleman's prize angus bull is nowhere to be found – and suspicion focuses on the Sydney–New England line that rockets through the biggest paddock on the property every day. The cattleman insists that the bull must have been hit by the train and he wants to be reimbursed the animal's market value.

When the cattleman turns up at the small country courthouse, the railway's lawyer, a fully fledged QC, tries to get him to settle out of court. And finally the old codger agrees to take half of the $6000 he's been asking. The bull was, after all, a fine stud animal.

After he's signed the release and accepted the cheque, the city lawyer can't resist gloating.

'I hate to tell you this, old fella, but I put one over you. I couldn't have won the case. We've discovered that the driver was asleep at the controls when the train went through your property that morning. I didn't have one witness to put on the stand. So I'm afraid I bluffed you.'

To which the old cattleman replies, 'I was worried about the case myself. I didn't think I had a hope of winning it.'

'Why not?'

'Because I found that old bull this morning. In the paddock next door.'

## More Computer Viruses . . .

**O**prah Winfrey Virus. Your 300 MB hard drive suddenly shrinks to 100 MB . . . then slowly expands to 200 MB.

**E**llen de Generes Virus. Disks can no longer be inserted.

**T**itanic Virus. Your whole computer goes down.

**D**isney Virus. Everything in the computer goes Goofy.

**Prozac Virus.** Screws up your RAM, but your processor doesn't care.

**Arnold Schwarzenegger Virus.** Terminates zome viles, leaves, but it vill be baaack.

**Lorena Bobbitt Virus.** Reformats your hard drive into a 3.5-inch floppy, then discards it through Windows.

A couple were looking back on a lifetime of TV viewing. In the middle 1950s, they'd had a little black and white set, a 16-inch Astor. Now, in the early days of the 21st century, they had a huge rear-projection set that filled half the lounge room. 'Have you ever noticed,' he said, 'that the more we watch, the bigger it gets?'

**M**um is preparing pancakes for her sons. One is six, the other three.

The boys argue over who should get the first pancake – and Mum, being a good Catholic, sees the opportunity for a moral lesson.

'You know, if Jesus was sitting here he'd say let my brother have the first pancake.'

The older kid turns to the younger brother and says, 'How would you like having the first chance at being Jesus?'

**I**t is the dawn of time and a couple of baby lung fish, with fins that are evolving into legs, have crawled from the ocean and are lying, blinking in the sunlight, on the sand. 'If Mummy catches us out here,' one says to the other, 'we'll be in real trouble.'

**T**he room was full of pregnant women and their partners, and the Lamaze class was in full swing. The instructor was teaching the women how to breathe properly, along with informing the men how to give the necessary assurances at this stage of the plan.

The teacher then announced, 'Ladies, exercise is good for you. Walking is especially beneficial. And, gentlemen, it wouldn't hurt you to take the time to go walking with your partners!'

The room went very quiet.

Finally, a man in the middle of the group raised his hand. 'Yes?' asked the teacher.

'Is it all right if she carries a golf bag while we walk?'

---

Two women in Kelly country had daughters, each of marriageable age. But due to shoot-outs with police, to brawls between competing gangs of bushrangers and accidents caused by being drunk in the saddle, there was a serious lack of prospective husbands.

The two mums pooled their resources and paid for an advertisement in the *Bulletin*, which was sent all over Australia. And they got an immediate result. Twin brothers, living in northern Queensland, were looking for wives. The two mothers sent for them.

On the last leg of their journey, close to Glenrowan, the twins met up with the Kelly gang. One twin was killed and the other escaped. And upon his bedraggled arrival the mothers began arguing as to whom the surviving twin belonged. It got to the point that they were going to kill each other over him. After all, each had a daughter's future at stake.

They took the case to the local judge. Though an alcoholic, he'd read his Bible and knew about the judgment of Solomon. So he ruled that the young man be chopped in half and one half awarded to each daughter.

The first mother was outraged. If the judge wasn't drunk or deranged, he was a diabolical monster for suggesting such a thing.

Whereas the second mother thought it was probably a good idea.

At this point the judge nodded at the second mother. 'Your daughter gets him. You are the real mother-in-law.'

### The Penguin Bumper Book of Australian Jokes

What follows are examples of the political dialect known as 'Poliranto'. It is spoken in Macquarie Street, Sydney, on Capitol Hill in Canberra, in Spring Street, Melbourne ... in the parliaments of every state and territory.

Poliranto: As head of the government, I denounce these scurrilous charges of sexual misconduct against my Minister – and will continue to support him.
Translation: How's the bugger got away with it for so long?

Poliranto: We are, however, conducting an independent inquiry.
Translation: We know what happened and will make sure you never will.

Poliranto: I thank the people for the election result, for this overwhelming mandate. We will never abuse your trust.
Translation: Bewdy! Now what was it that Kerry Packer wanted?

## The Penguin Bumper Book of Australian Jokes

Poliranto: It is with great regret that I announce the resignation of the Minister for the Armed Services. She will leave behind a proud record of achievements.
Translation: She was bloody useless. Thank Christ it was a minor portfolio.

Poliranto: It isn't appropriate to comment at this particular moment.
Translation: I don't think I've been briefed – and if I was I don't remember.

Poliranto: Yes, the electorate has sent us a clear message.
Translation: The ungrateful bastards.

Poliranto: I find my job as Treasurer demanding and fulfilling. I have no further political ambitions and will continue to give the Prime Minister my unswerving support.
Translation: I haven't got the numbers. Yet.

### PREGNANCY TESTING

**Q:** What's the easiest way to determine the date of your pregnancy?

**A:** Have sex once a year.

**Q:** My blood type is A-negative. My husband is O-positive. What does it mean if my baby is born type A-B positive?

**A:** It means you've been found out.

**Q:** I'm eight weeks pregnant. When can I expect my baby to move?

**A:** With any luck, a few years after he finishes university.

**Q:** My husband and I are regarded as very attractive. As a result, we expect our baby girl to grow into a very beautiful young woman. Whom should I contact about her modelling career?

**A:** Your psychiatrist.

**Q:** Does labour cause haemorrhoids?

**A:** Labour causes anything you want to blame it for.

**Q:** Where's the best place to store breast milk?

**A:** In your breasts.

# The Penguin Bumper Book of Australian Jokes

The blonde is in bed with her lover. Her lover is her husband's best friend. They bonk for hours, trying every imaginable position, and afterwards, whilst they're recharging their batteries, the phone rings.

She leans over and, with a naked arm, languidly picks up the receiver. The lover watches her and listens . . .

'Hello? Oh hi. I'm very, very glad you called. Really? Isn't that wonderful. And how big was it? That big! Marvellous. Well, have fun.'

She hangs up the phone and her lover asks . . . 'Well, who was it?'

'That,' she says, 'was my husband. Your best friend. Telling me about the great time he's having on his fishing trip. With you.'

A duck waddles into a bar. It waddles across the floor and, with a flap of its wings, manages to settle on a bar stool. The bartender looks at the duck and says, 'Yep? What would you like?'

'Some grapes,' said the duck, 'I want some grapes.'

'Sorry, but we don't have any grapes,' replies the bartender.

The duck is very annoyed, issues a succession of complaining quacks, and jumps from the bar stool. He waddles over the floor and out the door, leaving a few feathers in his wake.

Next night, the bar door is kicked open by an emphatic web foot and in waddles the duck. He crosses the floor, flaps his way onto the stool and before the bartender can ask for his order says, quite grumpily, 'I want some grapes!'

Again the bartender says, 'We don't have any grapes.'

Again the duck gets angry and exits.

The next night the door is almost kicked in as the duck, already indignant, comes waddling in. The bartender says, 'What do you want?'

Again the duck says, 'I want some grapes!'

'Look,' says the bartender. 'I've told you every night that we don't have any grapes. No grapes. None at all. Not one. And if you come in here one more night asking for grapes, I'm going to nail your fucking bill to this bar.'

The duck emits some indignant quacks and leaves.

A week later, the duck comes thundering through the door, across the floor and jumps onto the bar stool. The bartender gives it a menacing look. 'What ... do ... you ... want?'

The duck says, 'Do you have any nails?'

The bartender says, 'No.'

And the duck says, 'Fine. Then I want some grapes.'

**H**ow do French ladies hold their liquor?
*By the ears.*

**E**very night after dinner, he'd head for the local pub. And after a few dozen beers he'd head for home, pissed as a fart. Usually around midnight.

He'd have trouble getting the car into the garage. Trouble getting his key into the keyhole and even some difficulties with the door handle. So his wife would open up – and open up on him. She'd rage and rave and rant about his nocturnal activities and his drunkenness. But the bloke refused to vary his routine.

One day the missus was talking to a friend about her husband's recalcitrance and received the following advice. 'Why not treat him a little differently? Instead of blasting with both barrels, try some affectionate words. Give him a kiss.'

And the wife thought it was worth a try.

Next night, the bloke disappeared after dinner and, at about midnight, he could be heard trying to get the key into the lock. Whereupon she opened the door and gave him a warm, loving kiss. Then she took his arm and led him into the lounge. She sat him down in his favourite chair, plonked his feet on the ottoman and replaced his shoes with slippers. Then she sat on his lap and gave him a cuddle.

'It's pretty late, darling,' she said. 'I think we'd better go upstairs now.'

His response was: 'Well, we'll have to make it quick. Otherwise I'll really cop it when I get home.'

# The Penguin Bumper Book of Australian Jokes

**H**e tells his mum he's fallen in love and is going to get married.

She responds with mixed feelings and asks for the name of his betrothed.

'Look, just for a bit of fun, I'll bring home three sheilas and you try to guess which one I've proposed to.'

So the next day, he brings three very attractive women into the house and sits them, side by side, on the couch. And the five of them have a friendly conversation.

He then says, 'OK, Mum. Which one am I going to marry?'

And Mum says, 'The redhead in the middle.'

'Mum, that's amazing. You're absolutely right. But how did you work it out?'

'Easy. I don't like her.'

**T**he little boy was late for class. When he saw the door was closed he opened it very, very quietly and tiptoed to his desk.

Far from avoiding the scrutiny of the teacher, it made her very annoyed. 'Is that how your father would have come in? Late? And sneaking to his seat? Go outside and try it again.'

So the kid left the room and shut the door very quietly behind him. A second later he burst through the door, slammed it shut and, with a burning fag dangling from his lips, walked to the middle of the classroom. Then he dropped the cigarette onto the floor and ground it out with his foot. And said, 'G'day. You didn't expect ME, didya?'

A new monk arrives at a monastery famous for its illuminated manuscripts. He is assigned to help the other monks in copying the old text, using the finest of brushes for the calligraphy and the most beautiful pigments and gold leafing for the illustration. And he can't help but notice that his fellow monks are copying copies, not the original books. Surely this could lead to error. So he goes to the head monk and points out that they might, just might, be making mistakes.

Because if there was one in the first copy, that error would be continued in all of the others.

And the head monk says, 'We've been copying from copies for 300 years. Nonetheless, you have a good point.'

So the old religious man goes down into the deepest, darkest cranny of the archives to check the latest edition against the original.

Hours pass and nobody sees him. Finally the new monk clambers down the stairs to look for him. And he hears heartbroken sobs. And there's the old monk, beside the original book which is lit by a flickering candle.

'What's wrong?' he asks.

'The word isn't celibate,' says the head monk, 'it's celebrate.'

The old bloke was putting on his coat at the front door when his wife said, 'Are you going out?'

He said, 'Yeah.'

She said, 'Where?'

And he said, 'To the doctor's.'

So she said, 'Why? Are you crook?'

'No,' he said, 'but I want to get some of those Viagra pills they've been talking about on the telly.'

With that, his frail wife clambered out of her rocking chair and started climbing into her coat.

'Where are you going?' he asked.

'To the doctor's.'

And he said, 'Why? Are you feeling crook?'

And she said, 'If you're going to start using that rusty old thing again, I'm going to need a tetanus shot.'

The lawyer's dog escaped from its leash and headed straight for the local butcher. It ran through the door, scattering sawdust off the floor, and grabbed a leg of lamb off the counter.

The butcher went to the lawyer and said, 'If a dog, running unleashed, steals a leg of lamb from my shop, do I have the right to demand payment for it from the dog's owner?'

'Absolutely,' said the lawyer.

And the butcher said, 'Fine. Then you owe $12 for the leg of lamb your bloody dog nicked from me this morning.'

Without a word the lawyer wrote the butcher a cheque for $12.

And the next day, a courier delivered an envelope from the lawyer. The butcher read the contents. 'Consultation: $50.'

### DIFFERENCES BETWEEN YOU AND YOUR EMPLOYER . . .

If you take a long time, you're slow.
If your boss takes a long time, she's thorough.

If you don't do it, you're lazy.
If she doesn't do it, she's too busy.

If you make a mistake, you're a dill.
If she makes a mistake, she's only human.

If you do something without being told, you're overstepping your authority.
If she does the same thing, that's initiative.

### The Penguin Bumper Book of Australian Jokes

If you please your boss, you're sucking up.
If your boss pleases her boss, she's being co-operative.

If you're out of the office, you're wandering around.
If she's out of the office, she's on business.

If you take a day off, you're always sick.
If she takes a day off, she must be very, very ill.

If you ask for an hour off, you're going for an interview.
If your boss takes a week off, it's because she's overworked.

It was just after Christmas. Mum was cooking in the kitchen while her five-year-old played with his new Hornby train set. She heard the little engine stop and her son yelling, 'All you bastards who are getting off, get the hell off right now! And all you arseholes who are getting on board, get a bloody move on.'

Mum told her son, 'We don't use that kind of

language in this house. So go to your room and don't come out until you've learned your lesson. And the next time you play with your train, use nice language.'

An hour later the kid resumed playing with his train . . . and when the little engine stopped Mum heard him say, 'All passengers who are disembarking, please remember to take all your belongings with you. The railway company thanks you for your custom and hopes that you will ride with us again. For those of you boarding, we suggest you stow all hand language under your seat or in the racks overhead. Please remember there is no smoking, except in the carriage designated for that purpose. The company hopes you'll have a pleasant and relaxing journey. And for those of you who are pissed off because of the one-hour delay, complain to the bitch in the kitchen.'

**A**n interstate trucker, travelling from Queensland to Victoria, decides to pull his rig over and sleep for a while. Exhausted, he passes out. Only to be awoken by some loud knocks on the window of the cab.

It's a jogger wanting to know the time.

'Three forty-five,' grunts the trucker, who promptly falls asleep again. Ten minutes later he's woken by another jogger who wants to know the time. 'It's three fifty-five,' he yells. And determined to get some peace and quiet, he writes a note and hangs it on the door handle of the truck, a bit like a 'Do Not Disturb' sign on a hotel door.

It reads, 'I Don't Know the Fucking Time.'

A little while later another jogger wakes him. 'It's half-past five.'

---

Mum is walking to the shops with her little boy – and a flock of starlings whirls above them.

'Mum, are birds mechanical?'

'No, darling. Why do you ask?'

'Well, when I'm out walking with Dad he's always saying, "I'd like to screw the arse off that bird".'

**The Penguin Bumper Book of Australian Jokes**

**W**hat do you call a bloke with no arms or legs who swam the English Channel?
*Clever Dick.*

**R**esponding to a phone call about a 'domestic', the police arrive to find that the husband has hanged himself. His corpse, a belt around his neck, dangles in the doorway. The wife seems unperturbed. She's just sitting on the lounge, watching *Oprah*. 'Oh, don't take any notice of him,' she says, 'we had a row and now he's just trying to make me feel bad.'

**C**inderella is 80 years old. After a long and happy marriage with the late prince, she's sitting happily in her rocking chair, watching the world go by from the front porch of the palace, with a cat called Alan for companionship.

One arvo, out of nowhere, the Fairy Godmother appears.

'Fairy Godmother,' says Cinders, 'fancy seeing you after all these years.'

And the Fairy Godmother says, 'Well, Cinderella, you've lived such a good, virtuous life since we last met, so I've decided to grant you three wishes. Is there anything for which your heart still yearns?'

Cinderella is delighted with the offer and thinks about it for a few minutes. Then she whispers her first wish. 'I wish I was young and beautiful again.'

In a second, she is. And she feels energies and desires that she'd almost forgotten.

'And your second wish?' asks the Fairy Godmother.

'Well, we're a bit low on money. The kingdom wasn't very profitable and towards the end of his life, the prince couldn't raise enough taxes to pay for his health care.'

So the Fairy Godmother waves her magic wand and, lo and behold, there are bags of gold coins at Cindarella's feet.

'You have one more wish,' says the Fairy Godmother. 'What will it be?'

And Cinderella looks at the cat and says, 'I wish you to transform my old cat into a handsome young man.'

Another wave of the wand and the cat undergoes a miraculous transmogrification. And there stands before her a young man so beautiful, so fair, that the overcast skies are flooded with lights, and birds begin to fall from the sky at his feet.

'Congratulations, Cinders,' says the Fairy Godmother. 'Enjoy your new life.' And there is an intense glow of light and she disappears.

For a few long moments, the young man and Cinders looks into each other's eyes. She is transfixed by his gorgeousness. She has never seen anyone as perfect.

He then walks to the young Cinderella, who sits trembling in her rocker, and holds her close in his muscular arms. And he breathes the following words through her golden hair into her pretty little ear. 'And now you'll be really, really sorry that you sent me to the vet to be desexed.'

It's the Bob Jones University in the Deep South of the USA. Being segregated, the football team is entirely white. And not too bright.

The coach approaches the star player and says,

'Look we've got a bit of trouble. Although the Bob Jones University is a Christian college it does have to set minimum educational standards, otherwise it loses its tax breaks. And I'm not supposed to let you play since you failed your maths exam. So I have to ask you a mathematical question. But you have to get it right if you want to play.'

The player is nervous but agrees. And the coach, looking intently into his eyes, says, 'OK, now you have to concentrate. What is two plus two?'

The player thinks for a few seconds and then says, 'Four?'

'Four!?!?!' the coach shouts, delighted that he's got it right.

Whereupon all the other players in the team yell, 'Come on, coach, give him another chance!'

It was the Wild West and a couple of cowboys, Hank and Bert, were enjoying their sarsaparillas in the local saloon. Whereupon the swinging doors opened and a man walked into a bar with a Red

Indian's head under his arm. And the barman shook his hand and said, 'I hate redskins. Last week the bastards raided the farm of one of my best customers, burnt his barn to the ground, assaulted his wife, killed his kids and scalped him.'

He then turned to everyone in the bar and said, 'If anyone else brings me the head of an Indian, I'll give him $1000.'

The two cowboys looked at each other and decided to go hunting for a Red Indian. They wandered around for a while and suddenly spotted one. They hurled a couple of rocks at him and one hit the Indian right on the noggin.

He fell off his horse, toppled over a cliff and landed 70 feet down a ravine. And the two cowboys clambered down to the corpse and pulled their bowie knives from their sheaths.

While one of the cowboys worked on the decapitation, the other said, 'I think you should have a look at this.'

'Not now, I'm busy.'

'I really think you should have a look at this.'

'Not now, I'm busy! We're about to make a thousand bucks.'

'For Chrissake! Take a look!'

And there, standing at the top of the ravine, were 5000 Red Indians.

'Oh my God,' said the cowboy with the head in his hand. 'We're going to be millionaires.'


In the new, competitive world of deregulated banking, the customer is used to branch closures and the increased dominance of the ATM. But a customer was surprised to see that the ANZ had opened a new branch by the Crown Casino. Outside there was a large sign. TWENTY-FOUR HOUR MONEY LAUNDERING.


The little bloke had his first day at school. Mum was worried about how he'd get on and when she picked him up at the end of the day, she asked him how things went.

'Well, I came top of the class in spelling. I was chosen to be captain of our football team and I had sex with the teacher.'

The mother was aghast and sent him to his room. 'Just wait till your father gets home.'

But when his father came home and heard of his son's day at school he was very proud. Top of the class. Football captain. Sex with the teacher. 'That's my boy,' thought Dad, as he went upstairs to congratulate the child.

'Don't worry about Mum. She's a bit upset. But it sounds to me like you had a great day. In fact, I'm so pleased that I'm going to buy you that bike you wanted. I think I'll get it for you this weekend.'

'No, Dad. Don't. I won't be able to sit down for a while.'

**M**embers of the Ferrari racing team were recently hit by a virus. Fortunately the drivers were OK but the whole pit crew came down with the trots. So they were forced to employ some young blokes from Bankstown. They'd been inspired by a documentary about how young Bankstown blokes can take off a car's tyre within six seconds with only one spanner and a pair of pliers.

But there was a problem. The Bankstown boys not only changed the tyres in six seconds but 12 seconds later the car was resprayed and sold to the Maclaren team.

In the middle of the NRMA crisis, when relationships between board members were at their lowest ebb, Anne Keating was seen in the boutique of a prominent designer. She was fondling a cocktail dress and asking the anorexic sales lady. 'Do you have this in bulletproof?'

What's the difference between John Hopoate and a blow job?
*One makes your day and the other makes your hole weak.*

Hopoate is nothing but a shit-stirrer.

Trinity Grammar have expressed an interest in hiring Hopoate for six months. They think he'll fit in well.

You put your left finger in, you pull your left finger out.
You put your right finger in, and shake it all about.
You do the HOPOATE then you turn around,
that's what it's all about.

I think the criticism levelled at Hoppa is totally unfounded. He's been fingered for a crime he did not commit.

Hoppa has a segment on the 'Footy Show'. It's called Hoppa's Update.

John Hopoate, public enema number one.

Hoppa, the human thermometer.

Sara Lee have announced a sponsorship deal with the NRL. They're going to sell Hoppa's Sticky Date Pudding.

Hoppa is to star in the new James Bond movie *Brown Finger*.

**A** scientist shows his colleagues his latest effort – a tiny little Frankenstein monster. It still looks the same as Boris Karloff in the 1930s' films – but is just six inches high. 'Isn't nanotechnology remarkable,' he says proudly. 'Remember how big and clunky the first ones were?'

**H**umans make delightful pets. With proper care, they are also long-lived – for upwards of 70 to 80 years. As a cat, you will want to have your human pet house-trained as quickly as possible. So follow these simple instructions:

**Communication:** Human pets are unable to speak a proper language. Therefore, you should communicate every point loudly, repeatedly and, when possible, at about 2 a.m.

**Cleanliness:** Your pet will enjoy immersing itself in running water. Attempts to get humans to lick themselves clean have, thus far, failed.

**Feeding:** Morning feeding should start when your human pet is still fast asleep. A good time is three or four minutes before their alarm goes off.

**Recommended methods of waking your pet include:** Sitting on its face, miaowing in its ear and chewing its hair.

**Toilet training:** Your pet's natural tendency is not to change your litter box. Though experts in human behaviour believe it can be attributed to laziness, it can be corrected with 'shoe therapy'. Remember that a human shoe makes an excellent toilet.

It's a huge cattle property in the Kimberleys and a couple of blokes have been mustering herefords for weeks. In the middle of nowhere, one says to the other, 'This is where our trails divide. But you've got my email address, right?'

The scene, Crown Casino. Gamblers, exhausted by baccarat and/or the pokies are enjoying a magic show, fully imported from Las Vegas. On stage is a camel, the model with two humps. The magician drapes it in a black cloth and, after a roll of drums, whips the fabric away . . . and the camel has entirely disappeared.

'How the fuck did you do that?' calls a drunk in the audience.

'If I told you, sir,' the magician answers, 'I'd have to kill you.'

And the man yells back, 'OK, don't tell me. But tell my wife.'

**The Penguin Bumper Book of Australian Jokes**

In a country pub there's the local counterpart to the village idiot. Every night he can be found sitting on his bar stool mumbling amiably. And the drinkers invariably tease him – by offering him his choice of a 20 cent piece or a $2 coin.

And every time he takes the 20 cents. And the drinkers are immensely amused.

One day, after he'd grabbed the big silver coin the barman said, 'Look, these blokes are making fun of you. They reckon you don't know that the little gold coin is worth more than the big silver one. And that you've grabbed the 20 cents because it's bigger.'

The bloke gave a crooked grin and said, 'Nope, but if I took the $2, they'd stop doing it. And how would I pay for my beers?'

Grandma was in the local hospital for minor surgery. But she wasn't a happy Vegemite. She started complaining as soon as they got her into bed. About the temperature. The lighting. The hospital food. The mattress. The pillow. The lot.

But it got worse when she spotted a button at the end of an electric cord. 'What the hell's this?!' she demanded.

'Well, if you need something in the middle of the night, you just press that button.'

'And what happens? Does it ring a bell?'

'No, it turns on a light in the hall. For the nurse on night duty.'

'A light in the hall? Look, if the bloody night nurse needs a light in the hall, she can bloody well switch it on herself.'

### DIALOGUE FROM THE COURTROOMS

What is your date of birth?
*12 July.*

What year?
*Every year.*

Your medical condition. Does it affect your memory?
*Yes.*

And how does it affect your memory?
*Sorry, I forget.*

You forget. Can you give the court an example of something that you've forgotten?

What gear were you in at the moment of impact?
*Shorts, a T-shirt and a pair of thongs.*

How old is your son?
*Oh, 28, 29. Something like that.*

And how long has he lived with you.
*Forty years.*

Sir, have you had your IQ tested?
*Yes.*

What was it?
*Well, I can see fine without glasses.*

Did you blow your horn?
*After the accident?*

No, before the accident.
*Sure, I've been in the Salvation Army band since I left school.*

Were you present when this photograph of you was taken?

Was it you or your younger brother who was killed in the War?

How far apart were the cars at the time of impact?

And how many times have you committed suicide?

How was your first marriage terminated?
*By death.*

And by whose death was it terminated?

Is your appearance here this morning pursuant to a deposition notice sent to your lawyer?
*No, this is how I dress when I go to work.*

Doctor, how many autopsies have you performed on dead people?
*All of them.*

Doctor, before you performed the autopsy, did you check for a pulse?
*No, I didn't.*

Did you check for breathing?
*No, I did not.*

Did you check for blood pressure?
*No.*

So then it's possible the patient was alive when you began the autopsy?
*No, it isn't.*

And how can you be so sure?
*Because his brain was in a jar.*

Could the patient still have been alive, nonetheless?
*It's possible that he could have been alive. Practising law somewhere.*

You were not shot in the fracas?
*No, I was shot between the fracas and the navel.*

**A**ll the kids in the class had posed for a group photograph – and as the school received a percentage of the sales, the teacher was trying to persuade everyone to buy a print.

'Children, just think how marvellous it will be, in 20 or 30 years time, when you're all grown up. You can take out the photograph and show it to your children and say, "There's Betsy, she's now an MP. Or there's Bill, he's a merchant banker".'

And a little voice said, 'And there's our teacher, Miss Milburn. She's dead.'

**R**eturning home from the office, the bloke settles in his lounge chair and waits for the dog to deliver his slippers. But it's the cat who places them at his feet, explaining, 'The dog paid me.'

**A**n exec. couple – he an investment adviser and she a dot.com executive – are in their high-tech kitchen cooking together. Suddenly she stops and looks at him. 'Darling, I've just realised. Our relationship has moved from the bedroom to the kitchen.'

**I**t was the final examination for an introductory English course at Melbourne University. Like many such freshman courses, it was designed to weed out weak students.

The professor was very strict and told the class that any exam paper not on his desk in exactly two hours would not be accepted and the student would fail. Half an hour into the exam, a student came rushing in and asked the professor for an exam paper. 'You're not going to have time to finish this,' the professor stated as he handed one to the student. 'Yes I will,' replied the student, who took a seat and began writing.

After two hours, the professor called for the

exams, and the students filed up and handed them in. All except the late student, who continued writing. Half an hour later, the last student came up to the professor who was sitting at his desk preparing for his next class.

He attempted to put his exam on the stack of exam papers already there.

'No you don't! I'm not going to accept that. It's late.'

The student looked incredulous and angry. 'Do you know WHO I am?'

'No, as a matter or fact I don't,' replied the professor with an air of sarcasm.

'DO YOU KNOW WHO I AM?' the student asked again.

'No, and I don't care,' replied the professor.

'Good,' said the student as he quickly lifted the stack of completed exams, stuffed his in the middle, and walked out of the room.

**D**uring her annual check-up, the well-constructed miss was asked to disrobe and climb onto the examining table.

'Doctor,' she replied shyly, 'I just can't undress in front of you.'

'All right,' said the physician, 'I'll flick off the lights. You undress and tell me when you're ready.'

In a few moments, her voice rang out in the darkness. 'Doctor, I've undressed. What shall I do with my clothes?

'Put them on the chair, on top of mine.'

### WELCOME TO THE MENTAL HEALTH HOTLINE

If you are obsessive/compulsive, press 1 repeatedly.
If you have multiple personalities, press 5, 6, 7 and 8.
If co-dependent, please ask someone to press 2 for you.
If you are paranoid, stay on the line so we can trace your call.
If you are delusional, press 7 and you will be transferred to the Mother Ship.

If you are schizophrenic, listen very carefully. You will hear a small voice telling you which number to press.

If you are manic/depressive, it doesn't matter what number you press. You will get nothing but silence.

If you are dyslexic, press 4, 5, 4, 5, 4, 5, 4, 5, 5, 4, 4, 4, 5.

If you are having a nervous breakdown, please fiddle with the # key.

If you have amnesia, press 8 and state your name, address, phone number, date of birth, driver's licence number and your password.

If you have bipolar disorder, please leave a message after the beep. Or before the beep. Or after the beep. Please wait for the beep.

If you have short-term memory loss, press 9.

If you have short-term memory loss, press 9.

If you have short-term memory loss, press 9.

If you have short-term memory loss, press 9.

If you have low self-esteem, please hang up. All of our operators are too busy to bother with you.

**A**re you annoyed by the ads they put in the envelope with your bills? As if getting bills wasn't bad enough. Now they stuff all that crap in with them. Well, here's how to get back.

When popping your cheque in an envelope, include some garbage. Orange peel is good. As are used tea-bags.

Include a note saying, 'Could you please throw this away for me? Thanks.'

**D**ear Rev. Nile,

Like you, I believe the Bible is the word of God and that everything it says is true. And, like you, when someone defends the homosexual lifestyle, I simply remind them that Leviticus 18:22 clearly states it to be an abomination. End of debate.

However I need some advice from you regarding some of the specifics of God's laws and how to follow them.

**a.** When I burn a bull on the altar as a sacrifice, I know it creates a pleasing odour for the Lord (Leviticus 1:9). The problem is the people next door say the odour isn't pleasing to them. Should I smite them?

**b.** I would like to sell my daughter into slavery, as sanctioned in Exodus 21:7. In this day and age, what would be a fair price to ask?

**c.** I know I'm not allowed to have contact with a woman whilst she's in her period of menstrual uncleanliness (Leviticus 15:9–24). But how do I tell? I try asking, but most women take offence.

**d.** Leviticus 25:44 states that I may possess slaves, both male and female, provided they are purchased from neighbouring nations. A friend of mine claims this applies to Indonesians, but not New Zealanders. Can you clarify? Why can't I own New Zealanders?

**e.** I have a neighbour who insists on working on the Sabbath. Exodus 35:2 says he should be put to death. Am I allowed to kill him myself?

**f.** A friend of mine says that even though eating shellfish is an abomination (Leviticus 11:10), it is a lesser abomination than homosexuality. I don't agree and would be grateful for your adjudication on the issue.

**g.** Leviticus 21:20 states that I may not approach the altar of God if I have a defect in my sight. Trouble is, I wear reading glasses. Am I ruled out?

**h.** Most of my male friends get their hair trimmed, even though this is expressly forbidden by Leviticus 19:27. How do you recommend that I kill them?

**i.** My uncle has a farm and violates Leviticus 19:19 by planting two different crops in the same field, as does his wife by wearing garments made of two different kinds of material. (In her case, a cotton-polyester blend.) The farmer also curses and blasphemes a lot. Should I follow the advice of Leviticus 24:10–16 by organising the local town to stone them to death? Or could we just burn them to death at a private family affair, as Leviticus 20:14 recommends we do with people who sleep with their in-laws?

Again, thank you for reminding us that God's word is eternal and unchanging.

Yours sincerely,

Harry Knackers.

**A** penguin is driving down the road when his Falcon starts to sputter. Steam pours out of the bonnet and there's liquid splashing all over the road. The penguin pulls into a Castrol truck stop and asks the mechanic for help. The mechanic says it will take him a while to diagnose the difficulty – so the penguin goes into the cafe and sits at one of the tables, amongst the truckers, and has a cup of coffee.

He returns to the mechanic, who's still working on the problem – so the penguin goes and gets a Cornetto from the freezer. And as he licks away at it, he gets ice-cream all over his beak.

Now he returns to the mechanic who, still under the bonnet, looks up and says, 'Looks like you've blown a seal.'

And the penguin says, 'No! No, I haven't. I've just had an ice-cream.'


In the early days of Australian Federation, a wise politician said, 'When you discover that you're riding a dead horse, it's a good idea to dismount.'

In modern-day Canberra, however, a range of more advanced strategies are employed. The modern bureaucrat might recommend one or more of the following:

**1.** Buy a stronger whip.

**The Penguin Bumper Book of Australian Jokes**

**2.** Change riders.

**3.** Threaten the horse with termination.

**4.** Appoint a committee to study the horse.

**5.** Refer to other departments to see how they ride dead horses.

**6.** Reclassify the dead horse as 'living, impaired'.

**7.** Hire an outside contractor to ride the dead horse.

**8.** Harness several dead horses together to increase the speed.

**9.** Provide additional funding or retraining to increase the dead horse's performance.

**10.** Do a productivity study to see if lighter riders would improve the dead horse's performance.

**11.** Observe that the dead horse doesn't have to be fed, is less costly, carries lower overheads and therefore contributes substantially more to the departmental bottom line than live horses.

**12.** Rewrite the expected performance requirements for all horses.

**13.** Promote the dead horse to a supervisory position.

The ABC's 'Foreign Correspondent' reporter in Jerusalem rents an apartment overlooking the Western Wall. Every day she looks out and sees the same old Jew praying energetically. He stands there from dawn to sunset, nodding his head and, from time to time, resting his forehead on the ancient stones.

She wonders whether there might be a story for 'Foreign Correspondent' in this old gentleman's marathon praying – so introduces herself and says, 'You come to the wall every day. How long have you done this? And what do you pray for?'

And the old man replies, 'I've come here to pray every day for 25 years. In the morning I pray for world peace. Then I pray for the brotherhood of man. I go home and have a glass of tea at lunchtime and return to pray for the eradication of illness and disease from the earth. In the late afternoon, I pray for an end to anti-Semitism and other forms of bigotry.'

'And how does it make you feel to come and pray every day for 25 years for these worthy causes?'

And the old man says, 'Like I'm talking to a wall.'

It's not the increasing speed of life that concerns me. It's the sudden stop at the end.

Lead me not into temptation. I can find the way myself.

Ignoring the sign saying 'Trespassers Prosecuted', a blonde, a brunette and a redhead took a short cut through a farmer's paddock. Halfway across they heard him driving their way in his 4WD, and decided to hide in the three gum trees that provided shade for his cattle.

The farmer drove to the first tree and heard some rustling in the leaves. 'What's up there?' he called. And the redhead emitted a 'hoo-hoo, haa-haa' laugh. And the farmer said, 'Oh, it's just a kookaburra.'

Then he heard rustling in the second tree and called, 'What's up there?' The brunette went 'caw-caw'. And the farmer said, 'Oh, it's just a crow.'

Then he heard rustling in the third tree and said, 'What's up there?' And the blonde went, 'Moo!'

**A**n attractive flight attendant was checking boarding passes as customers boarded the Virgin flight to Brisbane.

Suddenly she was confronted by a flasher – a dirty old man who opened his raincoat.

'I'm sorry sir,' she said politely, 'but you have to show me your ticket, not just your stub.'

**T**wo New Yorkers were driving through South Carolina when they were pulled over by a state trooper – who walked up to their window and tapped angrily with his nightstick. The driver rolled down the window and the trooper hit him on the head with the stick.

When the driver came to, he said, 'What the hell was that for?'

And the trooper said, 'You're in South Carolina, son. And when we pull over a New Yorker, they better have their licence ready.'

Not wanting to make the situation any worse, the driver said, 'Sorry officer,' and proffered his licence.

The trooper ran a check and confirming that he was clean, returned the licence. Then he walked round to the passenger's side and tapped on the window. The passenger rolled the window down and the trooper smacked him with his nightstick.

And the somewhat dazed passenger said, 'Fuck! Why did you do that?' And the trooper said, 'I'm just granting your wish, boy.'

Rubbing his head, the passenger said, 'My wish?'

And the trooper said, 'I know how you Yankees are! A couple of miles down the road you're gonna say, "I wish that redneck motherfucker would have tried that shit with me!".'

**A** wife went to the local cop shop with her next-door neighbour to report that her husband, Freddie, was missing.

She was asked for a description.

'Well,' she said, 'he's mid-30s, very tall, has an athletic build, blue eyes and blond hair, is very soft spoken, kind to the kids and has a wonderful sense of humour.'

And the next-door neighbour said, 'But Freddie is little, fat, bald and beats you up.'

And the wife said, 'Yes. But who wants *him* back?'

Two eggs got married and went on their honeymoon. While they were lying on the bed, making love, the female egg pushed the male egg away and said, 'Excuse me, darling, I have to go to the bathroom. But I'll be back in a minute.'

Five minutes later the male egg saw the female egg return – wearing a slinky egglige whilst moving her hands over her smooth, oval body. Instantly the male egg slapped his hands on the top of his head, covering it protectively.

And the female egg said, 'What are you doing?'

He said, 'The last time I was this hard, someone cracked me on the head with a spoon.'

**A** farmer from Arkansas walked into his attorney's office. The attorney said, 'How can I help you?'

And the farmer said, 'I want one of them dayvorces.'

The attorney asked, 'Do you have any grounds?'

The farmer replied, 'Yeah, about 100 acres.'

And the attorney said, 'No, you don't understand. Do you have a case?'

The farmer replied, 'No, I don't have a case. I've got a John Deare.'

The attorney said, 'I don't think you understand. I mean do you have a grudge?'

The farmer said, 'Yeah, I got a grudge. That's where I park my John Deare.'

And the attorney said, 'No, sir. What I mean is – do you have a suit?'

The farmer said, 'Yes, I've got a suit. I wear it to church every Sunday.'

The attorney said, 'Look, sir. Does your wife beat you up?'

The farmer replied, 'No, sir, we both get up at the same time, 4.30 every morning.'

The attorney said, 'Sir, let me put it this way. Why do you want a divorce?'

And the farmer said, 'Well, I can never have a meaningful conversation with her.'

**D**ad 'n' Dave were visiting a shopping mall in Sydney. They were amazed by almost everything they saw – by all the things in the shops, by the escalators, by the plumbing in the toilets – but especially by the two shiny silver walls that moved apart and then moved back together again.

And Dave asked Dad, 'What is this, Dad?'

Dad said, 'Dave, I've never seen anything like it. I've no idea.'

While Dad 'n' Dave watched wide-eyed, an old lady in a wheelchair rolled up to the moving walls and pressed a button. The walls opened and the lady rolled between them into a small room. The walls closed and Dad 'n' Dave watched as a row of numbers lit up, one after the other. After a while the silver walls opened again and a beautiful young blonde stepped out.

And Dad said to Dave, 'Go and find your mother.'

**The Penguin Bumper Book of Australian Jokes**

**W**hat do you get when you mix a collie with a Lhasa apso?
*You get a collapso, a dog that folds up for easy transport.*

**W**hat do you get when you mix a Labrador retriever with a curly coated retriever?
*You get a lab coat retriever, the first choice of research scientists.*

**W**hat do you get when you cross a newfoundland and basset hound?
*You get a newfound asset hound, the perfect dog when you're investigating Alan Bond.*

**A**nd when you cross a bull-terrier and a Shitzu?
*Oh, never mind.*

An elderly couple are travelling between Darwin and Cairns. The woman is driving when she gets pulled over by the highway patrol. 'Madam, did you know that you were considerably exceeding the speed limit?'

The woman turned to her husband and asked, 'What did he say?'

And the old man yelled, 'HE SAYS YOU WERE SPEEDING!'

The highway patrolman then said, 'Please show me your licence.'

The woman turned to her husband and asked, 'What did he say?'

The old man yelled, 'HE WANTS TO SEE YOUR LICENCE.'

Looking at it closely, the patrolman said, 'I see you're from Brisbane. I spent some time there. Had the worst sex with a woman I ever had.'

The woman turned to her husband and asked, 'What did he say?'

And the old man yelled, 'HE SAYS HE THINKS HE KNOWS YOU.'

**An** Alaskan woodpecker and a Texan woodpecker met during the annual migration to Alaska and argued about which state had the toughest trees to peck. The Alaskan woodpecker said Alaska had a tree that no woodpecker could peck – but the Texan woodpecker instantly pecked a hole in it. The Alaskan woodpecker was very, very impressed.

Then the Texan woodpecker challenged the Alaskan woodpecker to try a tree in Texas that no Texan woodpecker had been able to successfully peck. And the Alaskan said that he'd have a fly and give it a try.

And when he tried, he found that he could peck the Texan tree quite easily. And the two woodpeckers couldn't figure out why the Texan woodpecker was able to peck the Alaskan tree and the Alaskan woodpecker was able to peck the Texan tree when neither was able to peck the same tree in their own state.

And they came to the same conclusion. 'Your pecker is always harder when you're away from home.'

**An** attractive woman walks up to the barman in a country pub – seductively signalling that he should bring his face to hers. When he does so, she begins to gently stroke his full, bushy beard.

'Are you the owner?' she asks, now stroking his beard with both hands.

'No,' he stammers.

'Could you get the owner for me? I need to speak to him.' And she runs her hands up from his beard and starts mussing his hair.

'I'm afraid he's not in at the moment,' breathes the barman, getting more and more aroused. 'Is there anything I can do?'

'Yes, there is,' she says softly. 'I need you to give him a message.' And she pops a couple of her fingers into his mouth and lets him suck them gently. 'Would you tell him,' she says, 'that there's no toilet paper or soap in the ladies room.'

**C**onfucius say that 'Man who walks through airport turnstile sideways going to Bangkok.'

## The Penguin Bumper Book of Australian Jokes

**A** cop pulled the car over and congratulated the driver because (a) he wasn't speeding and (b) both he and his passenger were wearing seatbelts. 'In fact, you've won $5000 from our local Rotary Club.'

'Gee, that's bonzer,' said the driver.

'And what are you going to do with the money?' asked the cop.

'Well, I guess I'll get myself a driver's licence,' he answered.

'Oh, don't listen to him,' said the woman passenger, 'he's a smart-arse when he's drunk.'

Whereupon a bloke who'd been concealed beneath a rug in the back seat sat up and said, 'I knew we wouldn't get far in a stolen car.'

And there was a knock from the boot and a voice asked, 'Are we over the border yet?'

**A** bloke goes to a tattoo parlour in King's Cross and offers the artist a thousand dollars to tattoo a picture of a $100 bill on his dick. The artist is curious about the request. 'Why do you want to do this?'

'I've got my reasons. But I'd rather not tell you right now.'

So the tattoo artist goes ahead and does the job. It takes a lot of time and, because of the fine detail, must cause the customer considerable discomfort. And all the while he's curious about his motive. Why a $100 bill on his dick?

Finally he can't stand it. 'Look, you can keep your thousand dollars. I've completed the tattoo for nothing. But tell me why you want a $100 bill on your dick.'

The customer offers three reasons. 'Firstly, I like to play with my money. Second, I like to watch my money grow. Third and most importantly, the next time my wife wants to blow $100, she can stay home to do it.'

**A** man and a woman were sitting side by side in the hospital waiting room. 'What are you doing here today?' he asked her.

'I'm here to donate some blood. They're going to give me $5 for it.'

'Hmmm, that's interesting. I'm here to donate some sperm. But they pay me $25.'

A few weeks later the same man and woman met again in the hospital waiting room.

'Oh hello. Are you here to donate blood again?'

And the woman, her mouth firmly closed, shook her head.

A blonde got a job with Public Works. Her task was to paint white lines down the centre of a rural road. She'd be on probation for the first week – and must manage at least two kilometres per day to gain full-time employment.

At the end of the first day, the supervisor found she'd completed four kilometres. Which was double the daily average. On the second day, he was disappointed to find that she'd only accomplished two kilometres. But this was still the average and he didn't want to discourage her.

But on the third day, she only managed one kilometre. So he was forced to say something.

'Sorry, you were doing very well. Four kilometres the first day. Two kilometres the second day. But yesterday, just one kilometre. Is there a problem? An equipment failure? A back injury?'

And the blonde replied, 'No, it's just that each day

I keep getting further and further away from the paint bucket.'

Bill worked at a timber mill in Gippsland and whilst shoving a tree towards the saw, accidentally sheared off all ten of his fingers.

So he went to the ER at the Gippsland Base Hospital where the doctor said, 'Dear oh dear. What a mess. But don't worry. Give me the fingers and I'll have them sewn back on.'

And Bill said, 'But I haven't got the fingers.'

So the doctor said, 'What do you mean you haven't got the fingers? This is 2002. We've got one of the best microsurgeons in the country here. He could put them back on and make your hands like new. Why the hell didn't you bring your fingers?'

And Bill said, 'How could I, doc? How could I pick the bloody things up?'

**T**wo blondes were sitting side by side in a steam room and one couldn't help admire the perfection of the other's skin.

'Excuse me for asking, but what keeps your skin so soft and beautiful?'

'Well, once a week I fill the bath with milk and just bathe and soak in it.'

So the other blonde went straight to a local dairy farm and said, 'I'd like a whole lot of milk.'

'How much?' asked the dairy farmer.

'Well, quite a lot. Because I'm going to bathe and soak in it.'

And he asked, 'Pasturised?'

'No,' she said, 'just up to my tits.'

**A** couple are eating in a Chinese restaurant in Florida. At the end of the meal, the waiter hands them the bill and the ritualistic fortune cookies. The bloke breaks open the brittle crust, and pulls out the slip of paper. 'Christ!' he says, 'it's another vote for Al Gore.'

Did you hear about the bloke who forgot to pay his exorcist?
*He was repossessed.*


An Irishman in a timber yard. 'I need some four-by-twos.'

'You mean two-by-fours, don't you?'

He returned an hour later. 'You were right, I mean two-by-fours.'

'How long do you need them?'

'I'll go and ask.'

An hour later he returned. 'A long time. We're going to use them to build a house.'


Two Eskimos were fishing in a kayak and, as the fish were slow to bite, they were feeling colder and colder. So they lit a fire in the boat and it burnt a hole through the seal skin – and the kayak sank. Which proves, yet again, that you can't have your kayak and heat it too.

**T**wo boll weevils grew up in Southern Carolina. One went to Hollywood and became a famous actor. The other stayed behind in the cottonfields and never amounted to much. Inevitably, this stay-at-home became known as the lesser of two weevils.

**A** three-legged dog pushes aside the swinging doors of an Old West saloon. He waddles up to the bar and says, 'I'm looking for the bastard who shot my paw.'

**W**hen she told me I was just average, she was being mean.

# The Penguin Bumper Book of Australian Jokes

**A** chess tournament was being held in a resort hotel near Kosciusko. Between one of the major contests a group of enthusiasts were standing around in the lobby, by a huge open fire, discussing their winning strategies. After a while the manager came out of his office and asked them to break it up. If they wanted to, they could continue their discussion in the bar or the coffee shop.

Grumbling, they moved off. And the manager was heard to say, 'I can't stand chess nuts boasting in an open foyer.'


**I** keep seeing spots before my eyes?
Have you seen a doctor?
No, only spots.


**A**dvertisement in the *Australasian Post:* PENIS ENLARGERS. JUST $20. IF IT DOESN'T WORK, WE REFUND YOUR MONEY.

And when you send your $20 they'll send you a little plastic magnifying glass.

**W**hy did the blonde snort Nutrasweet?
*She thought it was Diet Coke.*

**A**n agitated patient, in the early stages of dementia, was raging around his psychiatrist's office. 'More and more of my memory's going! All gone! I can't remember my name. I can't remember my wife's name or my children's names. Or what kind of car I drive. Yesterday I couldn't remember where I worked. And today, it took me hours to find my way here.'

'And how long has it been like this?' asked the psychiatrist sympathetically.

'Like what?'

**I**t was the height of the arms race and the Americans and Russians were at their usual loggerheads. Finally, wise counsel prevailed and they realised that if they continued to behave so belligerently, so aggressively, they'd destroy the entire planet.

So the President of the United States and the General Secretary of the Soviet Union's Communist Party sat down and decided to settle the whole dispute with . . . one dogfight.

American and Russian scientists would have five years to breed the best fighting dog in the world . . . and after one, titanic dogfight either Washington or the Kremlin would be entitled to dominate the world. Absolutely and entirely unchallenged.

The Russians interbred the nastiest Dobermans and Rottweilers with huge Syberian wolves. They selected only the most savage puppies from each litter and kept breeding, breeding, breeding.

After five years, the most terrifying canine the world had ever seen had been produced – and had to be kept in a cage with titanium bars.

The Soviets were convinced that their dog couldn't lose.

But when the day came for the dogfight, the Americans showed up with a strange animal. It was an immensely long dachshund.

The Russians burst out laughing. They knew there was no way this silly looking animal could possibly go one round with the Russian monster.

The cages were pushed together by huge forklifts

and the scientists, using long poles, opened the titanium doors. The Russian dog snarled and leapt out of its cage. And the dachshund waddled out of its cage and, wagging its tail, moved towards the Russian dog.

And just when the Russian dog was about to rip at the dachshund's throat, it opened its mouth and swallowed the Soviet contender in one bite.

There was nothing left of the Russian dog. Nothing at all. The Russians shook their heads in disbelief. 'How could this have happened? We had our best people working for five years with the meanest Dobermans and Rottweilers and Syberian wolves.'

'That's nothing,' said an American scientist. 'We had the best plastic surgeons from California working for five years to make an alligator look like a dachshund.'

The Foreign Minister rushes into the Prime Minister's office. 'John, John, there's a terrible problem.'

'Calm down, Alexander. Calm down!' says the Prime Minister.

'I can't! I can't! It's too awful! You remember we gave George W. Bush our total support for his missile shield? You remember we promised he could use Pine Gap any way he wanted?'

'Yes, yes,' says the PM.

'Well, the Chinese have got very, very angry with us. And they've launched a whole lot of missiles at Australia in retaliation. And the American missile shield doesn't shield us from missiles. So I'm afraid we have only three minutes to live.'

'Good God!' cries the Prime Minister, 'is there time to do anything?'

'Well, I could boil you an egg?'

Mrs Finkelstein is fast asleep in her New York apartment. At 4 a.m. she receives a phone call.

'Hallo!?' she says loudly and with great consternation.

A deep husky male voice breathes into the phone and says, 'I know where you live. I'm going to come around to your apartment. I'm going to rip your clothes off. And I'm going to fuck you real good.'

Mrs Finkelstein remains silent for some moments and then says, 'All that from one "hallo"!?'

In pharmacology all drugs have a generic name. Tylenol is acetaminophen, Aleve is naproxen, Amoxil is amoxicillin, Avil is Ibuprofen, and so on.

The FDA has been looking for a generic name for Viagra, and announcd that it has settled on Mycoxafailin. Also considered were Mycoxafloppin, Mydixadrupin, Mydixarizin, Mydixadud and Alimpdixafixit.

### MORE BUMPER STICKERS

IMPOTENCE: NATURE'S WAY OF SAYING 'NO HARD FEELINGS'.

PLEASE TELL OUR PANTS IT'S NOT POLITE TO POINT.

## The Penguin Bumper Book of Australian Jokes

If that phone was up your arse, maybe you could drive a little better.

Don't be sexist – broads hate that.

Constipated people don't give a shit.

If you drink, don't park – accidents cause people.

To all you virgins: thanks for nothing.

If at first you don't succeed . . . blame someone else and seek counselling.

If you can read this, I've lost my trailer.

Honk if you love rear-end collisions!

The earth is full. Go home.

I have the body of a God . . . Buddha.

This would be really funny if it weren't happening to me.

So many pedestrians – so little time.

COVER ME, I'M CHANGING LANES.

IF SEX IS A PAIN IN THE ARSE, THEN YOU'RE DOING IT WRONG . . .

FIGHT CRIME: SHOOT BACK!

BOLDLY GOING NOWHERE.

HEART ATTACKS . . . GOD'S REVENGE FOR EATING HIS ANIMAL FRIENDS.

**A** famous Viking explorer returned home from a voyage and found his name missing from the town register. His wife insisted on complaining to the local civic official, who apologised profusely saying, 'I must have taken Leif off my census.'

**A** little bloke gets into a lift. He looks up and sees the biggest man he's ever seen looming over him. The giant looks down at the little bloke and says, 'Six foot

11. Three hundred and fifty pounds. Twenty-inch penis. A three-pound left testicle. A three-pound right testicle. Turner Brown.'

Whereupon the little bloke faints. The enormous man kneels down and begins gently shaking him. 'What's wrong with you?'

In a very weak voice, the little bloke says, 'Could you repeat what you just said?'

The giant says, 'Well, I saw the curious look on your face and decided I'd give you the answers to the questions everyone always asks me. So I told you that I'm six foot 11. Three hundred and fifty pounds. Twenty-inch penis. A three-pound left testicle. A three-pound right testicle. And my name is Turner Brown.'

And the little bloke says, 'Thank God! I thought you said Turn Around.'

The Barbie doll is a global pestilence. At last count, there were more Barbie dolls on earth than there are Indians on the subcontinent. They will soon exceed the entire population of China. In Australia, they are a greater pestilence than cane toads or the Crown of Thorns starfish. And if the current crop of Barbies weren't bad enough, there's a new lot about to be launched on the local market.

**1.** Bifocals Barbie. Comes with her own set of blended-lens fashion frames in six wild colours (half-frames too!), neck chain and large-print editions of *Vogue* and *marie claire*.

**2.** Hot Flush Barbie. Press Barbie's bellybutton and watch her face turn beet red while tiny drops of perspiration appear on her forehead. Comes with hand-held fan and tiny tissues.

**3.** Facial Hair Barbie. As Barbie's hormone levels shift, see her whiskers grow. Available with teensy tweezers and magnifying mirror.

**4.** Flabby Arms Barbie. Hide Barbie's droopy triceps with these new, roomier-sleeved gowns. Good news on the tummy front, too – muu-muus with tummy-support panels are included.

**5.** Bunion Barbie. Years of disco dancing in stiletto heels have definitely taken their toll on Barbie's dainty arched feet. Soothe her sores with the pumice stone and plasters, then slip on soft terry mules.

**6.** No-More-Wrinkles Barbie. Erase those pesky crow's feet and lip lines with a tube of Skin Sparkle Spackle, from Barbie's own line of exclusive age-blasting cosmetics.

**7.** Footy Mum Barbie. All that experience as a cheerleader is really paying off as Barbie dusts off her old high school megaphone to root for Babs and Ken Jr. Comes with mini-van in robin-egg blue or white and cooler filled with doughnut holes and fruit punch.

**8.** Mid-life Crisis Barbie. It's time to ditch Ken. Barbie needs a change, and Alonzo (her personal trainer) is just what the doctor ordered, along with Prozac. They're hopping in her new red Miata and heading for the Napa Valley to open a B&B. Includes a real tape of 'Breaking Up is Hard to Do'.

**9.** Recovery Barbie. Too many parties have finally caught up with the ultimate party girl. Now she does Twelve Steps instead of dance steps. Clean and sober, she's going to meetings religiously. Comes with a little copy of The Big Book and a six-pack of Diet Coke.

**10.** Post-Menopausal Barbie. This Barbie wets her pants when she sneezes, forgets where she puts things, and cries a lot. She is sick and tired of Ken sitting on the couch watching the tube, clicking through the channels. Comes with Depends and Kleenex. As a bonus this year, the book *Getting in Touch with Your Inner Self* is included.

**A**ustralians have a Wettex-like ability to absorb American influences – from reversed baseball hats to foreign policy. American films dominate our cinemas whilst American dramas clog our TV networks, and our appetite for their vernacular seems as insatiable as for their fast food. So here goes with a whole new language currently taking America by storm – as President George Dubya Bush (aka President Shrub) transplants Texas in Pennsylvania Avenue.

Be the first in your Australian street to use the following in your conversation and repartee.

The engine's runnin' but ain't nobody driving. (Meaning: He's not overtly intelligent.)

He's as welcome as a skunk at a lawn party.

Tighter than bark on a tree. (Not very generous.)

Big hat, no cattle. (All talk and no action.)

We've howdy'd but we ain't shook yet. (We've made a brief acquaintance, but not been formally introduced.)

He thinks the sun comes up just to hear him crow. (He has a pretty high opinion of himself.)

She's got tongue enough for ten rows of teeth. (That woman can talk.)

It's so dry the trees are bribin' the dogs. (We really could use a little rain around here.)

Just because a chicken has wings doesn't mean it can fly. (Appearances can be deceptive.)

This ain't my first rodeo. (I've been around a while.)

He looks like the dog's been keepin' him under the porch. (Not the most handsome of men.)

They ate supper before they said grace. (Living in sin.)

Time to paint your butt and run with the antelope. (Stop arguing and do as you're told.)

As full of wind as a corn-eating horse. (Rather prone to boasting.)

You can put your boots in the oven, but that doesn't make them biscuits. (You can say whatever you want about something, but that doesn't change what it is.)

**J**ust before it went belly up, and sold out to Qantas, Impulse was trying to inculcate its cabin crew with the latest, most customer-friendly approaches. But they didn't always work. Take the hostie who was having trouble with a passenger who kept insulting the lady sitting next to him. He was saying, 'Christ, that's the ugliest baby I've ever seen.' The young mother got very upset and screamed, 'This bastard is insulting my baby.'

So the hostie did her best to calm things down. 'Don't get upset. I'll have one of the stewards shift him to another seat. In the meantime, here's a drink of water for yourself and a banana for your monkey.'

The young merchant banker drove his new BMW 3 series into a tree. When he woke up he saw the paramedics bending over him and, looking around at the crushed metal and the splintered trunk, he started screaming, 'My BMW! My BMW! Christ, look what's happened to my BMW.'

It was at this moment the paramedics decided to break the really bad news. That he'd lost his right arm. And looking down where it used to be, the merchant banker started screaming, 'I've lost my Rolex, too!'

The sales rep walked into the office of an important client and there beheld his new secretary. She was astonishingly beautiful and he was instantly besotted. They talked for a while and she said, 'Would you mind if I made a rather unusual request of you?'

'No, not at all.'

'But you'll have to promise to keep it a strict secret. Just between you and me.'

'Of course, of course.'

'It's embarrassing to talk about and, as you know, my boss is a nice bloke. But he has, let me put it diplomatically, a certain physical weakness, a certain disability. Now, I'm just a woman and you're a real man.'

'That's right, that's right!'

'And since I've been wanting to do it for so long – will you please help me?'

'Yes! Yes!'

'Will you help me move this filing cabinet?'

**I**'m not feeling too good today. I got it this morning when I was shaving. I was dabbing my face with water and the toilet seat fell on my head.

**A** bloke was walking past a clothing store and saw a big sign: '25% off everything'.

He walked in and asked the sales lady. 'Is that right? Twenty-five per-cent off? Off everything?'

'Yes,' she said, 'because we're going out of business.'

'OK, I'll take a dozen shirts, five suits, six pairs of shoes, 50 pairs of socks, 100 pairs of underpants, 80 singlets, six belts, 24 ties, 12 hankies, eight cardigans, ten sports coats, four dinner jackets, four dressing gowns, two pairs of slippers, three raincoats, two overcoats and seven cravats. How much will that be?'

She added it up and said, 'That'll be $10 000.'

'Hang on, what about the 25% off?'

'That was when we were going out of business,' she said. 'Now you've bought this much, we're back in business again.'

**W**hy can't Frankenstein have kids?
*Because his nuts are on his neck.*

**A** New Zealand hunter kills a deer in the mountains and brings it back to his family in Auckland. He cleans and serves the venison for supper, but is reluctant to tell his kids exactly what it is they'll be eating. They have, after all, just been watching a video of *Bambi*.

They're halfway through the meal when his daughter asks him, 'Daddy, what is it we're eating?'

'Well,' says Dad, 'here's a hint. It's what your mum sometimes calls me.'

'Oh my God!' the child screams. 'We're eating arsehole!'

**A** woman from the Deep South and a woman from the North found themselves sitting side by side in a

Boeing. The woman from the South, being friendly and all, said, 'So where ya'll from?'

And the northern woman said, icily, 'From a place where they know better than to use a preposition at the end of a sentence.'

The woman from the South thought about this for a few seconds and then reformulated the question. 'So, where ya'll from, bitch?'


**S**he's sitting home alone, watching Stan Zemanek on 'Beauty and the Beast', when the bell rings. She opens the door and there's a rather unattractive bloke standing there. 'Hello, is your husband home?'

And she says, 'No, he's still at work. But he should be home in about half an hour.'

So they sit together watching Stan Zemanek. And after a while the visitor sounds a little like Stan: 'I reckon you must have great breasts. Any chance of seeing one? I'll give you a hundred bucks.'

She thinks about it for a few moments and, what the hell, unbuttons her blouse, drops her bra cup and shows him one. For a few seconds.

He is delighted and gives her $100.

Then he says, 'Look, that was great. But I've got to see both of them. If you let me see both of them at the same time, I'll give you another $100.'

And she thinks, what the hell. So she shows them both.

Then, looking at his watch, he excuses himself and leaves.

A few minutes later her husband gets home from work and she says, 'A friend of yours called into see you.'

'Yeah, that'd be Arthur. Did he drop off the $200 he owes me?'

## Popular oxymorons

Public servant
Exact estimate
Found missing
Legally drunk
Act naturally

# The Penguin Bumper Book of Australian Jokes

Resident alien
Airline food
Government organisation
Good grief
Sanitary landfill
Small crowd
Business ethics
Alone together
Soft rock
Military intelligence
Passive aggression
Clearly misunderstood
Extinct life
Plastic glasses
Computer security
Terribly pleased
Tight slacks
Political science
Pretty ugly
Definite maybe
Rap music
Working vacation
Microsoft Works
Religious tolerance

# The Penguin Bumper Book of Australian Jokes

## A COLLECTION OF AUTHENTIC EPITAPHS, GATHERED FROM THE WORLD'S HEADSTONES

ANNE MANN
HERE LIES ANNE MANN WHO LIVED AN OLD MAID
BUT DIED AN OLD MANN.
(LONDON, ENGLAND)

ANNA WALLACE
THE CHILDREN OF ISRAEL WANTED BREAD AND THE
LORD SENT THEM MANNA. OLD CLERK WALLACE
WANTED A WIFE AND THE DEVIL SENT HIM ANNA.
(RIBBESFORD, ENGLAND)

HERE LIES JOHNNY YEAST
PARDON ME FOR NOT RISING.
(RUIDOSO, NEW MEXICO)

HERE LIES BUTCH WE PLANTED HIM RAW
HE WAS QUICK ON THE TRIGGER BUT SLOW ON
THE DRAW.
(SILVER CITY, NEVADA)

### The Penguin Bumper Book of Australian Jokes

HERE LIES THE BODY OF JONATHAN BLAKE
STEPPED ON THE GAS INSTEAD OF THE BRAKE.
(UNION TOWN, PENNSYLVANIA)

SIR JOHN STRANGE
HERE LIES AN HONEST LAWYER
AND THAT IS STRANGE.
(ENGLAND)

I WAS SOMEBODY
WHO, IS NO BUSINESS
OF YOURS.
(STOWE, VERMONT)

HERE LIES LESTER MOORE
FOUR SLUGS FROM A 44
NO LES NO MORE.
(TOMBSTONE, ARIZONA)

JOHN PENNY
READER IF CASH THOU ART
IN WANT OF ANY
DIG SIX FEET DEEP
AND THOU WILT FIND A PENNY.
(WIMBORNE, ENGLAND)

## The Penguin Bumper Book of Australian Jokes

I TOLD YOU I WAS SICK.
(GEORGIA)

JONATHAN FIDDLE
WENT OUT OF TUNE.
(HARTSCOMBE, ENGLAND)

OWEN MOORE
GONE AWAY.
OWEN' MORE THAN HE COULD PAY.
(BATTERSEA, LONDON)

HERE LIES AN ATHEIST
ALL DRESSED UP AND NO PLACE TO GO.
(THURMONT, MARYLAND)

A bloke fronts a bar with an ostrich. The bartender asks for the order. The bloke says, 'I'll have a beer.' And, turning to the ostrich, 'What's yours?'

'I'll have a beer, too,' says the ostrich.

'That'll be $3.40,' says the bartender.

The bloke reaches into his coat pocket and pulls out the exact change.

The next day they come again. The bloke says, 'I'll have a beer.' And the ostrich says, 'I'll have a beer, too.' And once again the bloke produces the exact money from his pocket.

The same thing happens every day, sometimes with variations. For example, the bloke orders a large Scotch and the ostrich says, 'Same for me.' The bartender says, 'That'll be $9.50.' And once again the bloke produces the exact change. To the cent.

Unable to contain his curiosity any longer, the bartender says, 'Excuse me, but how do you manage always to come up with the exact change?'

'Well,' says the bloke, 'I went to a garage sale a few years back and bought this old, rusty lamp. When I rubbed it a genie appeared and offered me two wishes. My first wish? If I ever had to pay for anything, I'd just put my hand in the pocket and the right amount of money would be there.'

'That's very clever,' says the bartender. 'Most people would be greedy and ask for a million dollars. But you'll always have exactly the right amount of money as long as you live.'

'Exactly. Whether I'm buying an apple or an Aston Martin – all I've got to do is reach into my pocket.'

'Can I ask you another question?' says the bartender. 'How about the ostrich?'

The bloke sighs and says, 'My second wish? I asked for a chick with long legs.'

### THE GOOD, THE BAD AND THE UGLY

**G:** You agree, no more kids.

**B:** You can't find the condoms.

**U:** Your daughter borrowed them.

**G:** Your son spends a lot of time in his room.

**B:** You find some porn movies under his bed.

**U:** You're in them.

**The Penguin Bumper Book of Australian Jokes**

**G:** Your husband follows the fashions.
**B:** He's a transvestite.
**U:** He looks better than you.


**G:** Your son's maturing.
**B:** He's involved with the woman next door.
**U:** So are you.


**G:** You explain sex to your daughter.
**B:** She keeps interrupting.
**U:** And correcting you.

**G:** Your wife isn't talking to you.

**B:** She wants a divorce.

**U:** She's a lawyer.

**G:** Your son is dating someone new.

**B:** It's another man.

**U:** Your best friend.

**G:** Your wife is pregnant.

**B:** It's twins.

**U:** You had a vasectomy years ago.

# The Penguin Bumper Book of Australian Jokes

**A** multiple amputee is taken to Bondi Beach by his carer, who gently lowers him onto a Dickies towel and lavishly applies 30-plus sunscreen to his face and torso. He carefully positions his sunglasses, arranges the beach umbrella and puts a Beach Boys tape in his Sony Walkman. She then excuses herself while she goes to the loo.

No sooner has she departed than a preposterously beautiful young woman, in the most micro of bikinis, walks by. She looks down at him with sympathy and says, 'Excuse me asking you a personal question, but have you ever been hugged?'

'Yes, by my mum. But never by a beautiful woman.'

Whereupon she kneels beside him and gives him a big hug.

A few moments later another beautiful, bikini-clad girl walks by. She looks down at the poor bloke and says, 'Have you ever been kissed?'

Not believing his luck he says that, no, he hasn't.

And she kneels beside him and gives him a big, moist kiss, right on the lips.

Seconds later a third girl walks by and says, 'Have you ever been fucked?'

Heart palpitating, he says, 'No, no I haven't.'

'Well, you're fucked now,' she says, 'the tide's coming in.'

A bloke took a duck to his local taxidermist. He wanted it mounted. Two days later he went back to collect the bird but the taxidermist said, 'Sorry, I couldn't stuff your duck. It has a quack in it.'

A bloke was in Alaska studying polar bears. He would spend a week at a time out on the ice floes in subzero temperatures. Then he would return to the small town and spend a day or two in its only bar.

One day, when it was 40 below, he went into the bar and asked for a whisky.

'I dunno, pal. You've run up a really big tab.'

'I know, I know. But I'm flat broke until the cheque arrives from the zoo – and I desperately need a drink.'

'Alright,' said the barman, 'I'll write your tab

down on a piece of paper and pin it up by the coat rack.'

'Do you have to do that? I don't want everyone in town to see it.'

'Don't worry. I'll cover it up with your parka until it's paid.'


They were dating but, because of her religious scruples, she'd refused to have sex.

One day, as they headed down the F1, she was irritated by his slow driving. 'Look, I can't stand it,' she said, 'let's play a game. For every five kilometres per hour over the speed limit you drive, I'll whip off one piece of clothing.'

He enthusiastically agreed and pressed the accelerator. As he reached 115kph she took off her blouse. At 120 off came her pants. At 125 it was her bra and at 130 her knickers.

Seeing her naked he got wildly excited and lost control of the car. It veered off the freeway, rolled over an embankment and wrapped itself around a tree. She was thrown clear but he was trapped. She tried to pull him from the car but he was stuck.

'Go to the road and get help,' he moaned.

'But I don't have anything to cover myself with,' she said.

The bloke felt around but could only reach one of his shoes. 'You'll have to hold this in front of yourself,' he told her. So she did – and headed to the freeway for help.

Along came a semitrailer. The driver saw a naked woman and pulled over to see if she wanted a lift.

'My boyfriend! My boyfriend! He's stuck and I can't pull him out.'

The driver looked down at the shoe between her legs and said, 'Darlin', if he's in that far, I'm afraid he's a goner.'

**A**n atheist was walking through the woods admiring the wonders that evolution had provided. 'What majestic trees! What powerful rivers! What beautiful animals!' he said to himself. As he was walking alongside the river he heard a rustling in the bushes behind him. Turning to look, he saw a seven-foot

## The Penguin Bumper Book of Australian Jokes

grizzly bear charge towards him.

He ran as fast as he could up the path. He looked over his shoulder and saw the grizzly was closing in on him. Somehow, he ran even faster, so scared that tears came to his eyes. He looked again and the bear was even closer. His heart was pounding, and he tried to run faster. He tripped and fell to the ground. He rolled over to pick himself up but the bear was right over him reaching for him with its left paw and raising its right paw to strike him.

At that instant the atheist cried, 'Oh my God! . . .' Time stopped. The bear froze. The forest was silent. Even the river stopped moving. As a bright light shone upon the man, a voice came out of the sky. 'You deny my existence for all these years, teach others that I don't exist and even credit creation to a cosmic accident! Do you expect me to help you out of this predicament? Am I to count you as a believer?'

The atheist looked directly into the light. 'It would be hypocritical to ask to be a Christian after all these years, but perhaps you could make the bear a Christian?'

'Very well,' said the voice. The light went out. The river ran. The sounds of the forest resumed.

The bear dropped its right paw, brought both

paws together, bowed its head and spoke: 'Lord, for this food which I am about to receive, I am truly thankful.'

A child custody case; the judge couldn't decide which parent he should grant full custody to. So he asked the little boy, 'Would you like to live with your mother?'

'No,' said the boy.

'Why not?' asked the judge.

'Because she beats me.'

The judge said, 'OK, then you'll go to live with your father.

'Oh no,' cried the boy, 'he beats me, too.'

Dumbfounded, the judge asked, 'OK, who do you want to live with?'

'I want to live with the North Queensland Cowboys.'

'Why?' asked the judge.

'They never beat anybody.'

In 1990, Monash University funded a study to see why the head of a man's penis was larger than the shaft. Having expended $100 000 on the project, they concluded that the reason the head was larger than the shaft was to give the male more pleasure during sex.

After Monash published the study, in a refereed journal, RMIT decided to do their own study and expended $250 000 in three years of research on the project. They concluded that the reason was to give the female more pleasure during sex.

Unconvinced by the findings, James Cook University, in Queensland, spent $15 on some porn magazines and concluded that it was to keep a bloke's hand from flying off and hitting him on the forehead.

# THE PENGUIN BOOK OF AUSTRALIAN JOKES

## Collected by Phillip Adams and Patrice Newell

Jokes are a bit like electro-convulsive therapy. Laugher does to the brain what a good sneeze does to the nasal passages. If you read this entire volume in one sitting, it will be the equivalent of 10 years in psychoanalysis. *The Penguin Book of Australian Jokes* is a scandalous, subversive, hilarious collection of jokes, anecdotes, and distinctively Australian humour.

## THE PENGUIN BOOK OF JOKES FROM THE NET

**Collected by Phillip Adams and Patrice Newell**

When the printing press was invented, it promised literature. People read comics. When cinema was invented, it promised culture for the masses. We got *Xena*. When TV was invented, it promised education. We got *Sex and the City*. The Internet promised unprecedented access to information across the globe and an end to national barriers. What we got was 30 million net-heads – nerds, rock stars and your average punters – swapping politically incorrect jokes. Hundreds of which, we're unashamed to say, are contained within these pages.

# The Penguin Book of More Australian Jokes

**Collected by Phillip Adams and Patrice Newell**

This book is to the joke what a telephone directory is to the phone number. No taxi has been left unturned, no dunny wall unread, no pub unvisited in rounding up these funnies. The result is a naughtier, even more notorious volume than the bestselling *Penguin Book of Australian Jokes*. Of course, you should be reading serious fiction or uplifting works of theology – but if you don't mind feeling thoroughly ashamed of yourself, this is the book for you.

# THE GIANT PENGUIN BOOK OF AUSTRALIAN JOKES

## Collected by Phillip Adams and Patrice Newell

You asked for it – four bestselling joke books in one. This compilation volume of *The Penguin Book of Australian Jokes*, *The Penguin Book of More Australian Jokes*, *The Penguin Book of Jokes from the Net* and *The Penguin Book of Schoolyard Jokes* is the most giant joke book ever.

So enter at your peril.

## WHAT A GIGGLE!

### Collected by Phillip Adams and Patrice Newell

Before-school jokes! After-school jokes! Playground jokes! Jokes to tell instead of doing homework! *What a Giggle!* is bursting with snorts and giggles and hoots of laughter. Hundreds of jokes collected from kids all across Australia (including secret, naughty ones you should keep away from Mum and Dad).